Dialectics of the U.S. Constitution

Dialectics of the U.S. Constitution

Selected Writings of Mitchell Franklin

Edited by James M. Lawler

MEP Publications
Minneapolis

MEP Publications, an imprint of
Marxist Educational Press, Inc.
University of Minnesota, Physics Building
116 Church Street S.E.
Minneapolis, MN 55455-0112

MEP Publications Web site:
http://www.umn.edu/home/marqu002

Printed in the United States of America

Dedicated to the memory of
Virginia and Mitchell Franklin

Library of Congress Cataloging-in-Publication Data

Franklin, Mitchell, 1902-1986.
Dialectics of the U.S. Constitution : selected writings of Mitchell Franklin / edited by James M. Lawler.
p. cm.
Includes bibliographical references and index.
ISBN 0-930656-65-2 (cloth)
1. Constitutional law—United States—Philosophy. 2. Constitutional law—United States—Interpretation and construction. 3. Dialectical materialism. I. Lawler, James M., 1940– II.Title.

KF4550 .F68 2000
342.73'001—dc21

99—059254

CONTENTS

Acknowledgments

The editor wishes to thank the National Lawyers Guild for permission to republish the following articles: "The Judiciary State I," *National Lawyers Guild Quarterly*, vol. 2, 1940, 244–61; "The Judiciary State II," *National Lawyers Guild Quarterly*, vol. 3, 1940, 27–41; "Infamy and Constitutional Civil Liberties," *Lawyers Guild Review*, vol. 14, 1954, 1–10; "The Encyclopédiste Origin and Meaning of the Fifth Amendment," *Lawyers Guild Review*, vol. 15, 1955, 41-62.

The article "Brutus the American Praetor" was originally published in *Tulane Law Review*, vol. 15, 1940, 16–50, and is reprinted with the permission of the Tulane Law Review Association, which holds the copyright. All rights reserved.

Special thanks are due to colleagues who in one way or another supported me and this project, including Peter Hare, John Ryder, Tom Headrick, Andrew Schwartz, and Eileen McNamara, as well as the members of the Philosophy Department at SUNY Buffalo, who have provided a stimulating and gracious intellectual environment for both Mitchell Franklin and myself.

For keeping up a conversation with me on the substance of this work, I owe much to Gene and Virginia Grabiner, and to Terry di Filippo.

Thanks too for the patience and hard work of Doris and Erwin Marquit in helping me in the preparation of this manuscript.

For the home fires, both external and internal, love to Sharon, Hélène, Michael, Adrian, and Max.

Foreword

Many people know that the reversal of prior Supreme Court precedents by the Warren Court revitalized the Bill of Rights and the Civil War amendments to the Constitution. The Warren Court's influence is felt when justices continue to employ the "Second" (the Bill of Rights) and "Third" (the Thirteenth, Fourteenth, and Fifteenth Amendments) "Constitutions." These, of course, have been used to implement equality before the law; to ensure social justice for racial minorities, women, and other disenfranchised citizens; and to safeguard democracy by prohibiting the official suppression of free speech and political dissent.

But what is not widely known is that Mitchell Franklin anticipated the legal thought behind Warren Court actions; moreover, after its decisions were written, he disclosed their underlying assumptions. He revealed, first, that these decisions were based on authentic readings of the Constitution. They were not—as advocates of strict constructionism would have us believe—arbitrary political intrusions into the judicial process. Second, he noted that the Second and Third Constitutions were purposefully written as safeguards that could be expanded by future generations to defend civil liberty and political freedom. That these safeguards were conceived within the framework of capitalism is taken for granted. Yet Franklin's third point is that these safeguards defend the *democratic* form of our republican government and not just any government.

Franklin arrived at these and other insights with the aid of writings by Hegel and Marx. His analysis of constitutional texts eschewed the mechanical materialism of Charles and Mary Beard, who emphasized the undemocratic, class character of the Constitution. To the contrary, he insisted the Constitution was produced by complex class struggles and historical events that forced the slave owners and bourgeoisie to make significant concessions to democracy. His historical inquiry into how the Enlightenment and Roman law influenced the Jeffersonians demonstrated the utility of dialectical materialism for interpreting constitutional law.

Franklin's approach to the Constitution is as vital today as it was in his lifetime, and his view of the Constitution as a living document is shared by others. For instance, Justice Thurgood Marshall, appalled at the mindless bicentennial celebration of the Constitution, denounced the compromises made with slave owners at the first Constitutional Convention. But Marshall also insisted that the Civil War amendments repudiated these disgraceful compromises. The Constitution, in his view, represents a "living law" and not the words of dead men immutably carved in stone.

The same vision of our living law is held by innumerable social movements that continually express their belief in an open-ended Constitution. Together, these movements spend millions of dollars on test cases in the hope that a Supreme Court majority shares this belief. But, whatever the prevailing attitude of the Court at any given time, these movements have relied upon Franklin's Constitution and not the strict constructionist's to support affirmative action programs, stop political repression, safeguard humanity from ecological disaster, defend the right to privacy, achieve equal justice for all, and prevent the covert and illegal concentration of power in the executive branch of the government.

Among Franklin's achievements is the integration of philosophical-historical analyses and practical methodologies for interpreting Constitutional texts. In addition to learned scholastic arguments, we find in his writings an acute sensitivity to methods for making valid Constitutional interpretations. His articles are not passive reflections of legal events. They attempt to provide historical warrants and modes of reasoning for winning the day in court. His writings epitomize Marx's saying: The philosophers have only *interpreted* the world in various ways; the point, however, is to *change* it.

Yet even those parts of Franklin's writings useful for practical politics disprove that his work represents judicial activism in the sense that it represents an alien intrusion into the process of judicial review. Aside from the fact that judicial activists of every persuasion have been with us since the beginning of the Republic, Franklin's writings defy the facile dichotomy between "judicial activists" and "strict constructionists," upheld by militant conservatives like Robert Bork. In raising this issue, such conservatives claim their superiority in judging and being loyal to constitutional tenets. But Franklin's writings question the truthfulness of that claim. His work reveals that Supreme Courts can reverse precedent and actively introduce profound political changes while still remaining faithful to the spirit and meaning of the Constitution. In *Brown v. Board of Education*, for example, the Warren Court demolished the laws enforcing one of the most despicable forms of racial segregation. His Court condemned racial segregation in public schools by affirming the primacy of the Fourteenth Amendment in opposition to the undeniably activist stance of post-Reconstruction Supreme Courts. The Court opposed these nineteenth-century precedents culminating in *Plessy v. Ferguson* of 1896, which decreed that a *strict interpretation* of the Fourteenth Amendment did not best serve the interests of the South. Until the Warren Court's reversals, these precedents had subverted the Second and Third Constitutions by openly introducing racist politics into the process of judicial review.

Franklin defended the constitutional "rule of law" against attacks by some of the very officials sworn to uphold its principles. His writings show that members of all branches of the government including justices of the Supreme Court have subverted this rule of law. Take, for example, Justice Marshall's 1803 justification of judicial power superseding legislation based on the will of the people. Also, see the post-Reconstruction Supreme Court decisions nullifying constitutional safeguards against Jim Crow laws. And finally, notice that legislators and presidents subverted the Constitution when they suppressed freedom of speech and political dissent during the Truman presidency, the McCarthy period, and the Nixon administration.

More recently, in the 1980s, official subversion of the Constitution has relied heavily on secret operations. The Contragate hearings, for instance, showed how officials in the Reagan administration negated the constitutional system of checks and balances by secretly violating congressional mandates prohibiting the sale of arms to Nicaraguan counterrevolutionaries. Equally subversive was the sweeping covert investigation of CISPES (the Coalition in Support of the People of El Salvador), conducted by the Federal Bureau of Investigation from 1981 to 1988. Using techniques ranging from photographic surveillance to paid informants, the FBI allegedly searched for terrorists and Central Americans not registered as foreign agents. It activated personnel in fifty field offices and swept within their net every CISPES chapter and over 237 organizations working for peace and human rights in Central America. Enormous sums were spent investigating not crime or terrorism but rather peace demonstrations, trade unions, and political organizations engaging in the exercise of free speech and other kinds of lawful activity. More than two decades ago, the public was informed about the extensive FBI surveillance of civil rights activists and organizations opposed to the Vietnam War. FBI files released under the Freedom of Information Act have documented this massive surveillance of individuals and organizations opposed to the state terrorism and war in Central America backed by the U.S. administration. The indisputable fact established by this surveillance is that the FBI did not discover a single bit of evidence to publicly infame the people who opposed Reagan's Central American policies.

Franklin's writings show that the constitutional rule of law was designed to prevent the government from infaming people and denying them their rights as citizens. His articles make one realize why the executive branch and its enforcement agencies like the FBI show contempt for this rule of law when they investigate lawful organizations, engage in political harassment, and accumulate millions of files for infaming political dissenters. His works justify fighting to fulfill the recommendations of the Senate (Church Committee) and House committees that studied FBI intelligence operations. These committees upheld constitutional principles by proposing strict legislative guidelines for FBI domestic security and counterintelligence investigations.

Defending our political freedoms and civil rights against government subversion has never been easy. But it is vitally necessary. Franklin's distinguished writings map some of the constitutional parameters of this defense. He reminds us that we live in a society full of contradictions and that democracy requires an endless struggle to revitalize and enforce the *authentic* texts of the Constitution.

Herman Schwendinger
Sociology Department
SUNY at New Paltz

Introduction: Originalism, Moralism, and the Public Opinion State of Mitchell Franklin

by James M. Lawler

The forgotten man of American legal theory

The spring 1975 issue of the *Buffalo Law Review*, dedicated to Mitchell Franklin, calls the then recently retired Buffalo professor of law and philosophy "the foremost Marxist legal philosopher in the English-speaking world."[1] Recalling Franklin's earlier career at Tulane University, the *Tulane Law Review*, in the spring 1980 dedicatory issue of that journal, pays tribute to Franklin's "innovative and influential" studies on the U.S. Constitution. In a memorial special section of *Telos*, the editor recalls Franklin's influence on the founding of that journal, describing his presence during the days of student revolt of the late sixties as "an intellectual oasis in a dismal academic desert" (Delfini and Piccone 1986–87, 55).

Franklin's work has had a significant impact on the U.S. Supreme Court. In *Ullman v. United States*, 350 U.S. 422 (1956), Supreme Court Justice William O. Douglas invoked the Fifth Amendment as applicable to circumstances in which "public opinion casts a person into outer darkness as happens today when a person is exposed as a Communist," and when "the government brings infamy on the head of the witness when it compels disclosure. That is precisely what the Fifth Amendment prohibits." In support of the Fifth Amendment as an anti-infamy amendment, Douglas wrote: "The Fifth Amendment was designed to protect the accused against infamy as well as against prosecution. A recent analysis by Professor Mitchell Franklin of Tulane illuminates the point" (457).

Mitchell Franklin (1902–1986) received the J.D. at Harvard in 1925, and the S.J.D. in 1928. Founder of the program of comparative law, he was the W. R. Irby Professor of Law at Tulane, where he taught from 1930 until his retirement there in 1967. Tulane awarded him the LL.D. in 1978. In 1967 he received a joint appointment in the philosophy department and in the law school at the State University of New York (SUNY) at Buffalo, where he retired in 1974.

In addition to his distinguished academic career he had a notable career outside of the university. From 1925 to 1928 he was law secretary for the Supreme Judicial Court of Massachusetts, and served at the trial of Sacco and Vanzetti (where he wrote a legal brief for acquittal). During the aftermath of World War II, as Legal Officer for the U.N. Secretariat, he wrote the original legal draft for the Nuremberg trials of Nazi war criminals. He was also founder and president of the New Orleans Progressive Party, which ran Henry Wallace for President in 1948. He was a founding member of the National Lawyers Guild, of which he was a vice president for many years.

Franklin's theory of the Constitution has been applied to criminology and African American studies, to education, race relations, and labor studies (Grabiner 1980, 1982, 1983, 1985). However, despite this diverse influence, including on the leading theoretical figure of the Warren Court, Justice Douglas, it can still be said that Mitchell Franklin remains "the forgotten man of American legal theory" (Fraser 1986–87, 42). Part of the reason for this neglect is the need to "overcome obstacles of [Franklin's] style and hard to locate publications" (D'Amico 1986–87, 6). Franklin was an essayist whose usually lengthy essays, which sometimes approached the length of a book, must be retrieved from scattered law journals and essay collections. The "difficulty of style" results mainly from the fact that Franklin would often recapitulate his previous work in a highly condensed form before addressing the particular issue in question. Over time this resulted in articles involving a complex interweaving of issues in philosophy, general legal theory, history, and more specific matters such as those dealing with the U.S. Constitution. Without sufficient background from the more amply expounded earlier presentations, the reader may find later articles a formidable challenge. This problem is remedied by reading his articles in chronological order, as this volume permits readers to do with five important early essays.

But Franklin's isolation both as a philosopher and theorist of the U.S. Constitution is not to be explained primarily on grounds of style. The originality and complexity of his thought might have achieved for him the prominence of thinkers whose writings are far more obscure had it not been for the fact that his ideas always flew in the face of deeply held convictions of his potential audience. In the first place Franklin was a critic of the common law in a country dominated by the legal methodology of the common law. Franklin taught comparative law at Tulane University in New Orleans, in Louisiana, the only state in the United States that maintains the civil law tradition of France, and of the European continent generally. In North America, only Louisiana and Quebec maintain a civil law system. In the American revolutionary context, Franklin has argued, it was the French Enlightenment tradition and its civil law orientation that gained decisive influence over the legal thinking of the constitutional founders, above all Jefferson.

The principal effect of this influence was the existence of the Constitution itself. England did not and does not have a written constitution. The creation of a written code of law, organized according to rational principles, was a central objective of the continental *philosophes* who eventually succeeded in embodying this aspiration in the French Civil Code. Although U.S. Enlightenment thinkers never succeeded in creating a fully developed legal code covering the civil law, they did take one decisive step in that direction by writing a code of public law, the U.S. Constitution. Franklin argued that a correct understanding of a body of codified law such as the U.S. Constitution requires a type of legal formation that is generally lacking in U.S. law schools, which follow the common law legal method stemming from British heritage. A historically objective conception of the U.S. Constitution, however, requires an understanding of civil law methodology, which is a method of implementing a rationally organized code of law, including its application to changing, unforeseen, and/or novel circumstances.

One would have supposed that a radical critic of the American legal establishment would have found favor at least in leftist intellectual circles. But Franklin's civil law reform proposals did not coincide with the nihilistic tendencies of many radical critics of the U.S. legal system. Franklin rejected the notion, classically expressed by Charles and Mary Beard, that the U.S. Constitution was a narrowly bourgeois document. Franklin argued that knowledge of the historical conditions of the American Revolution should lead to a recognition of the deeply democratic character of that revolution. If the U.S. Constitution was a bourgeois document, it was the work of a revolutionary bourgeoisie, leading a broader popular struggle in the name of exalted democratic ideals. The Constitution reflects high-water marks in U.S. democratic history, particularly if one integrates both the Bill of Rights and the Civil War amendments into this history. Once the revolutionary fervor subsides, and the American bourgeoisie turns to the more mundane businesses of life, the Constitution remains as a written testimony, endowed with force of law, to that more exalted period—for those, at least, who are able to read its authentic historical meaning. Throughout his career Franklin attempted to uncover this authentic historical meaning against subjective and unhistorical methods of legal interpretation that distort or limit that meaning, or cryptically introduce spurious meanings.

A Marxist whose thought matured during the twenties and thirties, Franklin had to endure the Cold War hostility toward Marxism as an alien and "un-American" ideology. And yet, when Marxism burst onto the North American scene once more in the late sixties, Franklin was perceived disparagingly by some of his radicalized students, attracted by subjectivist tendencies of existentialism, phenomenology, and the Frankfurt school, as a "rationalist" and a "hard-line Stalinist" (Delfini and Piccone 1986–87, 57). But Franklin's work was scarcely appreciated in the Soviet Union. Stalin's influence on Marxism in the Soviet Union conflicted with much that is central to Franklin's thought, especially the prominent place of Hegel's dialectical methodology, and Franklin's defense of the U.S. Constitution as a profoundly democratic, not a narrowly bourgeois, document.[2]

Bork on original understanding and "capital" punishment

Perhaps the times are now more favorable to a rereading of Mitchell Franklin's work. Recently there has been a wealth of writings on the Constitution involving complex and intellectually sophisticated philosophical and methodological theories. Philosophy has invaded the academic law schools in all its complex variants, for better or for worse. In *The Tempting of America*, Robert Bork writes disparagingly:

> To understand the new constitutions being built in the law schools, it is necessary to be a philosopher, at least an amateur one. If the literature is to be taken seriously . . . it would be necessary to read widely in moral philosophy, hermeneutics, deconstructionism, Marxism, and who-knows-what-will-come-next. The reader is supposed to be familiar with utilitarianism, contractarianism, Mill, Derrida, Habermas, positivism, formalism, Rawls, Nosick, and the literature of radical feminism. It turns out, though previously it had never been suspected, that in order to understand the American Constitution ratified in 1787, one must study not John Locke or even James Madison, but a modern German Marxist [presumably Jürgen Habermas]. (1990, 134)

Robert Bork was a Reagan-appointed candidate for the Supreme Court whose interpretation of the Constitution became subject to intense scrutiny during the 1987 Senate hearings in which he was ultimately rejected. Bork's book is a defense of "the orthodoxy of original understanding" (7) of the Constitution, the idea that Supreme Court judges are to base their decisions on the "meaning understood at the time of the law's enactment" (144). The primary targets of Bork's attack are liberal and/or leftist professors of law and philosophy, the "theorists of liberal constitutional revisionism" (187–221), who, he claims, dominate the major law schools. They propound a variety of constitutional approaches that either directly abandon the notion that the original meaning of the Constitution is binding on judges, or find indirect ways to distort or displace the idea of objective and binding constitutional meaning. The result of such freedom from constitutional determination is the possibility they have created of reading their own favorite moral or political positions into law. Such law-making by an unelected judiciary, Bork argues, effectively supplants the democratic will of the American people as exercised through the elected congress and presidency. Such nonoriginalist or moralist approaches were at the bottom of the sweeping constitutional revolution that took place during the time of the Supreme Court headed by Justice Earl Warren (1953 to 1969). In particular, Bork singles out Justice William O. Douglas as a proponent of what he calls "disguised activism" (70)—i.e., active intrusion of his own subjective preferences disguised as an objective reading of the Constitution.

I have noted that Douglas cited Franklin as the theoretician of the anti-infamy character of the Fifth Amendment. Franklin was both a proponent of the original, objective historical meaning of the Constitution as well as a proponent of the major decisions of the Warren Court—though not always of the actual reasoning or methodology behind those decisions. As a philosopher, Franklin wrote detailed critical analyses of many of the complex epistemological concepts that inject themselves into juridical method. He was also a critic of the theory of "strict constructionism"—Bork's originalism—an approach that interprets the meaning of the Constitution narrowly and suspiciously, as exhausted by the immediate purposes and limited intentions of its framers and ratifiers.

Strict constructionist methodology has much in common with the Anglo-American common law method. The common law judge claims to base a decision on past precedent, following the doctrine of *stare decisis:* let the decision stand. However, because past decisions are numerous and varied, and because they are interpreted narrowly so as to apply to a very limited number of cases, the judge can pit one decision against another and by this means become freed of obligation to past decisions while at the same time claiming to be bound by them. Similarly, if the Constitution is read merely as a collection of various independent clauses with narrow application, the judge can treat them, on a market analogy, as competing values that have to be "balanced." In this way, even in the name of "strict construction," the judge can be freed from following the legal text, both in letter and in spirit, so as to make law independently of the legislature.

But a rationally organized code of law is not a collection of independent clauses. It is a coherent, interconnected text that derives its authority from the legislature or legislatures that adopt it. In addition to this interconnected textual meaning, there is the context in which the text must be placed. Knowledge of this context too is essential to an authentic or objective conception of the Constitution, especially in the case of the United States, where the fundamental code of law is over two hundred years old. In his examination of the "original meaning" of various constitutional provisions, Judge Bork ignores the relevance of the fact that the U.S. Constitution, including the Bill of Rights, was the legal expression of a revolution.

It is important to have some idea of the nature of this revolution. It was not merely a national revolution, as some have argued, but also a social one, according to Franklin. The American revolutionaries opposed England's attempt to impose an absolutist, neofeudal regime on its colonies, similar to that which Spain imposed on its colonies in Latin America. The understanding of such a context is important if we are to grasp both the spirit in which the Constitution was written and the meaning of certain aspects of the written text. This objective social-historical context provides a key to understanding the ideological presuppositions of the text. In the light of this context, Franklin emphasizes the crucial importance of Jefferson, whose influential correspondence with Madison establishes a direct link between the formulation of the Bill of Rights and the Enlightenment philosophers—Rousseau, Diderot, Voltaire, the Abbé de Mably, Beccaria, etc. Reading the intellectual background narrowly, Bork cites Locke and Madison, but not Rousseau and Jefferson, among others, as important for an understanding of the Constitution.

It is on the basis of such intellectual background that Franklin examines the history of infamy, which illuminates the otherwise obscure text of the Fifth Amendment: "No person shall be held to answer for a capital, or otherwise infamous crime, unless. . . . " It was Franklin's work on the subject of infamy that influenced Justice Douglas in the reference to Franklin cited above. Bork cites this same passage of the Fifth Amendment against Ronald Dworkin's defense of a constitutional basis for outlawing capital punishment, stating that the Fifth Amendment "three times assumes the availability of the death penalty" (1990, 213). In terms of the passage just cited, this may be an example of narrow isolation of a single word in the name of "originalism" that fails to explore the whole text of the amendment and its larger historical meaning. Can we read into the word "capital" a simple reference to the death penalty? But the complete constitutional phrase is "capital, or otherwise infamous crime." The term "capital" is associated directly with the concept of infamy. The essential thrust of the text is not to affirm a right of the State to the death penalty, but to subject the potential tyranny of the State in its most threatening manifestations to the judgments of two juries of citizens. If the Constitution does not outlaw the death penalty absolutely, neither does it merely assume its existence. It takes the power to impose the death penalty away from the State and gives it to the individual's peers. If the Constitution does not ban the death penalty outright, its authentic historical spirit may be incompatible with the way the death penalty can become the weapon of "hanging judges."

The main term in this amendment is not "capital," but "infamous crime," which is the larger genus of crime under consideration. To understand the authentic meaning of this amendment, it is not enough to observe the existence of the word "capital"—whose meaning, as will be explained below, is not as obvious as it may seem. Franklin focused on the meaning of the phrase "infamous crime." Unless we understand that seemingly obscure phrase, we do not understand the full meaning of the text. Furthermore, a larger conception of the relation between the State and its citizens is implicit in this text, a conception of a society in which the last word is placed with the decisions of the informed people.

Hegel and the U.S. constitutional struggle

In their struggle against England's effort to impose a feudal-like colonial regime, the leaders of the American Revolution and founders of the U.S. Constitution were thrust into the general antifeudal struggles of continental Europe, especially of France, where these struggles came into sharpest focus. In this way, the Enlightenment thought of continental Europe came to exert a decisive influence on the constitutional thought of the intellectual leadership of the American Revolution. To understand the legal significance of that revolutionary period, as it is embodied in the U.S. Constitution, Franklin turns to the thought of Hegel. Summarizing the significance of the French Enlightenment, and in particular its legal theory, Hegel wrote:

> What the philosophers brought forward and maintained was, speaking generally, that men should no longer be in

> the position of laymen, either with regard to religion or to law; so that in religious matters there should not be a hierarchy, a limited and selected number of priests, and in the same way that there should not be in legal matters an exclusive caste and society (not even a class of professional lawyers), in whom should reside, and to whom should be restricted, the knowledge of what is eternal, divine, true, and right, and by whom other men should be commanded and directed; but that human reason should have the right of giving its assent and its opinion. (Hegel 1974, 379, 397–98)

That the law should not be the obscure and sacrosanct possession of an elite body of lawyers, that it should be accessible and understandable to ordinary educated persons, that, furthermore, it should respect their own "liberty of conviction" and even tend to reflect it—this great demand of the French Enlightenment, which Hegel called "subjective freedom," was embodied not only in the creation of the French Civil Code, but in the U.S. Constitution as well. Hegel continued the spirit of eighteenth-century revolutionary Enlightenment, especially French Enlightenment, in early nineteenth-century Germany, during the period which led to the German bourgeois revolution of 1848. Since the authentic historical meaning of the U.S. Constitution presupposes this European revolutionary tradition, Hegel's understanding of that tradition, reflecting his own participation in it, should be added to a list of philosophies with historically authentic constitutional relevance.

The notion of an "American Enlightenment," with a close connection to the French Enlightenment, has profound practical political relevance for understanding the U.S. Constitution. The idea that "strict construction" or the original meaning of the Constitution does not justify the constitutional revisions of the Warren Court, Franklin argues, stems from constitutional conceptions in which intentions are read not strictly, but narrowly or abstractly, undialectically and unhistorically, out of context and in separation from the social-historical and ideological presuppositions implicit in them. In this sense, Franklin would reject Bork's abstract "originalism" for the very reason that Bork rejects its supposed alternative—for giving great play to subjectivist readings.

The rejection of so-called originalism does not require an acceptance of what Ronald Dworkin calls "the moral reading of the Constitution" (1996a). Dworkin argues that many abstract constitutional clauses embody certain general moral principles whose practical import may be perceived differently today from the way they were perceived at the time of the founders. The post–Civil War Fourteenth Amendment right guaranteeing equal protection of the laws to all citizens was not originally intended to imply a rejection of segregated schools, Dworkin argues. But because it was the general principle, and not the specific applications of it, that received constitutional expression, it is legitimate for us today, in accord with our current understanding of what the moral principle of legal equality requires, to interpret this clause as condemning school segregation.

While Franklin would agree that the U.S. Constitution embodies general principles, the significance of these principles should not be determined by appealing to unhistorical moral principles intuited independently of their constitutional formulations. Dworkin recognizes that such moral principles can, with some limitations, be interpreted in widely different ways depending on the political orientation of the Court. However, if we grasp the historical and ideological context of the formulations in which general principles are expressed, we will see that they express richer and far more determinate meanings than imagined, and these meanings cannot be legitimately undermined by the intuitions of different political forces interpreting abstract moral principles differently. Central to this historical understanding is the fact that the U.S. Constitution is really three constitutions, each one summing up a different phase of U.S. revolutionary history.

The First Constitution

Of fundamental importance for an authentic understanding of the U.S. Constitution is therefore the revolutionary context that gave rise to the American prolongation of the French Enlightenment. The implications of this context for an understanding of the legal method of the Constitution are suggested by Hegel in the passage cited previously, where he condemns the elitism of feudal legal practice. The English common law method of legal decision making, involving reference to what may be a mass of contradictory opinions found in legal precedent, turns the law over to an "exclusive caste" of lawyers, in the words of Hegel, and thereby deprives the rational citizen of the right to his or her educated opinion. In Roman law, and in the French civil law derived from it, judges must base their decisions on a rationally codified body of law, which in the case of the French Civil Code, derives its authority from the revolutionary convention, and possible subsequent legislation, that produced it.

Similarly, the U.S. Constitution is a written code of law, a succinct, rationally organized document describing the powers of the branches of government, and certain basic rights of the citizens. It therefore expresses a repudiation of the English feudalistic, common law form of judicial interpretation, connected with the notion of an "unwritten constitution." It anticipated the French Civil Code by several years, while reflecting the same body of legal thought that demanded a form of law that is rationally structured and so comprehensible to an educated public. The young student of Hegel Karl Marx once expressed this idea in saying that "A statute-book is a people's bible of freedom" (1975b, 162). However, outside of Louisiana and Quebec, private law in North America continues to follow the English method, and legal education, including education in constitutional law, reflects this fact. As a result, U.S. judiciary and legal scholarship both generally lack the theoretical means for understanding the legal method appropriate to a rationally formulated constitution.

The text of the constitutional document that emerged from the deliberations of 1787 in Philadelphia was supposed to create harmonious checks and balances between three independent powers of government. Because this was a chief idea of Montesquieu, Franklin calls this text the "Montesquieuan Constitution." For the general significance of this Montesquieuan Constitution, Franklin turns again to the analysis of Hegel, who argued that what is supposed to be a harmony of mutual checks and balances turns out in reality to be a struggle between the separated and independent powers.

In fact the structure of the Montesquieuan Constitution reflects underlying social tensions—including the weighty presence of the broader masses of the people which was not without determining influence on even the most conservative elements of the convention, such as Alexander Hamilton. The text that emerged from the revolutionary context, significantly influenced by the external pressure of an armed citizenry that had just won its independence, was rather a compromise in which no branch is dominant, and rival social forces have the possibility of gaining influence in the different branches of government. The outcome of this rivalry is often a secretive, and sometimes a terroristic, struggle for hegemony. The impeachment proceedings against President Nixon revealed the extent to which one branch of government, reflecting particular social forces, would go to remove its "enemies" in the other parts of government.[3] Franklin also calls this "Montesquieuan Constitution" the "Ambiguous Constitution," because it does not establish a definite center of governmental power. The ambiguity, however, is resolved during the further course of U.S. constitutional history.

The Second Constitution

If the Constitution must be situated in history, it also has its own history. The Ambiguous, or Montesquieuan, Constitution was only the "First Constitution," quickly succeeded by a "Second Constitution"—the first ten amendments or Bill of Rights. Without the addition of the Bill of Rights, the Constitution would not have been adopted in the states' ratifying conventions. Appealing to deep democratic sentiment and hostility to any reestablishment of a North American dictatorship after the English tyranny was defeated in battle, the Second Constitution implies recognition of a new power of government, a fourth power, which ought to have ultimate hegemony—the power of educated, enlightened, unalienated public opinion.

Franklin cites a letter from Jefferson, who evokes Rousseau while underscoring this legal-philosophical realignment of the American Enlightenment: "I deride with you the ordinary doctrine, that we brought with us from England the *common law rights*. This narrow notion was a favorite in the first moment of rallying to our rights against Great Britain. But it was that of men who felt their rights before they had thought of their explanation. The truth is, that we brought with us the *rights of men;* of expatriated men" (1854, 65). Jefferson is here echoing Rousseau, who said, "Man is born free, and everywhere he is in chains" (1983, 17). The Second Constitution resolves the ambiguity of ultimate power characteristic of the First Constitution by establishing what Franklin calls the "Enlightened State," or the "Public Opinion State." This is the State in which, Enlightenment thinkers believed, native or essential human freedom is finally recovered or realized, in which humanity at last finds its true homeland.

The effective force of this Second Constitution was tested in the struggle over the Alien and Sedition Acts at the end of the eighteenth century. By his electoral victory of 1800, Jefferson defeated the threat posed by these acts, which was to intimidate and silence public opinion. In this case it was the popular presidency that stood for the democratic meaning of the Constitution, while the Supreme Court under Justice John Marshall attempted to undermine the Public Opinion State. In *Marbury v. Madison*, Justice John Marshall argued that the Supreme Court had the power of "reviewing" and reversing the decisions of the executive and legislature by declaring them unconstitutional. Franklin, agreeing with Jefferson's own criticisms, regarded *Marbury* as the enunciation of "the Judiciary State"—the State in which the unelected judiciary is the supreme power of government. In a context in which the Supreme Court was attempting to overturn the New Deal legislation of President Roosevelt, Franklin argues in great detail that Marshall's decision was unconstitutional.[4]

Congressional hearings of the 1950s recall the time of terror of the Alien and Sedition Acts of the 1790s. In Franklin's writings of the time, this 1950s Congressional terror was the incentive for exploring the terrorism of the feudal institution of infamy and its repudiation by the Constitution. The antiterrorism of Enlightenment thought sought to subordinate arbitrary State power to the rule of enlightened or educated public opinion. This Enlightenment antiterrorism is reflected in various ways in the U.S. Constitution, which was the first legal expression of the eighteenth-century struggle against arbitrary, despotic government. Crucial concepts embedded in the Constitution are lost, and others are profoundly distorted, without an understanding of the real historical context, including the Enlightenment intellectual presuppositions, the *Encyclopédiste* theoretical formation of the founders of the Constitution.

The foundation or keystone of the Public Opinion State is the First Amendment.[5] Judicial opinion of the 1950s, which upheld the imprisonment of U.S. Communists for educating public opinion, attempted to justify such action by a pragmatic theory of "balancing" First Amendment rights to freedom of press, association, and speech, considered as private rights (or, perhaps, "minority" rights), with the right of the public to safety. But if the Second Constitution establishes a Public Opinion State, such rights are public, not primarily private, rights. They are not merely or not only rights of the individual, as a private person, against government interference in private life, but rights of the individual as a citizen in public life to determine government—rights of active political life that must be safeguarded against the great potential of State power tyrannically to suppress those rights.

The Jeffersonian Public Opinion State gives a democratic solution to a central contradiction of Enlightenment thought. In his famous third thesis on Feuerbach, Marx explains this contradiction as arising from the limitations of the Enlightenment mechanical materialist theory that ideas and character are shaped by environment (1976, 7). If the masses of people appear debased, and incapable of governing themselves, said the Enlightenment *philosophes,* this is not, as feudalist ideology alleged, because of the innate inferiority of the masses, but because of the feudal environment itself, because of imposed ignorance and superstition. Change that environment, alter the processes of education, and the people will be able to govern themselves. But then this problem emerges: if character and ideas are the product of feudal environment, how can antifeudal, democratic ideas possibly arise? If the required response to feudal alienation—what Jefferson called the world of expatriated men—is to provide scientific education for the public, how is it possible for true educators to emerge in an untrue world? The Enlightenment materialist doctrine is inconsistent in supposing that some individuals are not the products of their environment. It forgets, as Marx wrote, that "the educator must himself be educated."

Because of this exception for the educator, the danger arises that society will once again be divided into two parts—the masses of the population who are passive products of the environment, and an elite body of educators who escape this determination and are somehow able to shape the environment. In contradiction to mechanical materialist theory, the philosophers tended to relapse into an idealism so as to rise above the influence of the alienating environment, to grasp the natural freedom of human beings, and, on this basis, to provide the education required for an authentically human society.

In the thought of Alexander Hamilton, who in the Constitutional Convention "experimented" with the idea of a monarchic presidency, an unelected, supposedly enlightened senate was held to be the educative force, able to check the supposed irrationalities of the popular House of Representatives. Or, this failing, Hamilton hoped to rely on an "independent" judiciary. For Jefferson, however—whose position here approaches Marx's own solution—self-determined public opinion must be the final arbiter of government. If the public that is debased by the feudal environment requires education for it to fulfill this essential political role in a democracy, the educators of the public must be free to engage in scientific education without danger of control by the State. Franklin writes that "Jefferson himself held, as against the judiciary State, which regards the people as 'not enlightened enough to exercise their control with a wholesome direction' that a regime of 'the people themselves' whose 'discretion' had been informed 'by education . . . is the true corrective of abuses of constitutional power'" ("Brutus the American Praetor," this volume, 113).

The Second Constitution, which establishes the Public Opinion State, dialectically subordinates the First or Ambiguous Constitution. The struggle between the powers of government that is sanctioned by the Montesquieuan Constitution must be subordinated to the purpose of the Bill of Rights, which is to create the Public Opinion State. But just as there is no mechanical harmony of the powers of government, so there is no mechanical or automatic establishment of the power of educated or scientific public opinion. Such opinion can be alienated or dominated by one or another of the State powers, representing underlying social forces. On the other hand, by upholding the conditions of authentic democratic life expressed in the Second Constitution, one or another of the State powers can become the vehicle of self-determining public opinion.

Constitutionally legitimate activism

The McCarthy period of American history was one in which the legislature, through a congressional committee, sought to thwart the Public Opinion State by silencing its free educators. This was not a denial of the private rights of a minority in order to safeguard the public rights of the majority, as the Court decided in *Dennis v. United States*. It was the suppression by an elite minority, entrenched in one of the governmental powers, of the Public Opinion State of the majority, a suppression that took the form of silencing of the political educators of the public. In reaction to this antidemocratic usurpation of power by the legislature, the Supreme Court, by restoring the authentic historical significance of the Bill of Rights, became a sort of tribune for the people of the Public Opinion State. In this way the struggle between the powers of the State, which is the subject of the First, or Montesquieuan, Constitution, was resolved democratically and in the spirit of the hierarchically superior Second Constitution. The tribunitial activism of the Warren Court was in this way in accord with the historical meaning of the Constitution.

In his defense of New Deal legislation against the Supreme Court, Franklin had previously argued that the First Constitution, contrary to Marshall's argument in *Marbury v. Madison*, does not give the judiciary the power to review legislative or executive decisions. But in his defense of the constitutionally legitimate activism of the Warren Court, Franklin argues that the Second Constitution does contain a foundation for judicial review—through the Ninth Amendment. This connection of thought establishes the Supreme Court as a tribune of enlightened public opinion. This tribunitial function of the Supreme Court does not justify unconstitutional invention of new rights, let alone of private rights against the rights of the public. But it does justify the recovery of the authentic meaning of the Constitution in new situations, through reasoning by analogy, in accord with civil law methodology.

This line of thought is further strengthened by the Fifth Amendment, which was narrowly invoked during the McCarthy hearings mainly in connection with the clause that guarantees that individuals not be forced to incriminate themselves. Franklin's work explores the rich significancc of the entire constitutional text, which also requires that persons accused of a "capital, or otherwise infamous crime" must be indicted by a grand jury and convicted by jury trial. In connection with the notion of infamy, Franklin, citing Buckland, writes that infamed persons "appear in Justinian's law as a sharply defined group who, by reason of wrongful or unseemly conduct, are subjected to serious disabilities. Shameful trades, condemnation in certain actions and criminal charges, dismissal in disgracc from the army, and misconduct in family relations are the chief cases" ("Infamy and Constitutional Liberties," this volume, 116–17).

The concept of infamy is closely connected to that of capital crimes, which are of different types. In the Roman law context—which emerges in the United States. because of its revolutionary orientation to continental legal and philosophical sources—deprivation of citizenship is *capitis deminutio media* (literally, medium diminution of one's head). President Eisenhower once unconstitutionally proposed such infaming punishment through loss of citizenship as a means of silencing politically active educators. An action deserving of such punishment would be a "capital" crime. "When enslavement or deprivation of freedom is added to such loss of citizenship," Franklin wrote, "*capitis deminutio media* becomes *capitis deminutio maxima*, virtually civil death" ("Infamy and Constitutional Liberties," this volume, 136). Consequently "capital" crimes do not necessarily involve loss of life, but do involve loss of social status by the socially infamed.

Jefferson, through correspondence with Madison, was the guiding spirit in the formulation and understanding of the Bill of Rights. But this meaning would have been stillborn without what Jefferson called "the revolution of 1800," the peaceful, electoral revolution that politically vindicated this understanding, establishing the freedoms of the First Amendment as absolute rights of republican self-government. It is only by this means that "opinion" can become enlightened or scientific opinion, which gives the people the ability to govern themselves. Without this capacity for free education, the people become vulnerable to control by elite social forces. The government can reestablish tyranny despite or even because of the checks and balances or ambiguity of the First Constitution regarding which branch of government has the power to exercise that tyranny.

Franklin summarizes this meaning:

> The theory of the First Amendment, therefore, is a theory guaranteeing the position of the self-determined political educator, or political party, that of the self-determining political student, or people, and securing the means of access by the consciousness of the self-determining political student. It is not surprising that the First Amendment consecrates the theory of the self-determined educator instead of a theory by which society is divided into two parts, the dominant educator and the dominated, alienated, or fettered people, who are to be educated. ("Infamy and Constitutional Liberties," this volume, 122)

Infamy: The Sartrean stare

The First Amendment is strengthened by its connection to the Fifth Amendment. By infaming individuals as Communists, Senator Joseph McCarthy used the power of the State to brand or infame and thereby to chill or silence the contemporary Enlightenment educator. But the historical meaning of the Fifth Amendment, linked dialectically to the First Amendment, is to protect individuals from the State-imposed infamy that was part and parcel of the arsenal of feudal despotism. The language of the Fifth Amendment goes beyond reference to the English jury system to reflect continental European Enlightenment opposition to feudal methods of infamy—methods of branding, stigmatizing, ostracizing, excommunicating, shunning—of turning individuals or entire groups into "objects" by what Franklin, in an article on *Brown v. Board of Education*, calls a "Sartrean stare":

> "Thus Hegel's brilliant intuition," Sartre has said, "is to make me depend on the Other in *my* being. I am, he said, a being for-itself which is for-itself only through another. Therefore the Other penetrates me to the heart. I cannot doubt him without doubting myself since 'self-consciousness is real only in so far as it recognizes its echo (and its reflection) in another.' . . . [I]n my essential being I depend on the essential being of the Other, and instead of holding that my being-for-myself is opposed to my being-for-others, I find that being-for-others appears as a necessary condition for my being-for-myself."
>
> This means that being-for-self is jeopardized if recognition is withheld for the other. If a racist interpositionist declares the Negroes infamous or civilly dead, if he seeks to veer a Negro subject of the Constitution into an object of the Constitution by a Sartrean stare, he correspondingly limits, excludes, separates, or segregates his own being-for-self from the real world of subjectivity, a weird world of his imagination. The struggle to recreate the world of the *Dred Scott Decision* has created the world of William Faulkner. (1958, 191)

Franklin mobilizes the philosophy of Jean-Paul Sartre, with its prominence for the Hegelian conception of being-for-others, on behalf of an authentic interpretation of the Constitution. The Sartrean stare that turns individuals into things, isolating them from the social bonds with others that make them truly human and that enables them to rule themselves politically, is a modern expression of infamy. Franklin's work meticulously unearths the rich history of the problem of infamy that has its own American history, but that achieved sharpest theoretical and legal expression in the thought of the European Enlightenment. Through European influences, the theory of infamy was mastered by such a decisive influence on the Bill of Rights as Thomas Jefferson.

The constitutional significance of infamy was elaborated by Franklin in connection with the unfolding drama of political life in the United States during the fifties, sixties, and seventies. In his defense of the freedom of the educator of public opinion during the height of the McCarthy "witch hunts," the governmental power that reflected most adequately U.S. constitutional democracy was the Supreme Court. Franklin's writings at this time called upon the Court, legal scholars, and progressive lawyers to recover the buried or "narcotized" force of the Constitution. If the texts of the First Constitution relative to the judicial power give the Supreme Court no authority to set itself above the other branches of government, those of the Second Constitution, which include an outline of judicial methodology in the Ninth Amendment, imply, as Jefferson himself suggested, a special role of the Court in upholding civil rights.

The Third Constitution

Brown v. Board of Education, in 1954, was a turning point in judicial activism. This decision was judicial activity not aimed at burying the Constitution by an extraconstitutional theory of balancing self-styled private rights against a presumed public one. Its task was rather to reveal its actual historical meaning after this meaning had long been ignored. Evoking the Fourteenth Amendment to overturn the decision of *Plessy v. Ferguson* (1896), the Court held that segregated educational facilities could not in the nature of things be equal. The Thirteenth, Fourteenth, and Fifteenth Amendments, arising out of the Civil War and the destruction of slavery, establish the "Third Constitution." The blatant contradiction of early U.S. democracy, sanctioning slavery and the infaming of Black Americans, was thereby overcome, and the democratic character of the Constitution was deepened and made more specific.

Franklin evokes dialectical theory in explaining the connection between the three major stages of the Constitution:

> In *Ullman v. United States* Justice Frankfurter, writing for the majority of the Supreme Court in a case concerning the Fifth Amendment, said that "As no constitutional guarantee enjoys preference, so none should suffer subordination or deletion." Hence he demanded an "Appeal . . . to the Constitution—to the whole Constitution, not to a mutilating selection of these parts only which for the moment find

> favor." (*Ullman v. United States*, 350 U.S. 422, 428 [1956]). Of course as the texts of the Constitution reflect each other, all of them should be studied in their relationships. This is fundamental. Nevertheless, what is called the Constitution of the United States is in reality three Constitutions, each of which states in legal formulations the outcome of vital historic changes in American social history. This means that old constitutional texts may be overcome or subordinated by later constitutional texts, unless they strengthen or deepen the force of the new constitutional provisions. (1958, 70)

In stating that "All persons born in or naturalized in the United States . . . are citizens of the United States and of the State wherein they reside," the Fourteenth Amendment declares the primary citizen relation to be national citizenship. It subordinates state citizenship as secondary, derivative, or a mere consequence of residence. The Fourteenth Amendment repeats the language of the Fifth Amendment, while specifically asserting its application to state governments, declaring that no state shall "deprive any person of life, liberty, or property without due process of law." The Fourteenth Amendment thereby rejects previous Southern interpositionist efforts to interpret the Constitution as sanctioning a "states' rights" theory of government. Most famously, it forbids a state to "deny to any person within its jurisdiction the equal protection of the laws." This makes it clear, for example, that the First Amendment, which is directed explicitly to acts of congress, also applies to state governments. A whole era of judicial struggle in which federal governmental power was "interposed" or "nullified" in the name of states' rights, i.e., the rights of Southern slavery, was thereby brought to an end. In the passage cited above, Franklin refers to the neo-interpositionism of the defenders of U.S. racial segregation. Martin Luther King, in his "I Have a Dream" of 28 August 1963, evokes the same language.

> I have a dream that one day, down in Alabama, with its vicious racists, with its governor having his lips dripping with the words of interposition and nullification, that one day, right there in Alabama, little black boys and black

> girls will be able to join hands with little white boys and white girls as sisters and brothers. I have a dream today! (1986, 219)

The meaning of the Third Constitution, and in particular the Fourteenth Amendment, is also rendered more specific by reference back to the Second Constitution, which condemns State-directed infaming of individuals or whole sections of the population, while nevertheless inconsistently continuing to tolerate the mass infamy of slavery. The old constitutional text in this way strengthens or deepens the force of the new constitutional provision. While the First Constitution tolerates the existence of slavery, the Second Constitution implicitly condemns slavery because the slave, without due process of law, including the double protection of two juries, is deprived of life, liberty, and property for what amounts to the "capital, or otherwise infamous" crime of being Black. Through State-sanctioned means, an African American is turned by a Sartrean stare into a thing, an object, a pariah in the eyes of the divided and alienated public opinion of non-Blacks. By sanctioning slavery and racial segregation, the State infames a group of individuals without the rational procedure outlined in the Fifth Amendment in which evidence for committing a legally defined crime must be presented to a jury of peers before the possibility of punishment and accompanying justified infamy. The public opinion that results from such infaming acts of the State is not the free, self-determining public opinion of the Enlightened or Public Opinion State. It is a manipulated or alienated public opinion because it is not based on the assertion of the human freedom of interconnected citizens mutually recognizing one another's freedom.

Does the Fifth Amendment really condemn slavery, given that the framers of this amendment tolerated slavery? Is it spurious interpretation to invoke the Fifth Amendment in this way? Franklin's complex historical conception of the Fifth Amendment makes it clear that its anti-infamy character is not primarily a matter of an abstract or general principle whose relevance to the issue of slavery is read into its meaning according to contemporary moral lights—illegitimately, according to proponents of strict construction or originalism, perhaps legitimately, according to the theory of the moral reading of the Constitution. The abstractness of the Fifth Amendment that enables it to condemn infamy in general while coexisting with slavery in particular is not a license for freedom from the historical meaning of the text through unhistorical moral readings. It is an expression of an objective historical contradiction that required a civil war to be resolved practically and a new stage of constitutional determinations to be resolved constitutionally.

The Civil War amendments, constituting the Third Constitution, bring out more fully and concretely the significance of the Second Constitution, confirming its dialectical subordination of the First Constitution. Strengthened by its clear reference to the Fifth Amendment, the Fourteenth Amendment implies that separate educational facilities are essentially infamous ones. Segregated schools isolate their inmates from contact with the rest of society, branding those who attend such schools as social outcasts. The child forced by law to attend a special racially designated school is in effect being accused by the State of "a capital or otherwise infamous crime."

The high-water mark left in the Third Constitution remained visible for those who wanted to look for it even after the tide of the democratic movement that produced it had receded. Reactionary forces were able to blunt and overcome the full force of the antiracist Civil War amendments. If the continuation of slavery after the Second Constitution reflects a kind of open contradiction in American life, the spurious doctrine of *Plessy v. Ferguson* that racial apartheid preserves the meaning of the Fourteenth and its attendant amendments constitutes the sort of self-deception that Sartre would call bad faith. The legitimate thrust of the Third Constitution became "narcotized" by racist social forces and by their expression in constitutional interpretations until this authentic meaning was recovered by the Warren Court in *Brown v. Board of Education* in 1954. The Warren Court, made up of Roosevelt appointees, was the delayed judicial expression of the democratic upsurge of the 1930s and 1940s.

The Ninth Amendment and constitutional methodology

A constitutional solution to the problem of applying the Constitution to novel or historically unforeseen circumstances, Franklin argues, is found in the Ninth Amendment. This states simply, "The enumeration in the Constitution of certain rights shall not be construed to deny or disparage others retained by the people." Franklin argues that this is a text of juridical method, not "a text consecrating natural rights without content, natural law with a variable content," as various constitutional theorists have argued (1958, 177).

Rather than fall back on common law methods of legal interpretation, Franklin argues for the constitutional requirement of referring to Romanist legal methodology. He explains that legal codes contain clauses that vary in degree of abstractness, from highly particularistic ones, such as the stipulation that the voting age be twenty-one years, to such general requirements as due process. What Franklin called "Stoic universals," and Dworkin calls general moral concepts, allow for application of the law to novel circumstances. Franklin explains:

> But as the Ninth Amendment is formulated under *Encyclopédiste* domination, it reflects the hostility of the Enlightenment toward the legal method of historically reprobated English feudal common law, which is antagonistic to formulated law, which upholds *stare decisis* in its various manifestations, which examines codified law narrowly and suspiciously, and which turns aside from and ignores the written text when the latter spends its immediate force. However, in place of such legal method of the feudal English common law, it is the mission of the Ninth Amendment to require and to justify the legal method of the Enlightenment, which here seized the legal method of Roman law. Roman law, as it had its outcome in the great Civil Codes of the eighteenth century, may employ formulated law by analogy to control the determination of historically novel problems, thus acknowledging historical development without justifying a new arbitrariness in such development.
>
> The great role of the Ninth Amendment thus becomes clearer. It requires the consistent judicial development of the first eight amendments to control novel situations which are not immediately subject to the Second Constitution. It recognized the general constitutional force of the

> first eight amendments, and makes them sources of constitutional law. It breaks any particularism in the first eight amendments. Thus, it excludes a counter-constitution or a paraconstitution. (1958, 177)

How does this Enlightenment understanding of the Ninth Amendment prevent the emergence of "natural rights without content, natural law with a variable content"? To answer this question it is necessary to be clear about the larger framework in which such abstract legal notions are embedded. This is not English common law, where positive legal provisions were often counterbalanced by appeal to an extralegal "equity," including English Chancery courts of equity evolving out of the prerogatives of the monarch. The larger framework, becoming operative because of the revolutionary circumstances out of which the U.S. Constitution was born, is the Romanist civil law as this was absorbed by French and American revolutionaries intent on creating a new kind of society. Franklin explains the significance of these circumstances:

> In the period before the French Revolution English equity, because of its negating character, was praised in France; for it essentially represented a way of overcoming the existing state of affairs in that country, and thus promised some relief from a miserable situation. The basis for the authority of equity was found, so far as France was concerned, in the good will of the prince and in natural law.
>
> In passing on to the conception of equity as it existed in France after the French Revolution destroyed feudal France, it might be said that this was a period in which those who before the Revolution had so much admired *l'adoucissement équitable* [the equitable softening or mitigation] of English equity and who had invited their prince to receive this negating equity of England, were themselves now transforming French society and preparing the *Code civil* that was to consecrate that transformation in legal terms. Nevertheless the English chancery, which they had once regarded as "most worthy of imitation by civilized nations," no longer interested these representatives

> of civilized France. Their task now was not that of negation, but that of protecting and deepening and furthering what had been newly established. Their interest in a negating equity ceased and passed over to an interest in an affirming equity. While equity for them is still based on natural law, the same natural law that had been perpetual and invariable, their basic interest is now not in destroying the new state of affairs by an appeal to heaven, but in protecting their heaven on earth. The new new equity is taken to be exactly this, and its is the precise opposite of what it had been. ("Brutus the American Praetor," this volume, 86–87)

In view of this circumstance, and in accord with the Romanist method of extending abstract Stoic universals to new circumstances, the Ninth Amendment declares that the formulations of the first eight amendments, narrowly understood, do not exhaust the meaning of popular rights necessary for political self-determination. But this is not to say that the people retain extraconstitutional moral rights that can be evoked against the Constitution. Rather, the rights of the first eight amendments, regarded as an approximate but not complete formulation of what is required for an Enlightened State, should be developed by analogy to meet new, unforeseen circumstances. It is this complex "conception," which rests on the meaning of the texts in their evolving entirety—with three, at least, major moments—that provides the touchstone for analogical reasoning to new circumstances.

A Fourth Constitution?

Arguing that his theory of the moral interpretation of the Constitution does not legitimize all possible moral readings of abstract formulations or principles, Ronald Dworkin holds that prior judicial practice, and perhaps reference to other elements of the Constitution, rule out, for example, an interpretation of the equal protection clause of the Fourteenth Amendment as requiring equality of wealth. From Franklin's perspective, however, past judicial practice, as in the famous case of *Plessy v. Ferguson*, can be reversed if it is found to be opposed to an authentic reading of the Constitution. And if, instead of focusing on isolated constitutional phrases, we take the rich conception of the Public Opinion State as the background conception for evaluating cases, a constitutional case might be made for requiring, if not equality of wealth, at least the guarantee of minimal economic conditions for participating in active political life. Unprecedented levels of economic inequality, the near monopolization of the means of communication, the danger of social ostracism or infamy of long-term unemployment, the subjugation of the electoral process to moneyed elites—conditions that might have appalled the framers of the Constitution—cripple the capacity of the people to rule themselves. In such circumstances should not the Court, together with jurists concerned with the real meaning of democracy, be obligated to fight for the authentic, historically required meaning of the Constitution and to express that meaning in legal decisions?

Perhaps for this purpose a new chapter in constitutional history would have to be written and a Fourth Constitution (an amendment or set of amendments) formulated in connection with political activism and unfolding social history. But just as the Third Constitution brought forward and concretized the meaning of the Second, such new constitutional development would confirm and concretize the radical implications of the present Constitution.

Marx wrote that ideas are material forces once they have become part of the thinking process of large masses of people, of nations, social classes, and influential social strata (1975a, 182). Mitchell Franklin was always confident that his own writings were also, in the long run, real forces sent out into the fray, to do battle with the opposing side. It would be wrong, however, to picture the contest in starkly unequal terms. Like Hegel and Marx, Franklin was an emphatic opponent of the separation in Kant's ethical theory (although not in his theory of history) of ideals from the real world. If an idea is worth expounding, it must already have some form of existence, some reality independent of the mind of the individual thinker. David must have help if he is to slay Goliath.

Franklin saw such an allied theoretical force in the U.S. Constitution. As Chronos devours his own children, the U.S. Constitution is the product of a time that leads, through internal evolution, to its revolutionary transformation. The ideas that watched over the birth of bourgeois society, and that express its heroic, world-historic achievements, turn against it in judgment in its period of decline. They do so, that is, if their real meaning is recognized, if the barriers to that recognition are removed, if a standpoint is established that gives access once more to the "narcotized" impulses of U.S. revolutionary democracy. Franklin, who always sought to etch his thought sharply in memorable expression, elaborated his own category of the "explosive possibility" in connection with a document which many today think, for opposite reasons, should be entombed.

Philosophy Department
SUNY at Buffalo

This introductory article is a revised and significantly shortened version of my article, "Originalism, Moralism and the Public Opinion State of Mitchell Franklin," published in the *Transactions of the Charles S. Peirce Society*, vol. 33, no. 2 (spring 1997): 446–87.

NOTES

1. For contending and detailed discussions of this topic, see Fraser 1986–87 and di Filippo 1986–87. The article by di Filippo contains an extensive bibliography of Franklin's writings.

2. Although Franklin cannot be called, in any theoretically meaningful way, a Stalinist, David Fraser is certainly correct in writing that "the Bolshevik Revolution was the central event of his life" (1986–87, 44). In his lectures and in writing (e.g., "Lenin as Historian," unpublished manuscript), Franklin always regarded Lenin as the philosophical heir of both Hegel and Marx.

3. See Franklin's articles on impeachment, 1973 and 1974.

4. See *The Judiciary State I* and *The Judiciary State II* in this volume. See also Franklin 1938, 357.

5. Franklin (1958) cites Justice Black in his dissenting opinion in *Dennis v. United States* (1951): "I have always believed that the First Amendment is the keystone of our Government, that the freedoms it guarantees provided the best insurance against destruction of all freedoms" (341 U.S. 494, 579, 580).

REFERENCE LIST

Bassham, Gregory. 1992. *Original intennt and the Constitution:* A Philosophical study. Lanham, Maryland: Rowman and Littlefield.

Bork, Robert. 1990. *The tempting of America: The political seduction of the law.* New York: Free Press.

D'Amico, Robert. 1986–87. Essays in memory of Mitchell Franklin. *Telos*, no.70 (winter): 6–10.
Delfini, Alex, and Paul Piccone. 1986–87. Our Mitchell Franklin. *Telos*, no. 70 (winter): 53–57.
di Filippo, Terry. 1986–87. Mitchell Franklin and Roman Law. *Telos*, no. 70 (winter): 11–25.
Dworkin, Ronald. 1978. *Taking rights seriously.* Cambridge, Mass.: Harvard Univ. Press.
——. 1996a. The curse of American politics. *New York Review of Books* 43, no. 1 (October): 19–24.
——. 1996b. The moral reading of the Constitution. *New York Review of Books* 43, no. 5 (21 March): 46–50.
Franklin, Mitchell. 1938. The constitutional struggle. *National Lawyers Guild Quarterly* 1:357–62.
——. 1940a. Brutus the American praetor. *Tulane Law Review* 15:16–50.
——. 1940b. The Judiciary State I. *National Lawyers Guild Quarterly* 2:244–61.
——. 1940c. The Judiciary State II. *National Lawyers Guild Quarterly* 3:27–41.
——. 1942. War power of the President: An historical justification of Mr. Roosevelt's message of September 7, 1942. *Tulane Law Review* 17:217–55.
——. 1952–53. The Kantian foundations of the historical school of law of Savigny. *Revista juridica de la Universidad de Puerto Rico* 22:64–89.
——. 1954. Infamy and constitutional civil liberties. *Lawyers Guild Review* 14:1–10.
——. 1955a. The *Encyclopédiste* origin and meaning of the Fifth Amendment. *Lawyers Guild Review* 15:41–62.
——. 1955b. Monadic legal theory and the perspectives for world law. *Philosophical and Phenomenological Research* 16:201-13.
——. 1956. The unconstitutionality of interposition. *Lawyers Guild Review* 16:45–60.
——. 1957. Laws, morals and social life. *Tulane Law Review* 31:465–78.
——. 1958. The relation of the Fifth, Ninth and Fourteenth Amendments to the Third Constitution. *Howard Law Journal* 4:170–92.
——. 1966. The Ninth Amendment as civil law method and its implications for republican form of government: Griswold v. Connecticut; South Carolina v. Katzenbach. *Tulane Law Review* 40:487–521.
——. 1973. Romanist infamy and the American constitutional conception of impeachment. *Buffalo Law Review* 23:313–41.
——. 1974. Further considerations relating to Romanist infamy and the American constitutional conception of impeachment. *Buffalo Law Review* 24:29–76.
——. 1975. Contribution to an explication of the activity of the Warren majority of the Supreme Court. *Buffalo Law Review* 24:287–543.
Fraser, David. 1986–87. Born in the U.S.A.: The civil law theory of Mitchell Franklin. *Telos*, no. 70 (winter): 41–52.

Grabiner, Eugene. 1980. "The *Bakke* decision: Its unconstitutionality and the intensification of white supremacy in higher education. *Research in Political Economy* 3:27–81.
——. 1983. Judicial subjectivism and judicial equivocation. *Journal of Curriculum Theorizing* 5, no. 3:55–73.
Grabiner, Eugene, and Virginia Grabiner. 1982. "Where are your papers?" and "Operation Zebra" and constitutional civil liberties. *Journal of Black Studies* 12, no. 3:333–50.
——. 1985. The self-determined educator and the expansion of the "labor-education thesis." *Journal of Curriculum Theorizing* 7, no. 1:39–61.
Hegel, Georg W. F. 1974. *Hegel's lectures on the history of philosophy.* Translated by E. S. Haldane and Frances H. Simson. New York: Humanities Press.
Jefferson, Thomas. 1854. *The Writings of Jefferson.* Washington's ed., VI.
——. 1896. *The Writings of Jefferson.* Ford's ed., VII.
King, Martin Luther Jr. 1986. *A testament of hope: The essential writings of Martin Luther King, Jr.* Edited by James Melvin Washington. San Francisco: Harper and Row.
Lawler, James. 1987. Freedom and the U.S. Constitution: Aspects of the Marxist legal theory of Mitchell Franklin. *National Lawyers Guild Practitioner* 44, no. 4 (fall): 111–23.
——. 1997. Originalism, moralism and the Public Opinion State of Mitchell Franklin. *Transactions of the Charles S. Peirce Society* 33, no. 2:446–87.
Marx, Karl. 1975a. Contribution to the critique of Hegel's philosophy of law: Introduction. In vol. 3 of *Karl Marx, Frederick Engels: Collected Works*, 175–87. Moscow: Progress Publishers.
——. 1975b. Debates on freedom of the press. In vol. 1 of *Karl Marx, Frederick Engels: Collected Works*, 132–81. Moscow: Progress Publishers.
——. 1976. Theses on Feuerbach. In vol. 5 of *Karl Marx, Frederick Engels: Collected Works*, 3–9. Moscow: Progress Publishers.
Moran, Philip. 1985. The Fifth Amendment's self-protection against self-infamy. *National Lawyers Guild Practitioner* 42, no. 3 (summer): 90–94.
——. 1986–87. Mitchell Franklin and the United States Constitution. *Telos*, no. 70 (winter): 26–40.
Rousseau, Jean-Jacques. 1983. *On the social contract. Discourse on the origin of inequality; Discourse on political economy.* Indianapolis: Hackett Publishing Company.

The Judiciary State I
(1940)

Marbury versus Madison . . . *so disconcerting to historians and observers trained in the principles of Roman Law.*

—Thomas Jefferson, quoted in *Thomas Jefferson: The Apostle of Americanism* by Gilbert Chinard

1

When the Supreme Court declared the unconstitutionality of democratic legislation during the first administration of Mr. Roosevelt it provoked the present constitutional crisis. The President's proposal to increase the number of justices, with the view of overcoming the crisis, was defeated; but not before the Supreme Court had abandoned the claim of judicial control of congressional legislation on the basis of the rule of law under the pressure of the proposal. Today there is an attempt to reestablish in the field of administration the principle of judicial supremacy which the Supreme Court abandoned in the field of legislation.[1] In effect, the claim to judicial control over all administration is even broader than the claim to control over all legislation; for since the rapid and comprehensive transformation of society has become a necessity for the continuance of our democracy, government must increasingly act through the administrative on which broad grants of political power are conferred.

Because of the intensity of the struggle against democratic administration on behalf of an expanded principle of government by judiciary, it has also become a necessity to discuss the validity of the conceptions from which the judiciary state (a state in which the judiciary is supreme) is believed to derive. It is not intended to present a tedious restatement of well-known and perhaps one-sided points of view, nor to discuss the vacillations of particular individuals; but rather to bring forward, as much as possible, neglected materials and opinions, so that the many-sidedness of the historical and jurisprudential background of the issue may be illuminated for those who are familiar only with the commonly accepted views, and who may be expected to reconsider them in the light of what is here presented.

Moreover, at the present time there is some basis for believing that the judiciary state, unless it is justified by genuine interpretation of the Constitution, might be questioned even within the Supreme Court itself. In a recent dissent, Mr. Justice Black, speaking of the Fourteenth Amendment, said, "A constitutional interpretation that is wrong should not stand."[2] A few weeks later the majority of the court, in the *Tompkins* case,[3] overthrew as unconstitutional the case of *Swift v. Tyson*[4] after it had held sway for nearly a century. Thus the Supreme Court itself has undermined the conception of the judiciary state as something resting on long usage or acquisitive prescription. The chief bulwark of the judiciary state, *Marbury v. Madison,*[5] today cannot be defended on the ground of practice alone.

There are three assumptions underlying the constitutional doctrines of the judiciary state that have to be kept separate in considering its theory, although these three as a unity constitute the judiciary state: (1) The separation of powers. (2) The supremacy of the judiciary. (3) The precept that the judiciary power should be exercised according to the juridical method of the common law. The last conception is usually derived from the second conception and affects it, but actually, as Mr. Pound has said, the idea of the supremacy of law and the conception of common law juridical method, based on the use of precedents, are different, and constitute two of the "distinctive institutions of the Anglo-American legal system."[6] The constitutional validity of these three conceptions is the concern of this paper.

Mr. Justice Holmes at one time virtually summed up dominant constitutional opinion as to the judiciary state by saying: ". . . research has shown and practice has established the futility of the charge that it was a usurpation when this Court undertook to declare an Act of Congress unconstitutional,"[7] although he himself was not disturbed at the thought of losing that power with regard to the legislation of Congress.[8] Moreover, Mr. Justice Holmes seems to have accepted the conception that constitutional law must include the common law doctrine of precedent. "If the Fourteenth Amendment were now before us for the first time," he once wrote, "I should think that it ought to be construed more narrowly than it has been construed in the past."[9]

Nevertheless there is the duty of actually referring to the text of the Constitution that yields these powers, for it is never to be conceded that there are invisible or concealed paragraphs in an American constitution, nor that there obtains, at least since the Tompkins case, a constitution based on practice or usucaption. It is proper to repeat what Paine once said of the English constitution: "If there were a constitution, it certainly could be referred to; and the debate on any constitutional point, would terminate by producing the constitution."[10]

2

The very essence of the conception of the American judiciary state is founded on the separation of powers under judicial hegemony; that is, the democratic state is split asunder in order that it may then be reunited in a way, through the rule of law, as the judiciary state. It is more than a century since Hegel foresaw something such as this as the necessary outcome of Montesquieu-ism. There would be a restless state, Hegel said, if the parts of it, because of their independence, did not constitute a unity, although it is true, he added, that the state had to be a unity of differences.

The state, he said, is an "organism" for "the development of the idea into its differences."[11] Indeed,

> the principle of the separation of functions contains the essential element of difference, that is to say, of real rationality. But as apprehended by the abstract understanding it is false when it leads to the view that these several functions are absolutely independent, and it is one-sided when it considers the relation of these functions to one another as negative and mutually limiting. In such a view each function in hostility to or fear of the others acts toward them as toward an evil. Each resolves to oppose the others, effecting by this opposition of forces a general balance, it may be, but not a living unity.[12]

Consequently "the idea that the functions of government should be independent contains the fundamental error that they should check one another. But this independence is apt to usurp the unity of the state, and unity is above all things to be desired."[13] If the different aspects were to be made independent, "the unity produced by the constitution is no longer established."[14] Therefore, it is improper, Hegel said, "To take the negative as the point of departure, and set up as primary the willing of evil and consequent mistrust, and then on this supposition cunningly to devise breakwaters, which in turn require other breakwaters to check their activity. . . ."[15]

Nevertheless, if the powers of state are actually made independent, Hegel says, "The state is, then, forthwith overthrown. . . . Or, in so far as the state is essentially self-contained, the struggle of one function to bring the other into subjection effects somehow or other a closer unity, and thus preserves only what is in the state essential and fundamental."[16] Indeed, he says, "It is clear as light that two independent things are not able to constitute a unity, but must rather introduce strife. As a result, either the whole world would be cast into disorder, or the unity would be restored by force. . . ."[17]

Thus in the American judiciary state it is conceived that there is a collection of supposedly isolated and disunited functions, nevertheless forced through the supremacy of law into an adequate working unity under the leadership of the undemocratic judiciary. The American judiciary state, however, remains a contradiction, for it makes disunity obligatory in order to establish its kind of obligatory unity. But what is the constitutional justification for the conception of the undemocratic judiciary state, if, as Justice Holmes seems to admit, it cannot actually be found in the text of the Constitution?

So far as the validity of the conception of separation of powers is concerned, Holdsworth is prepared to say that "The founders of the American constitution" under the influence of Montesquieu "were so convinced that liberty could only be secured by the separation of the legislative, executive and judicial departments of government, that they made it a fundamental principle of their constitution. . . ."[18] It is indeed true that Montesquieu was taken in *The Federalist* as the formulator of the "invaluable precept in the science of politics" that the "preservation of liberty requires that the three great departments of power should be separate and distinct."[19] However, it cannot be said, in general, that Montesquieu was accepted in America without reserve. Once Jefferson himself said of Montesquieu as a thinker that " I am glad to hear of everything which reduces that author to his just level,"[20] and on another occasion he said that "I had, with the world, deemed Montesquieu's work of much merit; but saw in it, with every thinking man, so much of paradox, of false principle and misapplied fact, as to render its value equivocal on the whole."[21]

Actually, some members of the Constitutional Convention, when they were embarrassed by the doctrine of separation of powers, distorted the orthodox conception. For instance, in an effort to consecrate judicial supremacy, Gouverneur Morris once said that "He could not agree that the Judiciary which was part of the Executive, should be bound to say that a direct violation of the Constitution was law."[22] When Wilson made his proposal that the judiciary should share in the "revisionary power" with the executive, Madison, supporting him, said that he "could not discover in the proposed association . . . any violation of the maxim which requires the great departments of power to be kept separate and distinct. On the contrary he thought it an auxiliary precaution in favor of the maxim."[23]

Indeed, the Constitution of the United States itself, as Livingston once pointed out, only has "strongly marked"[24] the separation of powers. In truth there is no explicit formulation of the conception in it, although this was done in some state constitutions, such as Massachusetts, where, to use Morison's word, it was "imposed"[25] on the state convention on the ground that the separation of powers would overcome "want of energy"[26] in government.

It is not absurd to believe that a text in the Constitution of the United States providing for an explicit conception of separation of powers would have been opposed by the American people. The Convention never lost sight of its task—as some have forgotten since—of preparing a Constitution that could be supported in the different states. The delegates were conscious of the need of rallying about the new Constitution the broadest possible following. It is not surprising, then, that Madison once said

> Another error has been in ascribing to the intention of the Convention . . . an undue ascendency in expounding it. Apart from the difficulty of verifying that intention it is clear, that if the meaning of the Constitution is to be sought out of itself, it is not in the proceedings of the Body that proposed it, but in those of the State Conventions which gave it all the validity and authority it possesses.[27]

Furthermore, it is incorrect to believe that the Convention was composed of completely intransigent delegates, planning a reaction against the revolution. Actually, democratic interests were represented, and indeed, the claims of democratic Americans were in the consciousness of even the reactionary delegates. Once Wilson proposed to join the judiciary with the executive in "revising" the laws and King expressed the view that the judges would "expound" the laws when they came before them. But the ancient Franklin, "well known to be the greatest phylosopher of the present age . . . the very heavens obey him,"[28] thought "it would be improper to put it in the power of any Man to negative a Law passed by the Legislature because it would give him the controul of the Legislature."[29]

It was consistent with this point of view for Franklin, representing the interest of the people, to urge the necessity for American unity on the basis of a democratic constitution. In one discussion

> He observed that in time of war a country owed much to the lower class of citizens. Our late war was an instance of what they could suffer and perform. If denied the right of suffrage it would debase their spirit and detach them from the interest of the country.[30]

On another occasion

> Doctr Franklin expressed his dislike of every thing that tended to debase the spirit of the common people. . . . This Constitution will be much read and attended to in Europe, and if it should betray a great partiality for the rich—will not only hurt us in the esteem of the most liberal and enlightened men there, but discourage the common people from removing to this Country.[31]

Once Gorham said:

> The elections in Phila., N. York & Boston where the Merchants, & Mechanics vote are at least as good as those made by freeholders only. . . . The people have been long accustomed to this right in various parts of America, and will never allow it to be abridged. We must consult their rooted prejudices if we expect their concurrence in our propositions.[32]

At the close of the Convention, Gerry declared

> . . . his fears that a Civil war may result from the present crisis of the U. S.—In Massachusetts, particularly, he saw the dangers of this calamitous event.—In that State there are two parties, one devoted to Democracy, the worst he thought of all

> political evils, the other as violent in the opposite extreme. From the collision of these in opposing and resisting the Constitution, confusion was greatly to be feared.[33]

Moreover, outside the Constitutional Convention, great leaders of popular feeling opposed the conception of separation of powers as anti-democratic. Thus, Samuel Adams

> had so little respect for the British Constitution, as interpreted by Montesquieu, that he was "always inclining to the most democratical forms, and even to a single sovereign assembly." Sam Adams had none of John Adams' fears that the people would abuse their power by making it a "Cloke for Licentiousness."[34]

John Adams also feared Paine who in

> *Common Sense* urged the "crude ignorant Notion" of one sovereign assembly ruled by means of appointed executive and judicial committees—a scheme of government which destroyed the sharp divisions between executive, legislative, and judiciary as well as the checks and balances which John Adams believed essential in a sound constitution.[35]

Once Paine said:

> To say that the Constitution of England is an union of three powers, reciprocally checking each other, is farcical; either the words have no meaning, or they are flat contradictions. To say that the Commons is a check upon the king, presupposes two things. First—That the king is not to be trusted without being looked after. . . . Secondly—That the Commons, by being appointed for that purpose, are either wiser or more worthy of confidence than the crown. But as the same Constitution which gives the Commons a power to check the king by withholding the supplies, gives afterwards the king a power to check the Commons by empowering him to reject their other bills; it again supposes that the king is wiser than those whom it has already supposed to be wiser than him. A mere absurdity![36]

In *The Rights of Man* Paine wrote:

> It has been customary to consider government under three distinct heads: The legislative, the executive, and the judicial. But if we permit our judgment to act unincumbered . . . we

> can perceive no more than two divisions of power, . . . namely, that of legislating, or enacting laws, and that of executing or administering them . . . So far as regards the execution of the laws, that which is called the judicial power, is strictly and properly the executive power.[37]

On another occasion Paine wrote:

> . . . there are but two powers in any government, the power of willing or enacting the laws, and the power of executing them; for what is called the judiciary is a branch of executive power.[38]

In thus treating judiciary power as executive power, Paine was not entirely alone. Dunning suggests that Montesquieu himself on occasion also regarded judiciary power as an aspect of executive power;[39] and so did Gouverneur Morris in the Constitutional Convention.[40] Hegel later certainly did in Germany.[41] It is, however, clear that in any event even Montesquieu was suspicious of paramount judicial power in the realm of private law, which was the only place he knew for it.

> The judiciary power ought not to be given to a standing senate; it should be exercised by persons taken from the body of the people at certain times of the year . . . in order to erect a tribunal that should last only so long as necessity requires. By this method the judicial power, so terrible to mankind, not being annexed, to any particular state or profession, becomes, as it were invisible.[42]

Indeed, even John Adams at one time himself asked: "Is not the constitution of the United States 'complicated with the idea of a balance'? Is there a constitution upon record more complicated with balances than ours?" After reciting eight balances, Adams exclaimed, "And here is a complication and refinement of balances, which, for anything I recollect, is an invention of our own, and peculiar to us. . . ."[43] On another occasion John Adams even went so far as to say that "I think the laws would be better framed and more duly administered, if the executive and judiciary officers were in general members of the legislature."[44] Yet Adams, as the great exponent of separation of powers, was "convinced that three branches of power have an unalterable foundation in nature."[45] He seemed to detest "M. Turgot's idea of a perfect commonwealth" with a single assembly "possessed of all authority, legislative, executive and judicial."[46] Turgot, indeed, seems to have noticed the closeness between his idea and that of the Articles of Confederation, which was the first constitution for the United States. But Adams replied that if "the people of America and their delegates in Congress were of opinion, that a single assembly was every way adequate to the management of all their federal concerns" this was "because congress is not a legislative assembly, nor a representative assembly, but only a diplomatic assembly,"[47] a distinction for which Adams was rebuked by Jefferson who said the sovereignty of Congress was "both legislative and executive" and "could have been judiciary also, had not the confederation required them for certain purposes to appoint a judiciary."[48]

3

Though he left it somewhat early John Adams played a great role in drafting the Constitution of Massachusetts,[49] which is slightly older than the Constitution of the United States. He prepared for it a paragraph, reading: "The judicial department of the State ought to be separate from, and independent of, the legislative and executive powers."[50] This was replaced by the world famous formulation, providing:

> In the government of this commonwealth, the legislative department shall never exercise the executive and judicial powers, or either of them; the executive shall never exercise the legislative and judicial powers, or either of them; the judicial shall never exercise the legislative and executive powers, or either of them; to the end it may be a government of laws and not of men.[51]

However, another paragraph by Adams allowed the executive and the legislature to call on the highest judicial court for "opinions . . . upon important questions of law."[52] This was accepted in substance as part of the constitution of the commonwealth.[53]

The provision in Massachusetts for the advisory opinion was an explicit departure for the conception of separation of powers. But *Marbury v. Madison* itself also violates the separation of powers unless the conception of the supremacy of law is also accepted.[54] For instance, in France where Montesquieuism also has had vogue, there has been no judicial supremacy because the "rule of law," in the sense attributed to Sir Edward Coke, is not recognized.[55] Actually, the great French problem has been that of finding a basis on which the courts could decide ordinary private litigation when the civil code did not provide for a solution. If *Marbury v. Madison* is not the inevitable result of a constitutionally sanctioned separation of powers it cannot stand, unless, as with the advisory opinion, it be explicitly consecrated, or unless the rule of law be accepted as a concomitant doctrine.

In a constitution that did not in precise terms provide for judicial supremacy (as distinguished from separation of powers on the basis of equality among them), a text providing merely for the advisory opinion in constitutional matters is the limit of judicial power over constitutionality. The giving of constitutional advice to the executive and to the legislature by the supreme judicial court could well have been the solution of the problem of constitutional determination entertained by Puritans who were intent on consecrating a separation of co-equal state powers in a democratic regime based on the conception that "all men are born free and equal,"[56] who, as such, organized a political body "by a voluntary association of individuals" in the form of a "social compact"[57] without explicitly recognizing the hegemony of any one social division of labor.

Thus it appears that while separation of power is indispensable to the judiciary state, it does not follow that the idea of separation of powers in itself must lead to the judiciary state. The rule of law notion, added to that of the separation of powers, accomplishes this. John Adams in consecrating the regime set out in the Constitution of Massachusetts thus emerges as one of the great opponents of the idea of judicial supremacy.[58] Indeed, the conception of the American judiciary state seems to dissolve under the blows of John Adams and of the revolutionary Constitution of Massachusetts.

Adams' point of view was powerfully brought forward against the idea of judicial supremacy in the federal Constitutional Convention. This was done through Gorham, a Massachusetts justice who participated in the drafting of both the Massachusetts and Federal Constitutions. In the Federal Convention, on July 21, Wilson, seconded by Madison, renewed the famous proposal that the "Natl Judiciary should be associated with the Executive in the Revisionary power," saying, "It had been said that the Judges, as expositors of the Laws would have an opportunity of defending their constitutional rights. There was weight in this observation; but this power of the judges did not go far enough."[59]

Madison then writes:

> Mr. Ghorum did not see the advantage of employing the Judges in this way. As Judges they are not to be presumed to possess any peculiar knowledge of the mere policy of public measures. Nor can it be necessary as a security for their constitutional rights. The Judges in England have no such additional provision for their defence, yet their jurisdiction is not invaded. He thought it would be best to let the Executive alone be responsible, and at most to authorize him to call on Judges for their opinions.[60]

Moreover, after the defeat of Wilson's plan, Pinckney of South Carolina, in opposing a new suggestion by Madison that proposed statutes should be submitted to the executive and judiciary departments for approval, said, on August 15, that he "opposed the interference of the Judges in Legislative business,"[61] and, on August 20, submitted for adoption to the Committee of Detail, the text of the Massachusetts constitutional provision relative to the advisory opinion.[62] Nothing more seems to be known of this proposal.[63] Nevertheless, consistently with Adams' views, more than a decade before *Marbury v. Madison*, President Washington through his secretary of state, Jefferson, called on the Supreme Court in 1793 to give him legal advice.[64]

The "government of laws and not of men," so much desired in Massachusetts, thus emerges not as the judiciary state, but as the conception that the activity of the three co-equal state powers, each acting within its sphere, which in the case of the supreme judicial court would include that of merely advising the democratic executive or the democratic legislative on matters of constitutionality when it was invited to do so by them, is, in their equality, the "government of laws."

4

What is the historic basis, then, for the conception of the judiciary state, if it is actually negated by such a decisive Constitution as that of Massachusetts, which established a democratic regime based on separation of power without judicial supremacy? There are attempts by American jurists to derive from phases of English history a theory of judicial supremacy according to the method of the English common law. In this connection much is often made of the struggle of Sir Edward Coke during the Seventeenth Century,[65] and in the controversy over the Supreme Court bill it was fashionable for lawyers to disguise themselves, by quotation at any rate, as this great English judge.

It is true that Coke said that ". . . in many cases the common law will control acts of Parliament and sometimes adjudge them to be utterly void,"[66] but, in the words of Plucknett, "the Revolution of 1688 marks the abandonment of the doctrine of *Bonham's Case*,"[67] and very lately Thorne even questions whether Coke intended to assert the supremacy of the courts, saying "Coke's ambitious political theory is found to be not his, but the work of a later generation of judges, commentators, and lawyers."[68] On the other hand, Coke did triumph when he held as against King James I that "The King is subject not to man, but to God and the law."[69] The actual effect, then, of Coke's position, so far as England was concerned, was the supremacy of the democratic Parliament over both the monarchy and the judiciary.

Yet there is, indeed, a certain value in referring to Coke's career,[70] for the United States of the Twentieth Century in some ways is paralleling English history of the Seventeenth Century. On both occasions, great social issues have been fought out in terms of the different powers of state. In this connection, Sir Edward Coke does deserve very close attention. Coke's victory over James I, his defeat at the hands of Parliament, and his defeat in his struggle with the English Chancery,[71] the court that best represented advanced legal demands, just as administration does currently,[72] give an exact picture of the human interests that succeeded in the English revolution. Even the avowed hostility of the Puritans to equity[73] and their preference for the common law counted for little when they actually attained state power. Holdsworth writes that "Parliament and the common lawyers were old allies, so that it was only natural that, when Parliament triumphed, the common lawyers should seek to reopen [the question of equitable jurisdiction]." Yet several efforts to destroy equity finally were defeated during the last half of the Seventeenth Century because "great hardships and injustices would arise, which the law would be powerless to prevent."[74]

Indeed, instead of consecrating the theory attributed to Sir Edward Coke as to the supremacy of the common law, the Constitution of the United States, it seems to me, actually records his great defeats, not only in his struggle against the Chancery, but also in his struggle against the Parliament. This seems to be the genuine meaning of the constitutional text setting out that the "judicial power shall extend to all Cases, in Law and Equity, arising under this constitution."[75] This is a provision rejecting the antagonistic point of view toward equity that, because of Puritan influence in America, denied or limited equity power in some states even into the Nineteenth Century. Equally so, this text would seem to be a formulation sufficiently precise to forbid the validity of the idea of judicial supremacy.

Yet Chief Justice Marshall, in *Marbury v. Madison*, turned this provision into one consecrating judicial supremacy, merely by the casual device of omitting the phrase "in Law and Equity" from his use of it. "The judicial power of the United States," he wrote, "is extended to all cases arising under the constitution. Could it be the intention of those who gave this power, to say that, in using it, the constitution should not be looked into? . . . This is too extravagant to be maintained . . . and if they can open it at all, what part of it are they forbidden to read or to obey?"[76]

Indeed, it is the constitutional phrase "in Law and Equity" that Chief Justice Marshall should have "looked into." In order to unveil the significance of Marshall's disregard of these four words, Pound's description of early American equity is essential:

> Over and above the hostility to all English law there was for historical reasons special hostility to English equity, so that the courts of Pennsylvania did not have equity jurisdiction as such till 1836 nor did the courts of Massachusetts have complete equity jurisdiction till the last quarter of the nineteenth century. Equity has never been popular in America. The Puritan has always opposed it. . . . It involves discretion . . . and that in the Puritan mind means that a magistrate is over us instead of with us. . . ."[77]

Hamilton devoted almost an entire number of *The Federalist* to discussing the varying power of equity in the different states.[78]

Hence it appears that the phrase "in Law and Equity" is a technical, historical phrase, repudiating, so far as our Constitution is concerned, the prevailing colonial backwardness in regard to

English equity power. Indeed, the constitutional text perhaps may even anticipate somewhat Nineteenth Century Anglo-American views as to "fusion" of courts of law and equity. The complete constitutional text under discussion thus seems to mean that the judicial power might comprehend substantially all private law power as it would have been understood in a plenary system of Anglo-American private law. The addition of the technical word "equity" to the judicial power was intended to consecrate the victory of Ellesmere over Coke. As a consequence the phrase "in Law and Equity" as a unity also necessarily discloses that the proper meaning of the word "law" as used in juxtaposing with the technical word "equity" is the likewise technical and narrow significance of the word "law" as understood in Anglo-American private law. This connotes, it seems to me, that the triumph of Locke and Parliament over Coke and the judges is also summed up in the phrase "in Law and Equity."

Moreover, the records of the Constitutional Convention also seem to indicate that Chief Justice Marshall may have misinterpreted the constitutional text on which *Marbury v. Madison* is partly based. This material should be closely considered.

On August 6, 1787, the Committee on Detail reported a proposed version of the Constitution. Section 1 of Article XI provided that "The Judicial Power of the United States shall be vested in one Supreme Court . . ." and Section 3 of Article XI provided that "The jurisdiction of the Supreme Court shall extend to all cases arising under laws passed by the Legislature of the United States. . . ."[79] These texts never would have justified *Marbury v. Madison.*

On August 27, Section 1 of Article XI was "taken up." On this occasion Madison writes that "Docr Johnson suggested that the judicial power ought to extend to equity as well as law—and moved to insert the words 'both in law and equity' after the words 'U.S.' in the 1st line of sect 1."[80] It is evident that the words "both in law and equity" in this proposal were meant in the technical and narrow sense; and hence do not sanction judicial supremacy.

This was the first proposal in a series of consistent and comprehensive basic textual changes, relative to the judicial authority, all of which were made on this one day. In this movement William Samuel Johnson, soon to be the first president of Columbia University, played a role of the utmost historical importance. This delegate of Connecticut was "a character much celebrated for his legal knowledge; he is said to be one of the first classics in America, and certainly possesses a very strong and enlightened understanding."[81] What was more notable concerning him is that, possibly due to his life in England, he had overcome American and even English prejudices against equity and stood out as a firm supporter of English chancery power.

In response to Johnson's suggestion, "Mr. Read," Madison wrote, "objected to vesting these powers in the same Court."[82] Read, a Delaware lawyer and judge whose "legal abilities are said to be very great,"[83] evidently also understood the phrase "both in law and equity" in the traditional narrow sense and opposed Johnson's proposal in the traditionally narrow way. Nevertheless, Johnson's proposal for amendment to Section 1 passed.[84] This meant that Section 1 now read: "The Judicial power of the United States both in law and equity shall be vested in one Supreme Court. . . ." This text would never have justified *Marbury v. Madison*.

In the second phase of this movement, also on August 27, Section 3 was "taken up." Johnson again made the necessary proposal. "Dr. Johnson moved," Madison wrote, "to insert the words 'this Constitution and the' before the word 'laws.'"[85] In other words, Johnson proposed to amend Section 3 to read: "The jurisdiction of the Supreme Court shall extend to all cases arising under this Constitution and the laws passed by the Legislature of the United States. . . ."

This formulation, if read in isolation from the newly amended Section 1, arguably might have been used as a basis for judicial supremacy. It was not surprising therefore that

> Mr. Madison doubted whether it was not going too far to extend the jurisdiction of the Court generally to cases arising Under the Constitution, and whether it ought not to be limited to cases of a Judiciary Nature. The right of expounding the Constitution in cases not of this nature ought not to be given to that Department.[86]

The importance of Madison's observations cannot be overstated, for in suggesting the need for clarification of the effect of Johnson's suggested amendment, Madison signified, it seems to me, that the matter of unassociated judicial supremacy despite some gratuitous statements earlier in the Convention, had never been decided previously by the delegates; and that the matter now indeed had to be settled.

The outcome of this statement by Madison as to Johnson's proposal was an authentic interpretation in which the theory of unassociated judicial supremacy was definitely repudiated. "The motion of Docr Johnson," Madison wrote, "was agreed to *nem: con*: it being generally supposed that the jurisdiction was constructively limited to cases of a Judiciary nature."[87]

Nevertheless, Coxe, a defender of the result in *Marbury v. Madison*, contends that Madison intended to adhere in this "construction" to the conception of judicial supremacy over constitutionality, provided only "that the judicial power of the United States should *not* extend to constitutional cases of an *extrajudicial* nature arising under the new Constitution."[88] This is the meaning he gives to Madison's statements.

Actually, however, Madison's own distinction is not between cases of a "judicial" nature and cases of an "extrajudicial" nature; but between two kinds of "judicial" cases. Madison himself said he was discriminating between "cases of a Judiciary Nature" and "The right of expounding the Constitution in cases not of this nature"; that is, between "cases" under the Constitution raising strictly traditional issues and "cases" under the Constitution raising constitutional issues. This is established by the context, both before and following Madison's "construction."

When Madison restricted power to "cases of a Judiciary Nature" he intended to limit jurisdiction to those cases which were within the "Judicial Power of the United States" as defined in Section 1, which had just been amended by Johnson to extend to cases "both in law and equity." The effect of Madison's authentic restrictive "construction" was that "the jurisdiction of the Supreme Court" in "all cases arising under this Constitution" (Section 3 as amended by Johnson) coincided exactly with "The Judicial Power of the United States both in law and equity" and as "vested in one Supreme Court" (Section 1, as amended by Johnson). In sum, the effect of Madison's "construction" was that Section 3 derived its content from Section 1, which, as has been shown, rejected judicial supremacy because of the use of the technical and historical phrase "both in Law and Equity."

It was not enough, however, that the delegates had "generally supposed" that Madison's "construction" was correct. Of necessity this "construction" had to be reduced to an actual text so that the

American people and the ratifying conventions of the states wouldknow definitively what the "construction" was. As a result of the consequent reformulation of the text to conform to Madison's "construction" it was impossible for Madison to have meant what Coxe attributes to him.[89] On the contrary these concrete changes indicate that Madison then determined to destroy the possibility of a conception of unassociated judicial supremacy.

The delegates almost immediately undertook action, under Madison's leadership, to make the constitutional text consistent with Madison's "construction" as it had been "generally supposed." This was accomplished on that very day by two further changes in the language of Section 3 (following a successful motion by Rutledge to include cases involving treaties within the jurisdiction of the Supreme Court).[90]

The realization of Madison's clarifying "construction" affecting Johnson's proposal was accomplished by transferring the necessary words from Johnson's amended first section to Johnson's amended and "construed" third section. As the first action in pursuance of these plans "Mr. Madison and Mr. Govr. Morris moved to strike out the beginning of the 3d section, 'The jurisdiction of the Supreme Court' & to insert the words 'The Judicial power' which was agreed to *nem: con*:"[91] This meant that Section 3 now read: "The Judicial power shall extend to all cases arising under this Constitution and the laws passed by the Legislature of the United States . . . ." This clearly linked Section 3 to Section 1 and established definitively that when, in his "construction," Madison spoke of "cases of a Judiciary nature,' he referred precisely to "the Judicial power . . . both in Law and Equity" as conceived in Section 1.

In the next and last stage of clarifying and formulating Madison's "construction," also accomplished on that very day, the tie between Section 1 and Section 3 was made even stronger. The *Journal* states that "It was moved and seconded to insert the words 'both in law and equity' before the word 'arising' in the first line, 3rd Section, 11 article . . . which was passed in the affirmative."[92] This meant Section 3 now read that "The Judicial Power shall extend to all cases both in law and equity arising under this constitution. . . ." Madison does not advert to this step,[93] but it clearly completely realizes his "construction." As a result of this change, Madison's "cases of a Judiciary nature" become explicitly "cases in Law and Equity." Hence Section 3 does not consecrate a system of judicial review as Marshall believed, but power for a plenary system of what might be called constitutional private law,as previously worked out by Johnson under Section 1, insofar as the Constitution permitted it.

As a result of these amendments, all of which were made on August 27, Section 1 of Article XI read that "The Judicial Power of the United States both in law and equity shall be vested in one Supreme Court . . ." and Section 3 read that "The Judicial Power shall extend to all cases both in law and equity arising under this Constitution. . . ."[94]

Save for changes in capitalization and punctuation and the elimination of the word "both" these formulations were retained by the Committee on Style,[95] composed, it should be noted, of Johnson, Hamilton, Morris, Madison and King.[96] Nevertheless, because of these borrowings by Section 3 from Section 1, there now was repetitiousness in the text; and the *Journal* appropriately records that subsequently the words "both in law and equity" were removed from Section 1.

This, then, was the way in which the Constitutional Convention seems to have excluded the conception of judicial supremacy from the Constitution. Actually the task confronting the Convention in formulating its conception of judicial power was more complicated than it has been necessary to indicate in this paper. The Convention was involved, when all sides of the problem of judicial power are considered, in a contradiction; and it is impossible to exaggerate the genius of Johnson and of Madison in sublating its difficulties through the formulation of the proper text. The contradiction which the delegates resolved was that of establishing a text relative to comprehensive judicial power sufficiently precise to exclude the conception of judicial supremacy and yet sufficiently indefinite in order that the judiciary would not be obliged to follow a backward system of English law, out of harmony with American democratic needs, as revealed, perhaps, in litigation or through American legal theory and legislation. The supremacy of American property relations was judicially established without the establishment of judicial supremacy.

As Madison said, it was necessary "to obviate pretexts that the separation from G. Britain threw us into a state of nature, and abolished all civil rights and obligations."[97] Nevertheless, it was offensive to accept the English common law without qualification, as he says, and it was also difficult to accomplish codification Madison made these things clear in a letter to Washington, a few weeks after the Convention ended, in which he discussed Mason's objections to the Constitution:

> What can he mean by saying that the Common Law is not secured by the new Constitution . . . What could the Convention have done? If they had in general terms declared the Common Law to be in force, they would have . . . brought over from G. B. a thousand heterogeneous and antirepublican doctrines, and even *the ecclesiastical Hierarchy itself*. . . . If they had undertaken a discrimination, they must have formed a digest of laws, instead of a Constitution.[98]

With this statement by Madison in view, it is possible to appreciate the genius with which the Convention overcame the difficulty in which it was involved.

The conclusion from this examination into the records of the Constitutional Convention seems to be that a system of judicial supremacy is actually negated by the words omitted from the very constitutional text relied on by Marshall to justify *Marbury v. Madison*.

Perhaps it is proper to speculate whether Marshall's method in this case was designed to avoid the contradictions into which Hamilton may have fallen when he sought to justify judicial supremacy in *The Federalist*. In *Federalist* 78 Hamilton asserted his claim of judicial supremacy. In *Federalist* 80 Hamilton attempted, it seems to me, to establish this judicial supremacy on the basis of the specific phrase "cases in law and equity, arising under the Constitution"; in this way seeking to make his case on the basis of the words later ignored by Marshall. Nevertheless, in *Federalist* 81 Hamilton contradicted this when he wrote that the doctrine of judicial supremacy "is not deducible from any circumstance peculiar to the plan of the Convention; but from the general theory of a limited constitution." As the latter view, which had been attempted somewhat in *Federalist* 78, was hopelessly untenable, it may be suggested that Hamilton had been compelled by the most weighty reasons, perhaps arising out of contemporary polemics over the adoption of the Constitution, to abandon his theory of *Federalist* 80.[99] This contradiction in *The Federalist* may have struck Chief Justice Marshall.

If it be possible to reconcile *Federalists* 78, 80 and 81, on the ground Hamilton consistently held that judicial supremacy need not be "deduced" from "the plan of the Convention," a new contradiction arises to the extent that Marshall actually attempted to "deduce" judicial supremacy from a specific text of the Constitution.

[TO BE CONTINUED]

NOTES

1. See Franklin, "The Constitutional Struggle: 1938" (1983) 1 *National Lawyers Guild Quarterly* 357.

2. *Connecticut Gen. Life Ins. Co. v. Johnson*, 303 U.S. 77, 85 (1938).

3. *Erie R. R. v. Tompkins*, 304 U.S. 46 (1938). See also Frankfurter, J., concurring in *Graves v. New York*, 306 U.S. 466, 487, 491-2 (1939).

4. 16 Pet. 1 (U.S. 1942).

5. 1 Cranch 137 (U.S. 1803).

6. 13 *Encyc. Social Sciences* (1934) 463.

7. *Blodgett v. Holden*, 275 U.S. 142, 147 (1927).

8. Holmes, *Collected Legal Papers* (1920) 295-6.

9. *Schlesinger v. Wisconsin*, 270 U.S. 230, 241 (1926).

10. Paine, *Life and Works* (Patriots' ed. 1925) 385.

11. Hegel, *Philosophy of Right [Law]* (Dyde's tr. 1896) §§ 269, 269 add.

12. *Id.*§ 272n.

13. *Id.* § 300 add.

14. *Id.* § 269 add.

15. *Id.* § 272n.

16. *Ibid.*

17. *Id.* § 272 add.

18. 10 Holdsworth, *History of English Law* (1938) 719. On the problem in general, see Sharp, "The Classical American Doctrine of 'The Separation of Powers'" (1935) 2 *U. of Chi. L. Rev.* 385 (1935).

19. *The Federalist* (1788) No. 47.

20. 5 Jefferson, *Writings* (Washington's ed. 1853) 539.

21. *Id.* at 566. See, for more detail, Chinard, *Commonplace Book of Thomas Jefferson* (1926) 31; Chinard, *Pensées choises de Montesquieu tirées du "Common-Place Book" de Thomas Jefferson* (1925).

22. 2 Farrand, *Records of the Federal Convention of 1787* (1937) 299.

23. *Id.* at 77.

24. 8 *Annals of Cong.* 2007 (1798).

25. Morison, *The Struggle over the Adoption of the Constitution of Massachusetts*, 1780 (1917) 50 *Prog. Mass. Hist. Soc.* 353, 385. Cf. Gardner, *Book Review* (1938) 52 *Harv. L. Rev.* 336.

26. "An address of the Convention, for Framing a New Constitution of Government, etc.," in *Journal of the Convention for Framing a Constitution of*

Government for the State of Massachusetts Bay (1831) 216, 217. But see Landis, *The Administrative Process* (1918) 10.

27. Letter to Trist, December 1831, 9 Madison, *Writings* (Hunt's ed. 1910) 477.

28. Pierce, *Character Sketches of Delegates to the Federal Convention*, in 3 Farrand, *op. cit. supra* note 22, 87, at 91.

29. 1 *id.* at 109.

30. 2 *id.* at 210.

31. *Id.* at 249.

32. *Id.* at 216. Mason "admitted that we had been too democratic but was afraid we sd. incautiously run into the opposite extreme. We ought to attend to the rights of every class of the people." 1 *id.* at 49. On slavery see 2 *id.* at 369-70.

33. 2 *id.* at 646-7.

34. Miller, *Sam Adams* (1936) 317-8; see 3 John Adams, *Works* (1851) 18.

35. Miller, *id.* at 317.

36. 2 Paine, *op. cit. supra* note 10, at 103-4.

37. 6 *id.* at 305-6.

38. 10 *id.* at 237.

39. Dunning, *Political Theories from Rousseau to Spencer* (1920) 115.

40. *Supra* at 247.

41. *Op. cit. supra* note 11, §§ 287, 290 add; Hegel, *Philosophy of Mind* (Wallace's tr. 1894) 541. See, for more exactness, Reyburn, *Ethical Theory of Hegel* (1921) 239.

42. 1 Montesquieu, *Spirit of Laws* (Nugent's tr., Pritchard's rev. 1900) 164.

43. 6 John Adams, *Works* (1851) 467-8.

44. *Id.* at 441.

45. 4 *id.* at 579.

46. *Id.* at 581.

47. *Id.* at 579.

48. *Id.* at 579, n. 1.

49. Wright, *American Interpretation of Natural Law* (1931) 120.

50. 4 John Adams, *Works* (1851) 230. Cf. Adams' role in 1772 after the Crown had assumed the payment of the salaries of the Massachusetts justices. The freeholders of Cambridge thereupon had stated that they were "alarmed with seeing the governor of the province made independent of the people, and the shocking report that the judges of the superior court of judicature and other officers, have salaries affixed to their offices, dependent on the crown and ministry, independent of the grants of the commons of this province." 3 *id.* at 513, 515.

51. *Mass. Const.* pt. 1, art. 30.

52. Adams, *op. cit. supra* note 50, at 255.

53. *Mass. Const.* pt. 2, ch. 3, art. 2 (chapter heading is "Judiciary Power").

54. Franklin, "Administrative Law in the United States" (1934) *Tulane L. Rev.* 483, 490-1.

55. *Id.* at 487-8.

56. *Mass Const.* pt. 1, art. 1.

57. *Mass Const.* Preamble.

58. In 1809 John Adams wrote Benjamin Rush concerning his own purpose in the Massachusetts constitutional convention. He said his own plans were very unpopular and that Cushing and Samuel Adams were "avowedly for a single assembly, like Pennsylvania." Then Adams wrote: "I had at first no support but from the Essex junto. . . . They supported me timorously, and at last would not go with me to so high a mark as I aimed at, which was a complete negative in the governor upon all laws." As a result of the convention Adams says that he acquired a reputation "scarcely compatible with republicanism and unpopularity among the democratical people in this State." 9 *Works* (1851) 616, 618. Boudin says that John Adams in his formal writings says "Literally and emphatically: Nothing" to justify *Marbury v. Madison*, 1 Boudin, *Government by Judiciary* (1932) 95-6, and John Adams himself wrote Jefferson in 1813 that his *Defense of Constitutions* and his *Discourses on Davila* "were all written to support and strengthen the Constitution of the United States," 10 *Works* (1851) 54. Cf. Haines, *American Doctrine of Judicial Supremacy* (2d ed., 1932) 224.

John Taylor and Boudin protest against the neglect, in American constitutional discussion, of John Adams, Madison and Jefferson; and the undue attention given to Hamilton. Taylor, *New Views of the Constitution* (1823) 213-4. Boudin, *supra*.

59. 2 Farrand, *op. cit. supra* note 22, at 73.

60. *Ibid.* It was Hamilton who seems to have realized that the legitimacy of judicial supremacy over the Federal Constitution could not be separated from the same problem as to the state constitutions. *The Federalist* no. 81.

61. 2 Farrand, *op. cit. supra* note 22, at 298.

62. *Id.* at 341.

63. Warren, *Making of the Constitution* (1928) 505.

64. See section 8 of this article.

65. E.g., "From Lord Chief Justice Coke to the Supreme Court of the United States is a long way, but a clear one." Humphreys, "The Rule of Law and the American Revolution" (1937) 53 *L. Q. Rev.* 80, 98.

66. *Dr. Bonham's Case*, 8 Co. 113a. 118a (1610).

67. Plucknett, "Bonham's Case and Judicial Review" (1926) 40 *Harv. L. Rev.* 30, 53.

68. Thorne, "Dr. Bonham's Case" (1938) 54 *L. Q. Rev.* 542, 552.

69. Quoted in Plucknett, *Concise History of the Common Law* (1929) 49.

70. See Goebel, "Constitutional History and Constitutional Law" (1938) 38 *Col. L. Rev.* 555.

71. Plucknett, *op. cit. supra* note 69, at 242.

72. See Frank, *Address, Administrative Flexibility or Industrial Paralysis?* Georgetown Law Alumni Club, Nov. 9, 1938.

73. Pound, *Spirit of the Common Law* (1921) 53; *Formative Era of American Law* (1938) 155.

74. 1 Holdsworth, *op. cit. supra* note 18, at 463, 464.

75. *U.S. Const.* Art. III, § 2. This was the view taken by John Taylor of Caroline in considering the question whether the phrase "cases in law and equity" justified federal judicial supremacy over state legislation: "A power to try cases in law and equity, has never been understood to comprise a power of common legislation, and much less the higher power of altering constitutions of forms of government. The English judiciary try cases in law and equity, but this does not comprise a power to alter the rights of the English political departments. . . . Controversies may arise under the Constitution between political departments, in relation to their powers . . . but they would not be cases in law and equity, nor is any power to decide them given to the federal judiciary. . . ." Taylor, *op. cit. supra* note 58, at 134. "The state courts may also try cases in law and equity, but this gives them no power to alter the mechanism or principles of constitutions, or to determine the controversies of political departments. Authorities might be cited in great number, to prove that such powers have never been considered as annexed to a jurisdiction in cases of law and equity." *Id.* at 138. For more detail, see *id.*, c. XII. For Jefferson's opinion of Taylor, see 18 *Writings* (Library ed. 1904) 312.

76. I. Cranch 137, 178-9 (U.S. 1803). On Marshall's juridical method in general, see Frankfurter, *The Commerce Clause* (1937) c. 1; and, on the setting in general, Lerner, *John Marshall and the Campaign of History* (1939) 39 *Col. L. Rev.* 396. *Cf.* with the point of view of this paper as to Marshall's method that of Coxe, *Judicial Power and Unconstitutional Legislation* (1893) 3, 52-67.

77. Pound, *Formative Era of American Law* (1938) 155.

78. No. 87 (1788).

79. 2 Farrand, *op. cit. supra* note 22, at 186.

80. *Id.* at 428; see also at 422.

81. Pierce, *supra* note 28, at 88.

82. 2 Farrand, *op. cit. supra* note 22, at 428.

83. Pierce, *supra* note 28, at 93.

84. 2 Farrand, *op. cit. supra* note 22, at 428.

85. *Id.* at 430, see also at 423.

86. *Id.* at 430. In 1788, Madison said it "was never intended and can never be proper to make the Judiciary Department paramount in fact to the Legislature." 5 Madison, *op. cit. supra* note 27, at 294.

87. *Ibid.* Johnson's biographer nevertheless believes that the text consecrates judicial supremacy. Groce, *William Samuel Johnson* (1937) 149-50; see also c. 2.

88. Coxe, *op. cit. supra* note 76, at 338. Actually, no one was more anxious than Madison to force "extrajudicial" texts on the judiciary. Several times he supported the idea that the judiciary should be associated in the "revisionary power" and in other schemes by which the judiciary might formally join in vetoing legislation. See Haines, *op. cit. supra* note 58, at 129, 131, 233 et seq.; Corwin, *Court over Constitution* (1938) 31-3; Beard, *Supreme Court and the Constitution* (1912) 30; 2 Farrand, *op. cit. supra* note 22, at 77.

89. Coxe attempts to justify his conclusion by "interpreting" Madison's "construction." Beard, *op. cit. supra* note 88, at 31, and Haines, *op. cit. supra* note 58, at 234, ignore it.

Madison's biographers have caught, perhaps, the full force of his role in excluding judicial supremacy over Congress. But *cf.* the mode of presentation in Hunt, *Life of James Madison* (1902) 132-3, with that in Burns, *James Madison Philosopher of the Constitution* (1938) 160. The main difficulty, however, has been overlooked: Madison's readiness to use the phrase "cases, in law and equity, arising under the constitution," to justify judicial supremacy over the states. Corwin, *op. cit. supra* note 88, at 36, calls this a "strange" distinction. Taylor, as a states'-rights advocate, criticized this interpretation, see note 75, *supra*, but could not point out Madison's contradiction, for Madison's records were not then public.

Madison's *Report on the Virginia Resolution* denied that the phrase "law and equity" effected a constitutional reception of the common law, in general; indeed, these words are considered "as a mere pleonasm or inadvertence." 4 Elliot, *Debates* (1836) 564. But he then holds this conclusion unnecessary because the constitutional phrase comprehends two situations: (1). "Cases growing out of the restrictions on the legislative power of the states." Here Madison in effect follows Hamilton's reasoning and "examples" in *Federalist* No. 80. Marshall, in *Marbury v. Madison*, also exploited *Federalist* No. 80, substituting his own "examples"—but against Congress,—without citing "law and equity." The Rhode Island legislature anticipated Marshall's method and conclusion, in 1799, in commenting on the Kentucky and Virginia Resolutions. Elliot, *supra*, at 533. Was Marshall exploiting Madison's vacillations? *Cf.* Boudin, *op. cit. supra* note 58, at 224; Burns, *supra*, at 156. In 1831, in condemning nullification, Madison said he had always held to the supremacy of the judiciary in questions of "the boundary of jurisdiction between the U.S. & individual states." 9 Madison, *op. cit. supra* note 27, at 476; see also *id.* at 383, 395, 351, 353, 141-2; cf. Boudin, *supra*, at 102n. *Cf.* also Jackson-Livingston, *Nullification Proclamation* (1832), 2 Richardson, *Messages and Papers of the Presidents* (1890) 643, and see Livingston, 6 *Cong. Deb.* 247, 264, 266, 267, 270 (1830) (Webster-Hayne debate). But many supporters of the Virginia Resolutions rejected the Federalist claim that exclusive power to determine constitutionality rested with the Supreme Court. See Jefferson, *infra*, Section 6 of this article. Bower, *Jefferson and Hamilton* (1925) 410; note discussion in Boudin, supra at 178. (2). "Suits between citizens and foreigners, or citizens of different states, to be decided according to the state or foreign laws, but submitted by the Constitution to the judicial power of the Untied States, the judicial power being, in several instances, extended beyond the legislative power of the United States." Therefore "cases in law and equity," Madison argued, not only excluded criminal cases, see *United States v. Hudson*, 7 Cranch 32 (U.S. 1812), but such cases were to be decided by the federal courts under state law, see *Erie R. R. v. Tompkins*, 304 U.S. 64 (1938). Cf. also Madison, *infra* at *xxx*. What may then be the significance of Brandeis' opinion in the Tompkins case as to the validity of *Marbury v. Madison*?

When Madison excluded unassociated judicial supremacy, he may still have hoped the Convention would accept some other kind of paramount control, see note 88, *supra*. Only when this wish had definitely failed did Madison seek new devices to subject the states to the Supreme Court. Cf. Taylor, *op. cit. supra* note 58, at 162-3. In the last week of the Convention, Madison seconded a proposal to permit the states to levy inspection taxes on exports, 2 Farrand, *op. cit. supra* note 22, at 588, saying that "perhaps the best guard against abuse of the power of the States" was congressional action under the commerce clause. When the question of the mode of relief against oppression by the states again was raised, Madison said: "The jurisdiction of the Supreme Court must be the source of redress. So far only had provision been made by the plan agst. injurious acts of the States. His own opinion was that this was insufficient. A negative on the State laws alone could meet all the shapes which these could assume. But this had been overruled." *Id.* at 589. These remarks are not entirely clear; nor is it even certain that Madison had in mind the "cases in law and equity" clause. In any event, it is notable that Madison's suggestion was repudiated by the Convention, and the present text adopted, according to which Congress is the source of redress. *U.S. Const.* Art. 1, 10 (2); Farrand, *supra*, at 597, 607, 624, 657. Hence, Taylor's subsequent attack was against both Hamilton and Madison, *supra*, at 44, 60, 162, 163. Taylor exploited relentlessly Madison's defeat on the inspection fee power, saying: "The negative given to Congress by the tenth section, over specified state acts, is an exception to the general principle of a mutual independence, quite sufficient to remove the obscurity into which mysteriarchs have endeavoured to plunge the constitution. . . . These limited negatives, prove that no general negative was intended to be given, either to Congress or the federal court, over state sovereign powers not prohibited. A prohibition upon some, demonstrates that the exercise of others was not prohibited. A special supremacy to Congress, demonstrates that no general supremacy was given to the federal court." *Id.* at 158.

90. 2 Farrand, *op. cit. supra* note 22, at 431.

91. *Ibid.* See also *id.* at 425.

92. *Id.* at 425.

93. See Coxe, *op. cit. supra* note 76, at 539.

94. 2 Farrand, *op. cit. supra* note 22, at 575-6.

95. *Id.* at 600.

96. *Id.* at 590, n. 8.

97. Letter to Washington, Oct. 18, 1787, 3 *id.* 129, 130.

98. *Ibid.*

99. See Corwin, *op. cit. supra* note 88, at 45-7.

The Judiciary State II

(1940)

5

Just as it may be questioned whether the original Constitution consecrates the opinion of Sir Edward Coke in support of judicial supremacy, it may also be doubted whether the Fourteenth Amendment embraces it.[100] Marshall attempted to embody Coke in the Constitution by omitting the phrase "Law and Equity" from it. By the same method it may be that Coke has been incarnated in the Fourteenth Amendment through disregard for its fifth section, which provided that "The Congress shall have power to enforce [the amendment] by appropriate legislation."

This section of the Fourteenth Amendment, it may be ventured, seems to give the power of enforcing it to Congress alone. This is not astonishing, considering that the Thirteenth, Fourteenth and Fifteenth Amendments, all of which state substantially the same thing as to Congressional power, are legal formulations for one of the basic social revolutions in the history of humanity, in which property relations founded on slavery were shattered, foreign financial intervention on behalf of slavery was defeated, and the conditions for reconstituting American social relations were created.

Moreover, the text of the Fourteenth Amendment, as Boudin has recently shown, in all its versions prior to adoption, consistently provided that Congress in some way or other should have power. The dominant personality in drafting much of the Fourteenth Amendment was the Republican Congressman, Bingham, one of the managers of the impeachment of President Johnson. He united, as did Lincoln, the struggle against slavery with the struggle against the Supreme Court because of his belief that slavery maintained itself through the judiciary state. On April 23, 1860, he said in Congress:

> The court has no power in deciding the right of Dred Scott and of his children to their liberty, to decide so as to bind this body . . . neither has that tribunal the power to decide that

> Five million persons born and domiciled in this land, "have no rights which we see bound to respect. ". . . With Jefferson, I deny that the Supreme Court is the final arbiter on all questions of political power, and assert that the final arbiter on all such questions is the people. . . .[101]

In 1867 Bingham proposed "sweeping away at once the Court's appellate jurisdiction in all cases," and in 1868 he supported the bill of the Judiciary Committee of the House to require two-thirds of the court to concur in declaring Congressional legislation unconstitutional "in a savage onslaught" urging that "Congress had full power over the Court."[102]

6

However, the greatest attack on the judiciary state in America came from the developed ideas of President Jefferson, who, with splendid comprehensiveness, opposed judicial domination. This is not in any way surprising, considering that the intellectual side of the American Revolution is rooted in the great philosophic thought of the Eighteenth Century, especially that of France, which had absorbed the best English thought before it. Indeed, French influence in America probably reflected back into France itself after the American Revolution.[103]

Hegel writes of this period:

> French philosophy does away with the lay or outside position in regard alike to politics, religion and philosophy. . . . What the philosophers brought forward and maintained . . . was, speaking generally, that men should no longer be in the position of laymen, either with regard to religion or to law; so that in religious matters there should not be a hierarchy, a limited and selected number of priests, and in the same way that there should not be in legal matters an exclusive caste and society (not even a class of professional lawyers), in whom should reside, and to whom should be restricted, the knowledge of what is eternal, divine, true and right, and by whom other men should be commanded and directed; but that human reason should have the right of giving its assent and

> its opinion. To treat barbarians as laymen is quite as it should be—barbarians are nothing but laymen; but to treat thinking men as laymen is very hard. This great claim made by man to subjective freedom, perception and conviction, the philosophers in question contended for heroically and with splendid genius, with warmth and fire, with spirit and courage, maintaining that a man's own self, the human spirit, is the source from which is derived all that is to be respected by him. . . . Thought was raised like a standard among the nations, liberty of conviction and of conscience in me. . . . Thus in another form they completed the Reformation that Luther began.[104]

This description of the great Eighteenth Century world point of view, so well put by Hegel, is reflected in our country by Jefferson's passionate democracy. It is to be taken for granted, then, that Jeffersonianism connotes unrelenting struggle against the rule of law as it is understood in American constitutional law. Edward Livingston, Jefferson's follower, put the matter thus:

> in all evils in government, it is among the greatest, that the laws . . . should be a mystery to the people, and the knowledge of them confined to certain designated classes or descriptions of men. They invariably make a property of them in the strictest sense of the word . . . and like other articles of commerce, is not always sold in a pure unsophisticated state.[105]

It is well to begin with Jefferson's general views as to the common law, because this discloses Jefferson's consistency. A well rounded attack on the judiciary state, which rests on the idea that the Constitution is subject to the English private common law, involves an attack on the supremacy of the common law not only over the Constitution but over private law as well. Jefferson represents exactly this kind of concerted attack on the supremacy of the common law.

English law had been seized on during the Revolution, he maintained, for agitational purposes and for nothing else. In his very important letter to Tyler he begins by saying:

> I deride with you the ordinary doctrine, that we brought with us from England the *common law rights*. This narrow notion

> was a favorite in the first moment of rallying to our rights against Great Britain. But it was that of men who felt their rights before they had thought of their explanation. The truth is, that we brought with us the *rights of men*; of expatriated men.

Jefferson then goes on to say that the common law is a received system of law.

> On our arrival here, the question would at once arise, by what law will we govern ourselves? The resolution seems to have been, by that system with which we are familiar, to be altered by ourselves occasionally, and adapted to our new situation.[106]

In a letter to Goodenow, ten years later, Jefferson said that there was no immediate constitutional reception of English common law. He asks:

> whether the common law (of England) makes a part of the laws of our general government? . . . as to the general government, the Virginia Report on the alien and sedition laws, has so completely pulverized this pretension that nothing new can be said on it. Still, seeing that judges of the Supreme Court, (I recollect, for example, Elsworth and Story) had been thought capable of such paralogism, I was glad to see that the Supreme Court had given it up. In the case of Libel in the United States district Court of Connecticut, the rejection of it was certainly sound; because no law of the general government has made it an offense.[107]

Jefferson, in the remainder of his letter to Tyler, considers the matter of the general place of the common law in America after the reception.

> I admit the superiority of the civil over the common law code, as a system of perfect justice, yet an incorporation of the two would be like Nebuchadnezzar's image of metals and clay, a thing without cohesion of parts. The only natural improvement of the common law, is through its homogeneous ally, the chancery, in which new principles are to be examined, concocted and digested.

There later follows, he says, the need of unifying the double system of law and of equity through legislation. When equitable conceptions are "rendered pure and certain, they should be transferred by statute to the courts of the common law, and placed within the pale of juries."

Finally, Jefferson soared beyond the conception of the common law to codification itself in one of the most interesting passages in American legal history:

> Whether we should undertake [in Virginia] to reduce the common law . . . to a text, is a question of transcendent difficulty. It was discussed at the first meeting of the committee of the revised code in 1776, and decided in the negative, by opinion of Wythe, Mason and myself, against Pendleton and Thomas Lee. Pendleton proposed to take Blackstone for that text, only purging him of what was inapplicable or unsuitable to us. In that case, the meaning of every work of Blackstone would have become a source of litigation, until it had been settled by repeated legal decisions. And to come to that meaning, we should have had produced, on all occasions, that very pile of authorities from which it would be said he drew his conclusions. . . . Thus we should have retained the same chaos of lawlore from which we wished to be emancipated. . . . We were deterred from the attempt by these considerations, added to which, the bustle of the times did not admit leisure for such an undertaking.[108]

In constitutional law, Jefferson consistently with this general view opposed the idea of the judiciary state as embodied in *Marbury v. Madison.* Frequently he resisted the power of the courts to declare constitutionality, sometimes interposing to the claim of the judiciary his conception of a system of separation of co-equal state powers in which there was no recognition of the rule of the judiciary.

In 1804 Jefferson wrote to Mrs. John Adams:

> You seem to think it devolved on the judges to decide on the validity of sedition law. But nothing in the Constitution has given them a right to decide for the Executive, more than to the Executive to decide for them. . . . [T]he opinion which gives to the judges the right to decide what laws are constitutional, and what not, not only for themselves in their own

> sphere of action, but for the Legislature and Executive also, in their spheres, would make the judiciary a despotic branch.[109]

In 1807 Jefferson wrote to George Hay:

> On this I shall ever act, and maintain it with the powers of the government, against any control which may be attempted by the judges, in subversion of the independence of the executive and the Senate within their peculiar department. . . . I have long wished for a proper occasion to have the gratuitous opinion in *Marbury v. Madison* brought before the public, and denounced as not law.[110]

In 1817 Jefferson wrote to W. H. Torrance:

> The second question, whether the judges are invested with exclusive authority to decide on the constitutionality of a law, has been heretofore a subject of consideration with me in the exercise of official duties. Certainly there is not a word in the Constitution which has given the power to them more than to the executive or legislative branches. . . . And, in general, that branch which is to act ultimately, and without appeal, on any law, is the rightful expositor of the validity of the law, uncontrolled by the opinions of the other co-ordinate authorities. . . . But there is another opinion entertained by some men of such judgment and information as to lessen my confidence in my own. That is, that the legislature alone is the exclusive expounder of the sense of the Constitution, in every part. . . . [T]his opinion which ascribes exclusive exposition to the legislature, merits respect for its safety, there being in the body of the nation a control over them. . . . Between these two doctrines, every one has a right to choose, and I know of no third meriting any respect.[111]

In 1819 Jefferson wrote to Judge Roane:

> In denying the right they usurp of exclusively explaining the constitution, I go further than you do, if I understand rightly your quotation from the *Federalist*, of an opinion that "the judiciary is the last resort in relation *to the other departments*

> of the government, but not in relation to the rights of the parties to the compact under which the judiciary is derived." If this opinion be sound, then indeed is our constitution a complete *felo de se* [self-destruction]. For intending to establish three departments, co-ordinate and independent, that they might check and balance one another, it has given, according to this opinion, to one of them alone, the right to prescribe rules for the government of the others, and to that one too, which is unelected by, and independent of the nation. . . . The constitution, on this hypothesis, is a mere thing of wax in the hands of the judiciary, which they may twist and shape into any form they please. It should be remembered, as an axiom of eternal truth in politics, that whatever power in any government is independent, is absolute also; in theory only, at first, while the spirit of the people is up, but in practice, as fast as that relaxes. Independence can be trusted nowhere but with the people in mass.[112]

In 1820 Jefferson wrote to Mr. Jarvis:

> You seem . . . to consider the judges as the ultimate arbiters of all constitutional questions; a very dangerous doctrine indeed, and one which would place us under the despotism of an oligarchy. . . . Our judges are as honest as other men, and not more so. They have, with others, the same passions for party, for power, and the privilege of their corps. . . . The Constitution has erected no such single tribunal, knowing that to whatever hands confided, with the corruptions of time and party, its members would become despots. When the legislative or executive functionaries act unconstitutionally, they are responsible to the people in their elective capacity. The exemption of the judges from that is quite dangerous enough. I know no safe depositary of the ultimate powers of the society but the people themselves; and if we think them not enlightened enough to exercise their control with a wholesome discretion, the remedy is not to take it from them, but to inform their discretion by education. This is the true corrective of abuses of constitutional power.[113]

7

Jefferson, moreover, attacked the third element on which the judiciary state depends, for he criticized the juridical method of the common law which is taken to accompany the theory of the supremacy of judge-made law.[114] Even if there were a constitutionally consecrated system of judicial supremacy, it does not follow that it must be a system of judicial supremacy according to the method of the common law. The idea of the supremacy of law indeed is ordinarily taken in America to compel reference to authoritative judicial materials; but this method as method is not constitutionally consecrated. Nor is the emerging juridical method of the expanded rule of law, based on a conception of freer legal determination, constitutionally consecrated. Actually, neither method is the necessary method, as the possibilities from the history of Roman law under the regime of codification or of authoritative texts, based on the exercise of state power, should show.[115]

The Constitution truly is one of the very first attempts in human history to codify public law. In this respect, the United States has been in the lead although so far it has been reluctant to codify private law. But the juridical method of the prevailing English common law is totally unsuited to the regime of the American Constitution, just as it would be unsuited to a regime of codification of private law. It is not astonishing, then that the juridical method of the English common law is no more embedded in the Constitution than is the English common law or the rule of law itself. In connection with the matter of juridical method it is proper to refer again to the genius of the constitutional formulation that "The Judicial Power shall extend to all cases both in law and equity arising under this Constitution. . . ." A modern phrase, such as "judicial power," connotes that English feudal legal ideas, even as to juridical method, have long since been left behind. Madison grasped this, though perhaps incompletely, when he once said:

> There has been a fallacy . . . in confounding a question whether precedents could expound a Constitution, with a question whether they could alter a Constitution. This distinction is too obvious to need elucidation. None will deny that precedents of a certain description fix the interpretation of a law. Yet who will pretend that they can repeal or alter a law?[116]

Really the question of the applicability of the English juridical method under the Constitution seems to have been an intense issue at the beginning of our constitutional history and it seems to have been fought over remarkably. It is not unexpected that the anti-democratic Hamilton should have supported the Anglo-American juridical method. As a result of his consistent, anti-democratic position, as revealed in *The Federalist,* Hamilton, although a member of the Committee of Style, contended also that somehow or other judicial supremacy over the Constitution had been provided for; and insisted on the separation of law and equity and against the extension of the jury to equity process; and maintained "I go further, and affirm, that bills of rights, in the sense and to the extent they are contended for, are not only unnecessary in the proposed Constitution, but would even be dangerous."[117]

Hamilton contended for English juridical method in *Federalist* 78, where he also set forth his conception of judicial power to declare constitutionality. He definitely perceived that the judiciary state rested both on the rule of law and on English juridical method. Hence he said:

> To avoid an arbitrary discretion in the courts, it is indispensable that they should be bound down by strict rules and precedents, which serve to define and point out their duty in every particular case that comes before them; and it will readily be conceived . . . that the records of those precedents must unavoidably swell to a very considerable bulk, and must demand long and laborious study to acquire a competent knowledge of them. Hence it is, that there can be but few men in the society, who will have sufficient skill in the laws to qualify them for the stations of judges. . . .

Jefferson, as the consistent representative of democracy, fought this aspect of the judiciary state also, just as he opposed these other views of Hamilton; Jefferson, contrary to Hamilton, rejected the conception that the Constitution should be subjected to the juridical method of the English common law. He made an effort to disclose the contradiction involved in permitting the judiciary to determine constitutionality, supposedly from the authoritative constitutional text, but actually by reference to its own body of authoritative judicial materials. The method of the English private common law resting on judicial decision was utterly inapplicable to the regime of American public law resting on a written Constitution; and it would be idle to pretend that the common law ever worked out a professional discipline, based on respect and good faith, suitable to a regime of constitutional and codified texts. Certainly it never has had to do so in English public law, and it never actually tried to do so in America. Yet the juridical method of a country which never had to solve the problem of the proper use of written texts has been casually forced on a people who previously "had never been permitted to exercise self-government" and who "when forced to assume it . . . were novices in its science," as Jefferson put it. But, as Jefferson also says, the Revolution looked forward, not backward:

> Our Revolution commenced on more favorable ground. It presented us an album on which we were free to write what we pleased. We had no occasion to search into musty records, to hunt up royal parchments, or to investigate the laws and institutions of a semi-barbarous ancestry. [118]

It is not surprising, then, for Jefferson, in 1823, to write:

> At the establishment of our constitutions, the judiciary bodies were supposed to be the most helpless and harmless members of the government. Experience, however, soon showed in what way they were to become the most dangerous . . . their decisions, seeming to concern individual suitors only, pass silent and unheeded by the public at large . . . these decisions, nevertheless, became law by precedent, sapping, by little and little, the foundations of the constitution, and working its change by construction, before any one has perceived that that invisible and helpless worm has been busily employed in consuming its substance. [119]

Moreover, Jefferson elsewhere complained that the American justices in constitutional matters went beyond this supposed historic limitation of the method of the common law, in that, according to him they even actually instituted planned campaigns for power: "We have seen, too," he writes, "that contrary to all correct examples, they are in the habit of going out of the question before them, to throw an anchor ahead, and grapple further hold for future advances of power."[120]

The lack of discipline in the juridical method of the common law has long been noticed. In the struggle with the historical school of Savigny over codification, Hegel adverted to this weakness of the English judge-controlled system. Hegel pointed out that under English law the results were legislative. "Since the unwritten law is contained in the decisions of law-courts and judges, the judges are continually the lawgivers," he wrote. But English judge-made law is an irresponsible system of legislation.

> The judges are both directed and not directed to the authority of their predecessors. They are so directed because their predecessors are said to have done nothing but interpret the unwritten law. They are not so directed, because they are supposed to have in themselves the unwritten law, and hence have a right to determine whether previous decisions are in keeping with it or not.

This results in "monstrous" confusion.[121]

Jefferson and Hegel had no illusions, then, that the rule of law was other than the rule of legislation on the basis of judicial supremacy. This is very well understood in the Twentieth Century. The rule of law perhaps has been already somewhat transformed through the popularization in the Twentieth Century of ideas such as these relative to common law juridical method. The conception of the supremacy of law originally was founded on the belief that the judges were beholding and administering a self-developing, antecedent body of legal doctrine. As this law was natural, it had to be supreme, and the judges therefore had to be independent. The problem of the judge was merely the modest one of adverting to the concept proper for the situation. Law was an impersonal body of dogma above and beyond the judges, and the doctrine of *stare decisis* seemed to demonstrate this. Hence it came to be believed that the judiciary alone, in the American state, was impartial, objective and mechanical. The prestige of the Supreme Court rested on the conception of the supremacy of law according to this juridical method.

However, American jurists of the Twentieth Century entertain a different conception of common law juridical method, for they have agreed in effect that the courts themselves are not entirely responsible in the traditional way to the existing law. This conception of juridical method, which swells to extreme proportion that aspect of the traditional juridical method which originally conceived of the antecedent materials as necessarily reflecting natural law and reason, is, of course, prominently in a period of social transformation. However, great changes in law, reflecting changes in society, have not been made in the past through mere changes in juridical method; but by the creation of completely new legal machines, different from the existing institutions, such as equity once was and administration now is. Similarly, changes in Roman social conditions led to Roman equity or praetorian law, and the breakaway from feudalism in France resulted in codification.

American legal discussion of the Twentieth Century has been devoted to establishing and justifying the essentially legislative nature of judiciary activity. The idea has become commonplace that a court should have a free hand because its tasks are creative. The judge has become inspired and exalted. He properly has "made" law. It has been fashionable to attack *stare decisis* in the name of law changing to meet changing conditions. In most instances the conception of the legislative power of the judiciary has been expressed with proper academic reserve and qualification; nevertheless it may be insisted that the different schools of American jurists have created the conditions for legitimating the opinion that the judges may be independent, in the strictest sense of the word, even of existing law itself.

The result, then, is that common law juridical method, as it is conceived in America today, frankly unites the antagonistic ideas that the judge should both follow precedent and reject precedent. If this development is considered in connection with the idea of judicial supremacy, the latter, which originally rested on the idea that the law bound the judges, now can be a conception that the law binds all except the judges. It can be a conception of unqualified judiciary power, masquerading as the old rule of law, in order to justify judicial supremacy and independence.

Naturally, under these circumstances there has developed burning interest in the political allegiance of judges, for a system exists in which *Marbury v. Madison,* for instance, might be justified on the ground of *stare decisis,* yet American administrative agencies, necessarily empowered under broad formulae, can be interfered with freely by reviewing courts, perhaps even to defeat legislative policy, and the course of the administrative even redirected, by judicial opinions and *dicta,* through development of a greater "directing activity."

Until the constitutional crisis it has not seemed necessary for Twentieth Century American jurists to consider the outcome of their theories of free decision. It must be firmly insisted that in most cases these schools, as they have flourished, have and can enjoy a progressive role. They often made excellent critiques of the present state of legal affairs (sometime disguised, of necessity, due to the then political isolation of these jurists). They often expressed desire for reformulation. They disclosed the relation of law to the other divisions of labor. They sometimes indicated transitions to new legal conditions. They disclosed the changing, and hence historical, nature of law. They sometimes raised basic questions relative to the explanation for legal change as well as to the necessity and inevitability of change. Their realistic conceptions of juridical method undermined the traditional explanation for the rule of law.

Nevertheless, if these progressive schools do not recognize the priority of the democratic state nor relate themselves to the concerns of democracy, their ideas could become the vehicle for a reactionary legal movement. If the transition from these schools were to a conception of law integrated to the democratic state, based on administration and codification, what has been accomplished so far in the Twentieth Century could be understood as a critique, preceding the negation, of judiciary supremacy. If, however, the transition were to the law of an anti-democratic state, based on the judiciary, what has already been done by Twentieth Century American jurisprudence could be taken to justify a new version of the rule of law based on the conception of the judiciary as having even fuller legislative powers.[122] Consistent with the latter purposes is the present struggle to subdue administration as well as the recent firm attempts to introduce into some states the idea that the judges should be appointed by the judiciary and bar associations.[123]

If American jurisprudence in the recent past has disclosed the legislative nature of judiciary power, the task of democratic jurists should be that of subduing the judiciary to democracy, whereas the task of anti-democratic jurists should be that of emancipating the judiciary from democratic responsibility. The latter can be the meaning of the expanded rule of law, and this could in time even develop into an American version of the leadership principle. "The

Justiciary of Aragon," Dickinson pointed out in the Constitutional Convention in discussing the conception of judicial supremacy, "became by degrees the law-giver." "He thought no such power ought to exist."[124]

8

It was not at all difficult for Jefferson to have the point of view, then, that judicial constitutional determination, far from being the detached working of the conception of the rule of law, was party political action. It is indeed true that Jefferson, as did John Adams, often gave his support to the conception of the separation of powers, the effect of which is to permit the different powers legally to express their independence of, or antagonism to, each other. He, too, criticized the Articles of Confederation for want of "separation of functions."[125] He once said: "The leading principle of our Constitution is the independence of the Legislature, executive and judiciary of each other, and none are more jealous of this than the judiciary."[126]

Nevertheless, also as did John Adams and the Massachusetts Constitution, Jefferson emphatically rejected the idea of separation of powers resting on judicial hegemony. "But would the executive be independent of the judiciary," he then asked, "if he were subject to the *commands* of the latter?[127] So he raised the question, whether the judiciary conception of what is proper separation of function is the definitive conception. The answer to this depends on whether the Constitution has consecrated the supremacy of the judiciary.

The judiciary idea of what was proper separation of powers certainly did not prevent Jefferson from inviting, on behalf of President Washington, the chief justice and the justices of the Supreme Court to give the executive advice during 1793 as to international and other law pertaining to a war-time crisis.[128] Actually the Supreme Court itself at different periods has also felt that the Constitution did not consecrate a system precluding historical development of the allocation of functions through legislation. The legality of administration is an indication.

Because he did not regard judicial supremacy as constitutional, Jefferson's acceptance of separation of powers does not have the ordinary signification given to it by those who support the rule of law as well as separation of powers. Thus, in his *Autobiography,* he said, "I would not indeed, make [the judges] dependent on the Executive authority, as they formerly were in England; but I deem it indispensable to the continuance of this government, that they should be submitted to some practical and impartial control."[129] In 1819 he complained that the "revolution of 1800," when the "nation declared its will by dismissing functionaries of one principle, and electing those of another, in the two branches, executive and legislative" failed to conquer the judiciary department which "has continued the reprobated system."[130] And in 1820 he wrote Ritchie that "A judiciary independent of a king or executive alone, is a good thing; but independence of the will of the nation is a solecism, at least in a republican government."[131] In 1821 Jefferson wrote Pleasants: "It is a misnomer to call a government republican, in which a branch of the supreme power is independent of the nation."[132]

9

Jefferson's attack on the judiciary state did not end with him. Edward Livingston, Jefferson's greatest follower, also fought the principle of judicial supremacy in Congress in 1798 in his speeches against the alien and sedition legislation. Although the conception of judicial determination of constitutionality was pressed on him in the House, he held that Congress had the duty of determining constitutionality even as to the Bill of Rights, and that in the last resort the people decided. So, when Otis asked him who should judge constitutionality, Livingston cried, "The people of the United States. We are their servants. When we exceed our powers, we become their *tyrants!*"[133] He entertained this view five years before the actual decision in *Marbury v. Madison.*

Jackson, under the influence of Livingston, who several decades later became his secretary of state, in the famous message vetoing the renewal of the charter of the Bank of the United State, refused to recognize the definitive authority of the Supreme Court over constitutionality, maintaining that for him the opinion of the Supreme Court only had doctrinal value:

> The opinion of the judges has no more authority over Congress than the opinion of the Congress has over the judges, and on that point the President is independent of both. The authority of the Supreme Court . . . have only such influence as the force of their reasoning may deserve.[134]

This in part is a conception of the constitutional role of the Supreme Court as founded on its ability to convince the President and Congress through reason, rather than to subordinate them through power. Indeed, the great constitutional conception of judgeship may be, not that judges should have state power nor that they should control the state through reason; but that they should persuade the state through convincing reasonableness. This may be the true rule of law, and it is a conception of judging that the Eighteenth Century, with its respect both for democracy and for reason, may represent in human history. A great conception of judging demands that the judge be both independent of the suitor before him, and loyal to the democratic American Constitution and legislation. Part of the statement of Jackson-Livingston, which unites some of the thought of Jefferson with the body of Eighteenth Century French philosophy, also reflects the essence of the doctrine of John Adams and of the Massachusetts Constitution, with its provision for the advisory opinion. This cannot be concealed, even though the advisory opinion may violate the conception that judicial action ordinarily should be grounded alone in litigation.

Finally, in his famous Springfield speech of 1858,[135] as well as in his first inaugural address,[136] Lincoln hurled Jefferson's and Jackson's hostile views regarding the supremacy of the Supreme Court against the *Dred Scott* decision. Lincoln thus pointed to the connection between the idea of judicial supremacy and the idea of slavery then existing, and it seems to me that the fifth section of the Fourteenth Amendment, providing for the supremacy of Congress, consecrates his victory over both the Supreme Court and slavery.

10

If the conception of the judiciary state is the result of the effort to subdue the American Constitution through the English private common law, the conception of the democratic state should lead to an effort to weaken the judiciary state by uprooting the English common law, even in its own realm. Consequently, in several ways other than that of constitutional determination the idea of the judiciary state was shaken in the early period of the United States. As early as 1786, Paine was suggesting that there were two kinds of law with different principles and effects, "Laws of universal operation," such as the "administration of justice," and laws relative to "matters of negotiation,"[137] which Mr. Dunning thought should be regarded as "administrative instructions."[138]

However, the great enemy of the idea of the judiciary state, which conceives that American constitutional law is a section of the English private common law, was the civil law during the period leading up to the Constitution. Jefferson, as has been shown, was impressed by the civil law and also noted the importance of comparative law.[139] In 1776, John Adams advised Jonathan Mason to study Coke, who "is justly styled the oracle of the law, and whoever is master of his writings, is master of the laws of England." Then Adams adds: "There is another science, my dear Sir, that I must recommend to your most attentive consideration, and that is the Civil Law. . . . The Civil Law will come as fast into fashion in America as the French language, and from the same causes."[140] The civil law had its own juridical method based on the value of doctrine and on a theory of proper judicial discipline before the written text.

As significant as the interest in civil law was the interest at the time in codification. This is important considering that France codified its law only in 1804. It has been shown that Jefferson considered codification as early as 1776.[141] In 1782, according to John Adams, a rumor swept the country that DeMably had been invited by the United States to give his aid to form a code of laws, and Adams as late as 1816 was denying that truth of the rumor.[142] In 1825 culminated the great Louisiana codification movement, in which virtually seven codes were prepared.[143] This exceptional action was headed by Edward Livingston, who was influenced by French codification as well as by Bentham's proposals for codification, and was linked, as well, to the constitutional ideas of Jefferson and Jackson.[144] In consequence of Livingston's work in Louisiana, Jefferson consistently renewed his own early interest in codification and united it with his theory of the Constitution. "One single object," he wrote Livingston, "if your provision attains it, will entitle you to the endless gratitude of society; that of restraining judges from usurping legislation." Moreover Jefferson wished "anxiously" that Livingston's great work would "obtain complete success, and become an example for the imitation and improvement of other states."[145] During the period when Livingston was Jackson's secretary of state, Bentham, under cover of Livingston's support of it, wrote Jackson to interest him in codification, so that the monopoly of what he called "the harpies of the law" could be broken.[146]

11

These materials, taken from the early phases of American legal history, may to some extent affect the validity of the idea of a judiciary state. They may be important in the present period of constitutional crisis, the outcome of which may decide the ultimate control over administration.

American administrative agencies represent more adequately the unification of different functions that Hegel desired so much and deemed so necessary in the state. Administration unites the essential but different functions of legislation and execution, concept and experience, theory and practice, formulation and action, in such way that they reciprocally interact, legislation guiding execution, execution in turn restating legislation. It is contrary to the doctrine of separate powers.

In America of the past there has been, as Hegel predicted, a working unification of the supposedly independent state powers, under control of the courts through the rule of law. This was not only undemocratic, but defective and barren, for the method of adjudication was an inadequate and incomplete way of utilizing paramount power. However, if the judiciary can gain control over administrative agencies it may have as its own this more effective unified system of legislation and execution. This is why administration is so furiously fought over today.

This is why it must be repeated that the contest is one over democracy. There will be either a democratic unification of the state, in which the administrative will be controlled by the popular executive and the popular legislative, or there will be a judiciary unification, in which administration will be controlled by the judiciary.[147] A judiciary state erected on control over the administrative arm of government probably would be vastly less democratic as well as more powerful than it ever was in the past.

NOTES

100. See, generally, 2 Boudin, *op. cit. supra* note 58, at 94 *et seq.;* Boudin, "Truth and Fiction About the Fourteenth Amendment" (1939) 16 *N. Y. U. L. Q. Rev.* 19; Note (1933) 33 *Col. L. Rev.* §54. See also Graham, "The 'Conspiracy Theory' of the Fourteenth Amendment" (1938) 47 *Yale L. J.* 371, 48 *id.* 171; Hurst, "Book Review" (1939) 52 *Harv. L. Rev.* 851.

101. *Cong. Globe*, 36th Cong., Ist Sess. (1860) 1939.

102. 3 *Warren Supreme Court in United States History* (1922) 171, 188–9.

103. See Chinard, *op. cit. supra* note 21, at 63–5; Becker, *Heavenly City of the Eighteenth-Century Philosophers* (1932) 33; Bowers, *op. cit. supra* note 89, at 97; Schapiro, *Condorcet and the Rise of Liberalism* (1934) c. 12; Jones, *America and French Culture* (1927) c. 14, 15.

104. 3 Hegel, *Lectures on the History of Philosophy* (Haldane's and Simson's tr. 1896) 379, 390, 397–8.

105. I Livingston, *Complete Works* (1873) 161; cf. Montesquieu, *supra* note 76, at 426. John Adams wrote Jefferson: "Your steady defense of democratical principles, and your invariable favorable opinion of the French revolution, laid the foundation of your unbounded popularity," 6 *Works* (1851) 52, 54. *Cf.* Chinard, *Thomas Jefferson* (2d ed. 1939) v-xvi.

106. 6 Jefferson, *op. cit. supra* note 20, at 65. If, to Jefferson, the common law served to arouse the first revolutionary feeling, to John Adams it seemed to serve the provisional purpose of temporarily organizing the revolution, 9 *Works* (1851) 390–1, and to Madison it served to protect relations from "the state of nature," *supra*, (1940) 2 *National Lawyers Guild Quarterly* 244, 260.

107. 7 *id.* at 251. The reference appears to be to the significant case of *United States v. Hudson*, 7 Cranch 32 (1812), which should be compared with *Marbury v. Madison*, decided only a few years before. On the relationship to the Kentucky and Virginia resolutions, see Chinard, *Thomas Jefferson* (1929) 345, 385–6. See also, letter to Randolph, Aug. 18, 1799, 7 *Jefferson, Writings* (Ford's ed. 1896) 383.

108. 6 *Jefferson*, *op. cit. supra* note 20, at 66–7. See also Jefferson's autobiography in I *id.* at 42–3; Chinard, *op. cit. supra* note 107, at 90, *Cf.* Hamilton, *infra* at 32–3. The omitted parts of this letter describe the wish to "uncanonize" Blackstone, and the feeling against Blackstone lawyers, "these ephemeral insects of the law." Note that Bentham's *A Fragment on Government* also appeared in 1776. See Waterman, "Thomas Jefferson and Blackstone's Commentaries" (1933) 27 *Ill. L. Rev.* 629.

109. 8 Jefferson, *op. cit. supra* note 107, at 311.

110. 5 Jefferson, *op. cit. supra* note 20, at 85.

111. 6 *id.* at 461–3.

112. 7 *id.* at 134.

113. *Id.* at 178–9.

114. See, generally, Boudin, "The Problem of Stare Decisis in Our Constitutional Theory" (1931) 8 *N. Y. U. L. Q. Rev.* 589.

115. Edward Livingston has been foremost in the English-speaking world (followed by Bentham) in addressing these problems; see Franklin, "Concerning the Historic Importance of Edward Livingston" (1937) 11 *Tulane L. Rev.* 163. "But the ultimate touchstone of constitutionality is the Constitution itself and not what we have said about it," Frankfurter, J., in *Graves v. New York*, 306 U.S. 466, 491–2 (1939).

116. Madison, *loc. cit. supra* note 27.

117. *Federalist* Nos. 78, 80, 81, 83, 84 (1788).

118. 7 Jefferson, *op. cit. supra* note 20, at 356; see Taylor, *Inquiry into the Principles and Policies of the Government* (1814) 224.

119. 7 Jefferson, *op. cit. supra* note 20, at 322. "It is as tyrannical, that a court, by precedents, should make laws and constitutions, as that a legislature should render judgments. The English judges corrupted the English laws by precedents. . . . Would not the federal judges corrupt our constitution, if invested with a power to alter it by precedents? They would thus acquire power for themselves. . . ." Taylor, *op. cit.* note 58, at 149.

120. 1 Jefferson, *op. cit supra.* note 20, at 82. Jefferson, in emphasizing the legislative role of the judiciary, continues a great line of thought that possibly begins with Bacon and includes Hobbes and Bentham. In Jefferson's school, Livingston is of course paramount. See note 114, *supra.* Hardly less important is John Taylor of Caroline: ". . . the judicial power, in its capacity to disallow or repeal the acts of legislature, is made a greater legislative power. . . . [A] power of construing is nearly equivalent to a power of legislating; why should construction of law be quite independent of sovereign will, when law itself is made completely subservient to it. . . . [T]he power of construction is a supremacy over the legislature and the sovereign. . . . But judicial power has seized upon a quality peculiar to the American policy, to transform itself into a political department, and to extend its claims far beyond precedent. . . . [S]uch is the connexion between legislating and judging, that one may be easily run into the other; and that it is impossible to keep these powers separate and distinct, as our theory requires." Taylor, *op. cit. supra* note 118, at 204, 206, 208, 224.

In 1800, Madison, in condemning the claim that there had been a general federal reception of the common law, said that this "would confer on the judicial department a discretion little short of a legislative power. . . . [I]t is manifest that the power of the judges over the law would in effect, erect them into legislators. . . ." Elliot, *op. cit. supra* note 89, at 566.

121. Hegel, *op. cit. supra* note 11, ss 211 n. See Kantorowicz, "Savigny and the Historical School of Law" (1937) 53 *L. Q. Rev.* 326.

122. "Yet the judicial process involves also an administrative element. One form which this administrative element takes is . . . something at least very like discretion in the choice of starting points for judicial reasoning, or choice of premises in cases where no authoritative precept exists to require one starting point or one premise rather than another. As said by the Supreme Court of the United States: 'The rule of *stare decisis,* though one tending to consistency and uniformity of decision is not inflexible. Whether it shall be followed or departed from is a question entirely within the discretion of the court. . . .' It means an ability to choose, but the choice must be made by applying an authoritative technique to authoritative legal materials." *Report of the Special Committee on Administrative Law,* Advance Program, 61st Annual Meeting, *ABA* (1938) 159.

Also Hegel long since pointed out that each of the different powers of state "involves" or has in itself the elements of the other powers, *op. cit. supra* note 11, §§ 272, 273, 300, *cf.* 275; and he made it possible to ask, what, if each of the divisions of power contains the elements of the others, is the rational basis of three powers, each containing the elements of the others; and to inquire why the undemocratic power should have supremacy over the democratic power.

123. See "Committee Reports" (1937) *I National Lawyers Guild Quarterly* 63; (1938) I *id.* 319.

124. 2 Farrand, *op. cit. supra* note 22, at 299.

125. 1 Jefferson, *op. cit. supra* note 20, at 78.

126. 5 *id.* at 103.

127. *Ibid.*

128. 4 *id.* at 22.

129. 1 *id.* at 81.

130. 1 *id.* at 133–4.

131. *Id.* at 192; see also *id.* at 256.

132. 10 Jefferson, *op. cit. supra* note 107, at 199.

133. 8 *Annals of Cong.* 2104 (1798); see Bowers, *op. cit. supra* 89, at 378–9.

134. Richardson, *op. cit. supra* note 89, at 582. *Cf.* Bowers, *Party Battles of the Jackson Period* (1922) 219.

135. 3 Lincoln, *Complete Works* (Nicolay's and Hay's ed. 1905) 177–81.

136. 6 *id.* at 180.

137. 4 Paine, *op. cit. supra* note 10, at 235–6.

138. Dunning, *op. cit. supra* note 39, at 116.

139. 7 Jefferson, *op. cit. supra* note 20, at 209.

140. 9 Adams *op. cit. supra* note 34, at 432–3. On the civil law in the early period of American law, see Aumann, "Influence of English and Civil Law Principles upon the American Legal System during the Critical Post-Revolutionary Period" (1938) 12 *U. of Cinn. L. Rev.* 289; Radin, "Rivalry of Common-Law and Civil-Law Ideas in the American Colonies," in 2 *Law: a Century of Progress 1835–1935* (1937) 404; Pound, *op. cit. supra* note 77, at 107.

141. *Supra* at 29–30.

142. 5 Adams, *op. cit. supra* note 43, at 491; 10 *id.* at 226.

143. On other phases of the early codification movements, see Murrow, *Codification Reappraised: The Significance of Civilian Technique in Anglo-American Codification* (Unpublished MS. in Yale Law School Library). See also Pound, *op. cit. supra* note 77, at 152–3; Pound, *Outlines of Lectures on Jurisprudence* (4th ed. 1928) 80.

144. Harris, *Introduction to Pound*, *op. cit. supra* note 77, at ix-x.

145. 7 Jefferson, *op. cit. supra* note 20, at 403–5.

146. 4 Jackson, *Correspondence* (1929) 150. Livingston introduced proposals for codification in Congress, 6 *Cong. Deb.* 247 (1830); 7 *id.* 209 (1831).

147. See Gellhorn, "Improvement of Public Administration" (1939) 2 *National Lawyers Guild Quarterly* 20.

"Is it not then a rather strange reversal of form for the house of delegates of the American Bar Association to come out so strongly for a system whereby the exercise of legislative power is vested in the courts? That the point did not escape them is clear from the report on the hill." Lane, Address, National Lawyers Guild Convention, *Chicago Daily Law Bull.*, Feb. 11, 1939, p. 2, col. 5.

Brutus the American Praetor
(1940)

"... *le pretêur expliquoit, corrigeoit, ou suppleoit ce qu'il trouvoit obsucur & defectueux dans le Droit écrit...."*
"... the praetor explains, corrects or supplements that which he finds obscure and defective in the written law."—*Encyclopédie, ou dictionnaire raisonné des sciences, des arts et des métiers,* XIII (1765) 340.

1

Those who presently demand inquiry into the abuses of administration also demand for themselves the administration of abuses; for their research into the administration of power is also their search for the power of administration. Thus the struggle over the American judiciary state has taken a new turn, for it is now intended that administration, which developed in part from the need for unity between democratic legislation and democratic execution —between theory and practice—shall be virtually surrendered to the undemocratic judiciary power. Administration could be made practically independent of democratic control through a system in which expert administrators would be given over to independent administrators of experts.[1]

There is a certain importance, then, in calling attention to and in examining some of the *Letters of Brutus,* as they have been republished by Mr. Corwin in the appendix of his late book on the Constitution.[2] These articles were first published in New York in the spring of 1788 during the controversy there over the adoption of the federal Constitution, and are devoted to the question of the constitutionality of the judiciary state, to which the author, Brutus, was opposed. Here then is an occasion to consider the somewhat neglected text of the Constitution itself, apart from the gloss, particularly that of the *Federalist,* which has gathered about it; and thus to indicate somewhat the one-sidedness of the dominant conception of the American judiciary state.

Brutus[3] was Robert Yates,[4] subsequently a chief justice of New York. Yates was a leading Clintonite and therefore was described by Madison as a "zealous partisan" and "the representative of the portion of the State of New York which was strenuously opposed to the object of the [Constitutional] Convention."[5] Yates-Brutus was a delegate from New York to the Constitutional Convention, and as such belonged to the group of three that also included Hamilton-Publius. Brutus quit the Philadelphia Convention, in Madison's words, "on the 5th of July before it had reached the midway of its session, and before the opinions of the members were fully developed into their matured practical shapes."[6] Yates-Brutus not only left Philadelphia prematurely, but in the New York ratifying convention opposed and voted against the adoption of the Constitution;[7] and so came in conflict with Hamilton-Publius in a struggle eventually won by the latter, 30 to 27.[8] Therefore, it is proper to consider the *Letters of Brutus,* which were written at this time, beside the slightly later *Federalist* papers of Hamilton-Publius. Yates-Brutus was also the author of the well known *Secret Debates,*which was his report of the Philadelphia Convention,[9] and which Madison condemned as unreliable.

In the articles by Yates-Brutus as reprinted by Mr. Corwin, Brutus conceived of the Constitution as consecrating the judiciary state, and it was his purpose, in the view of Mr. Corwin, "to inflate judicial review to the dimensions of a bugaboo, and thereby convert the case for it into an argument against the Constitution."[10] Indeed, the full development of Brutus' position leads him to conceive of the Supreme Court as a dispensing or praetorian body; and in a curious way he even may have been among the first to consider a question of present American concern as to whether the judiciary power could be transformed into legislative power.[11] It is obvious that the very great importance of Brutus' articles derives from his discussion of the constitutional basis for this judicial supremacy.

Brutus' conception of paramount judicial power, designed to prevent the adoption of the Constitution, is, however, only important to the extent of its convincingness, because Brutus himself had no share in preparing the specific text of the Constitution he interpreted in his essays; for he had left the Constitutional Convention long before it was formulated.

Brutus based judicial supremacy on the part of the Constitution providing that "The judicial power shall extend to all Cases, in Law and Equity, arising under this Constitution. . . ."[12] He directed particular attention to the phrase, cases "in law and equity." This in itself is notable because Chief Justice Marshall subsequently omitted these words in his discussion of this very constitutional text in *Marbury v. Madison* [13] and so grounded the judiciary state in part in a Constitution from which he excluded the words "in law and equity."[14]

Brutus begins by holding fast to the very text of the Constitution. Speaking of the phrase "cases in law and equity," Brutus wrote that "At first view one would suppose that it meant no more that this, that the courts should exercise, not only the power of courts of law, but also that of courts of equity, in the manner in which those powers are usually exercised in the different states."[15] This interpretation Brutus rejects, saying that the word "law" authorizes the judiciary "to determine all questions that may arise upon the meaning of the constitution in law" and that the word "equity" empowers it "to explain the constitution according to the reasoning spirit of it, without being confined to the words or letter."[16] He elsewhere says the judges "will determine, according to what appears to them, the reason and spirit of the constitution."[17] Consequently Brutus concluded

> that the supreme court under this constitution would be exalted above all other powers in the government, and subject to no controul. . . . I question whether the world ever saw, in any period of it, a court of justice invested with such immense powers, and yet placed in a situation so little responsible. [18]

Brutus thus maintained in effect the position that if the Constitution provided for judicial supremacy over the Congress,[19] it also provided for judicial supremacy over the Constitution itself, so that the judges could "mould the government, into almost any shape they please."[20] Brutus stated that the "spirit" of the Constitution would be derived from its preamble[21] and believed that the states as a result probably would be "subverted" by the judiciary power.[22]

As he himself recognized,[23] Brutus' position rested entirely on the assumption that the constitutional phrase "law and equity" had a special meaning different from its ordinary acceptation. "Equity" thus is made to mean, not chancery power under the Constitution, but a general power to dispense with the constitutional text itself.

Brutus purported to rest on a conception of equity transmitted to him by Grotius and Blackstone.[24]

It should be apparent that Brutus did take hold of the vital words of the Constitution relative to the judiciary state. But instead of consecrating the judiciary state, the phrase "cases in law and equity" is in truth the fundamental fetter on the judiciary power, for the words "law and equity" do not remove a barrier to the exercise of judicial power, but constitute a limitation on the exercise of that authority. Brutus' conception fails, and with it the case for the judiciary state as it has been understood in the United State seems to go down.[25]

The phrase "cases in law and equity" was introduced into the Constitution by the Constitutional Convention, largely under the leadership of Madison, on August 27, 1787, that is, several weeks after Brutus had left Philadelphia, at a time when "the opinions of the members were fully developed into their matured practical shapes."[26] It was formulated for the very purpose of expelling the conception of judiciary supremacy from the Constitution. Brutus therefore seeks to interpret the decisive text of the Constitution so that it means its precise opposite.

On August 27, on the motion of Johnson, the Constitutional Convention considered extending the judicial power "to all cases arising under this Constitution."[27] Thereupon Madison said he "doubted whether it was not going too far to extend the jurisdiction of the court generally to cases arising Under the Constitution, and whether it ought not to be limited to cases of a Judiciary Nature. The right of expounding the Constitution in cases not of this nature ought not to be given to that Department."[28] As a consequence of Madison's statement, an authentic interpretation was accepted, Madison writes, in which "The motion of Docr Johnson was agreed to *nem. con:* it being generally supposed that the jurisdiction was constructively limited to cases of a Judiciary nature."[29]

However, this authentic interpretation would have been a secret to the state ratifying conventions which gave the Constitution "all the validity and authority it possesses."[30] Subsequently before the day was out it was agreed to introduce an explicit limitation on the judicial power so that it would extend "to all cases in law and equity arising under this constitution. . . . "[31] It seems to the writer that the definitive text publicly concretizes Madison's authentic "construction" excluding the judiciary state and that it repels Brutus' conception of a judiciary with praetorian power over the Constitution.

Furthermore, it appears to the writer that the constitutional text reflects amazingly well the solution by the Constitutional Convention of grave problems relative to the judiciary power. In part the task of the Convention was that of overcoming, so far as the federal Constitution was concerned, Puritan animosity to traditional equity power which existed in several states.[32] In this respect, the constitutional formulation brought the United States, as far as possible, abreast of England, where the Puritan revolution had failed to destroy equity despite Coke's desire to conquer it.[33]

In part also the Constitutional Convention had the task of excluding the content of English law in general because of its "antirepublican doctrines," as Madison called them.[34] It was intended at a time when codification was impossible that there should be no reception, so far as the Constitution was concerned, of English common law (including equity) or English criminal law.

In part also, the Constitutional convention had the task of formulating a text that would exclude the notion of the judiciary state. This is the meaning of Madison's construction.[35]

Under these contradictory circumstances it is necessary to notice the great precision with which the Constitution described the judiciary authority. It speaks carefully of the judicial "power," and extends it to "cases in law and equity" with the result that the entire formulation based on the introductory words "the judicial power shall extend to all cases in law and equity" is at once sufficient to fetter and exclude judicial supremacy as well as to overcome antagonism to a substantially plenary—and perhaps unified—conception of private law in general without necessarily receiving it with its English content or as an independent power.

2

Brutus admitted that he would have to overcome the fettering effect of the phrase "cases in law and equity" as a limitation on the expansion of the judicial power, if his conception of the praetorian judiciary were to prevail.[36] He sought in essence to unlimit this limitation by a theory based on an exploitation of the dialectical word "equity" as it was used by natural law jurists in the eighteenth century. When existing law has to be made to conform to natural law, "equity" has the task of overcoming the existing law. In part this has been precisely the role of Roman praetorian and the English chancery "equity" during the period of their expansion. The task of both Roman and English "equity" has been partially that of negating an existing legal system; and when the basis for the negation is grounded on extra-legal conceptions, "equity" may be identified with natural law. This negating "equity," which then may lead to an inner dialectical development, is essentially the conception that Brutus exploited in discussing the limit of judiciary power under the Constitution.

But equity may have another meaning in natural law, according to which it rectifies, by extension, the existing law, when the matter is itself an incomplete rendition of natural law. In Roman law, this often means the practice of employing legislation analogically. The existing law is taken to be an imperfect expression of natural law and the written text may be "interpreted" to include more than the text itself says, so as to mirror more perfectly the natural law.

Indeed, the two kinds of "equity" are in relation not only to the specific positive law, but are themselves in relation. The first meaning of "equity"—that of contradicting the existing law in the name of higher law—may be the reflection of a struggle between entrenched human interests and new human interests, arising from economic change and fighting to be recognized. The first sense of "equity" accomplishes this. The second meaning of "equity"—that of projecting the existing law—may be the reflection of the actual conquest of the state itself by the new human interests. If the state has indeed been made over by the new forces, "equity" then becomes a weapon with which to defend the victory and to extend the conquest to every part of the society. In this situation its task is to enforce the policies of the new regime by excluding overthrown, archaic and archaistic legal conceptions when they present themselves unexpectedly for recognition, as well as to deepen or to advance the new policies into new and unanticipated situations. This may be accomplished by regarding the fresh body of existing law as the starting point for legal decision. This is the second meaning of "equity."

The historic context in which "equity" appears becomes, therefore, vital; and it may lead to confusion to disregard the underlying basis on which each "equity" rests. It will be shown, for instance, that the first conception of "equity" was admired in France during the feudal period leading up to the French Revolution; and that the second conception of "equity" obtained in France after the Revolution destroyed feudalism and after the ensuing *Code civil* established the triumph of the new social relations.

Hence if "equity" had been used in the Constitution in any unusual sense it legitimately would have been the second conception of "equity," perhaps, for instance, as regards the bill of rights, because the American Constitution, just as the *Code civil,* is the legal and written form of a basic democratic revolution. To hold that either the American or French text gave a general negating power to the judiciary is to say that each text deliberately provided for an invisible counter-text and for its own destruction by the judiciary. The American Constitution, in order to bring the United States fully abreast of the English legal system did, it is true, provide for a limited judicial negating power in the traditional sense in which "equity" negates "law," so that they constitute a unity of opposites. But this limited judiciary negating power is also a determination so precise that it negates any general power of judiciary negation, such as Brutus, in essence and without regard to his own mode of expression, suggested existed on behalf of the judiciary power as to the Constitution itself.

Because of the dialectical character of "equity" there is then a certain interest in considering the Constitution and the *Code civil* together and in adverting to the fact that much the same position as Brutus' relative to the meaning of "equity" was asserted about fifteen years later in France during the preparation of the *Code civil.*[37] The issue in France, however, was fought with more clarity; and the point of view corresponding to that of Brutus was condemned.

If this comparison between the Constitution and the *Code civil* as to the conception of "equity" is to be appreciated in full it is perhaps also proper to give as well some hint of French ideas concerning "equity," especially English equity, in the period before the French Revolution. For it will be discovered that the "equity" of the *Code civil,* which embodied the French Revolution, was fundamentally the equity of projection and development; and that, on the contrary, the "equity" admired before the Revolution in feudal France, which suffered from an intolerable state of affairs, was English equity, because this was fundamentally the equity of negation.

French ideas of equity, in the eighteenth century, both before and after the French Revolution, rested firmly on a natural law base, and in accordance with natural law conceptions French jurists generally—only generally—regarded equity as perpetual and invariable. "Nature," Diderot and d'Alembert said, "is always the same."[38] The passing back and forth from negative or negating equity to positive or affirming equity in general was not admitted; and hence the dialectical or historical character of equity or of natural law in general was ignored. This was possible because both types of equity were simply explained by reference to a natural state of affairs in such way that it was the positive law that was negated or prolonged, depending in fact on what the underlying state of human affairs required. It was the positive law that either was overthrown because it did not reflect natural law, or deepened because it did reflect natural law even though only somewhat incompletely. The equity or natural law itself did not change.

Consequently under cover of these unchanging conceptions, concrete historical processes could well up, develop and pass over into new forms, and yet not violate the ideological position of natural law. "This natural law being founded on principles so essential," the Encyclopaedia said, "is perpetual and invariable; it cannot be derogated by any agreement, nor can the obligations which it imposes even be dispensed by any law."[39] It was then the historical function of French natural law to recognize the necessity of the movement of history, while at the same time it deprived history of its necessary movement. Such was the cunning of history; but the separation of theory from practice was fatal.

In the period before the French Revolution English equity, because of its negating character, was praised in France; for it essentially represented a way of overcoming the existing state of affairs in that country, and thus promised some relief from a miserable situation. The basis for the authority of equity was found, so far as France was concerned, in the good will of the prince and in natural law.[40]

In passing[41] on to the conception of equity as it existed in France after the French Revolution destroyed feudal France, it might be said that this was a period in which those who before the Revolution had so much admired *l'adoucissement équitable* [the equitable softening or mitigation] of English equity and who had invited their prince to receive this negating equity of England, were themselves now transforming French society and preparing the *Code civil* that was to consecrate that transformation in legal terms. Nevertheless the English chancery, which they had once regarded as "most worthy of imitation by civilized nations," no longer interested these representatives of civilized France. Their task now was not that of negation, but that of protecting and deepening and furthering what had been newly established. Their interest in a negating equity ceased and passed over to an interest in an affirming equity. While equity for them is still based on natural law, the same natural law that had been perpetual and invariable, their basic interest is now not in destroying the new state of affairs by an appeal to heaven, but in protecting their heaven on earth. The new equity is taken to be exactly this, and it is the precise opposite of what it had been.

In the preparation of the *Code civil* the nature of the new equity was considered. *Lex* 11 of a proposed text on interpretation of the *Code civil* provided that "in civil matters the judge in default of a precise statute is a vicar of equity. Equity is a resort to natural law or received usages in the silence of the positive law."[42] This text was not received in this form in France.[43] Some French jurists seem to have opposed the proposed text on the ground that the reference to "equity" would justify English equity so that the French courts could dispense with or negate the new *Code civil.* The reasoning for this position must have been similar to that of Brutus almost two decades earlier in relation to the meaning of "equity" in the Constitution. But Portalis, the *orateur* for the government, answered that equity under the new regime consecrated an affirming equity, and not a dispensing equity. What he says[44] is important not only in considering the historical character of equity, but also in considering the historical character of Montesquieuism, with its theories of independent powers within the state.

This, then, is the way in which natural law conceptions of equity passed, under the cover of the invariability of natural law, from negative equity into positive equity through the pressure of the French Revolution and the ensuing *Code civil.* Hegel[45] gives a somewhat similar account of the effect of the pressure of the English revolution on English political conceptions, and this is also of some importance here because of the direct light it casts on the conception, derived from Coke and the rule of law, that the judiciary state legitimately descended from the English revolution into the American Constitution.

3

Edward Livingston was the American point of contact between both Brutus and Portalis, between both negating and affirming equity. Livingston originally emerged from the struggles in New York that involved Brutus-Yates and Publius-Hamilton, and from New York entered the struggle between Jeffersonian democracy and the federalists. He led the fight in the Congress of the Jeffersonians against the alien and sedition legislation, in the course of which he opposed the judiciary state years before it had been created by Chief Justice Marshall in *Marbury v. Madison*. Several decades later, when Livingston was Secretary of State for Andrew Jackson, the President rejected the idea of exclusive judicial supremacy over the Congress and the President in the controversy concerning the Bank of the United States. Almost at the same time, Livingston collaborated also in President Jackson's anti-nullification proclamation, at a period when the courts supported them; and during it took a position that seems essentially Madisonian in its conception of the control by the judiciary of the states through the phrase, "cases in law and equity."[46] Livingston was known as the "Montesquieu of the Cabinet" and Jackson's nationalism was attributed to him. Through Livingston, then, democratic Jeffersonism sought to become nationalist; for Jefferson had made Livingston his political heir.[47]

In Louisiana, Livingston directly confronted Portalis' conception of "equity," when he encountered the Louisiana Civil Code, for this Code explicitly received the French idea of equity in its positive, post-revolutionary conception. Thus Livingston at different periods in his career became immediately involved both with Brutus' negating "equity" and Portalis' affirming "equity." He resisted the former and surpassed the latter.

Livingston came to Louisiana, influenced by French encyclopaedism and Jeffersonian democracy, as well as by the English legal thought of Bacon, Hobbes and Bentham. He grasped the Louisiana Civil Code as a weapon with which to undermine the judiciary state, even in its own domain of the private law. He put himself at the service of Louisiana, which seized on the French Civil Code to expel medieval Spanish law and to repel medieval English law, seeking admittance into Louisiana after it had been purchased for the United States by Jefferson and Robert Livingston.[48] Under these circumstances, Edward Livingston was responsible for virtually seven new codes, not all of which were adopted.

It is well to compare somewhat the Louisiana Civil Code with the Constitution of the United States, because each was concerned with the similar problem of excluding unwanted law, especially English law. The fact that the Louisiana Civil Code is a code and that the Constitution is not entirely a code corresponds precisely to the ideological resources available in each situation, and reflects ultimately the unequal legal development of France and England. Louisiana had at its disposal the *Code civil,* which was the cultural product of the French Revolution. The American Constitutional Convention, representing a new country that was not even completely abreast of England as to equity power, had at its disposal only the detested labyrinthine common law; and this Convention must have realized that it lacked the resources for codification. Jefferson had refused in 1776 to introduce codification into Virginia, although it was desirable, for it was intolerable that codification should rest on the disliked, perhaps "insect," Blackstone.[49] In the Constitutional Convention, Madison knew that the "antirepublican" English law could have been repelled by a "digest of laws,"[50] and he probably knew as well that the Convention lacked the resources to produce such a "digest." Under these circumstances, the excellent constitutional phrase "cases in law and equity," in so far as it is in any respect positive, is the exact reflection of the cultural poverty of the United States, brought about by the cultural backwardness of England, for the constitutional expression consecrates some of the power of English courts, but would repudiate its English content. On the contrary, the Louisiana Civil Code is the exact reflector of the cultural wealth of Louisiana, due to the *Code civil*. This aspect of the phrase, "cases in law and equity," was therefore of no interest to Livingston or Louisiana, for Louisiana prevented the reception of the English common law by its own Civil Code, with its specific, antifeudal content.

But Livingston was very much interested in the text of the Louisiana Civil Code consecrating French affirming "equity," as received from Portalis.[51] In this text, Portalis had remitted that protection and development of the *Code civil* to "equity," based on natural law, as it was understood in the French courts. Although Portalis had contemplated only an affirming "equity,"[52] and although the French courts were never independent in the American constitutional sense, nevertheless, the French courts were able through their freedom and the neglect of the French lawmaker during the subsequent century to negate parts of the *Code civil* under the pressure of further economic development. To this extent, Brutus' conception of praetorian "equity" later came quietly to obtain in practice in France.

The Jeffersonian Livingston, as the antagonist of the judiciary state, sought, in Louisiana, to overcome this weakness of French affirming "equity" based on the French courts, long before the weakness actually appeared. Livingston conceived of legislation as permanent, that is, as always developing historically on the basis of the unity of theory and practice, and proposed, without success, that the democratic legislature should itself constantly reformulate its codes on the basis of the continued unfolding of history, including, of course, judicial experience.[53] This is not without importance today in considering the theory of American administration, which envisages more clearly the conscious making of history. In this Livingston had the full approval of Jefferson, who not only denied the courts the power to "usurp the function of exclusively explaining the constitution," but wished that Livingston's Louisiana codification should "become an example for the imitation and improvement of other states."[54] "One single object," Jefferson told Livingston, "if your provision attains it, will entitle you to the endless gratitude of society; that of restraining judges from usurping legislation."[55] This, then, was the way in which Livingston, with his consciousness of historical development, surpassed the "equity" of Portalis, the jurist of natural law; and because of Livingston, it might be said that Louisiana legal thought attained a level not reached either in the rest of the United States or generally in France.

4

Brutus' conception of constitutional "equity" is a failure, but the importance of his papers is not destroyed thereby. He rightly perceived that the decisive constitutional text was the one stating that the judicial power should extend to "cases in law and equity." He understood that his position depended on giving a new sense to the historic phrase "law and equity."[56] If "equity" were to receive his meaning, "law" also might have a new and a political meaning, involving that of judicial power to declare the constitutionality of legislation. But if Brutus' conception of "equity" failed, as it did, his novel meaning of "law" would have to shrink to exclude judicial determination of constitutionality. For if "equity" does not sanction praetorianism, the phrase "law and equity" degenerates into a description of ordinary judicial power, largely as it is understood in Anglo-American private law, and amounting to a specific unity of specific opposed powers, "under" but not over, the Constitution. This is exactly what the constitutional words say and mean. Hence, because of this failure to establish the praetorian sense of "equity," Brutus in a sense becomes a remarkable opponent of the judiciary state as understood in *Marbury v. Madison.* This is important at the present time.

It may be therefore proper to speculate as to the possible impact of Brutus' theory on various American jurists. The main interest naturally will center on Chief Justice Marshall. It may be recalled[57] that Chief Justice Marshall in part established judicial supremacy in *Marbury v. Madison* on the basis of the very constitutional text referred to by Brutus. But he erased the limiting phrase "law and equity" from his use of the Constitution, so as to say that "The judicial power shall extend to all cases arising under this constitution." If he knew of Brutus' conception at all, Chief Justice Marshall might have slighted the phrase "law and equity" provided the effect of puncturing a conception of the word "equity" such as Brutus held was that of reducing the words "law and equity" to a conception of substantially plenary judiciary power without, however, judicial supremacy. Moreover, if he knew of Brutus' theory and agreed that it was correct, Chief Justice Marshall might not have cared openly to agree with Brutus' conception of praetorian "equity," although *Marbury v. Madison* may be a praetorian decision.[58]

However, it would be one-sided to consider the possible relation of Chief Justice Marshall to Brutus without considering at the same time the role of Hamilton, with whom Brutus seems to have been primarily engaged. It may appear that Chief Justice Marshall was attempting in *Marbury v. Madison* to avoid the difficulties which assailed Hamilton in contending for the judiciary state in the *Federalist* papers. Hamilton-Publius belonged with Yates-Brutus to the New York delegation to the Convention; and they were opposed to each other during the ratification controversy in New York.[59] Hamilton wanted the Constitution adopted and he was also prepared to hold that it provided for judicial supremacy. Brutus, on the other hand, was against ratification and in effect tried to defeat ratification by showing that the Constitution, if it consecrated judicial supremacy, also consecrated a judicial system with praetorian powers, so that the democratic Constitution itself disappeared, leaving only unmitigated judiciary power. It is proper to speculate as to the impact of these men on each other.

In order better to understand Hamilton's problem in presenting his conception of judiciary power in the *Federalist* it is best to sketch somewhat Hamilton's thought in the period of the Constitutional Convention that preceded the *Federalist;* for it may be significant, as Mr. Corwin indicated in 1913, that Hamilton perhaps became a "convert" to the judiciary state "between the time of writing *Federalist 33* and *Federalist 78.*" [60]

Gouverneur Morris—contrary to Ellsworth[61]—once said that Hamilton "had little share in forming the Constitution. He disliked it believing all Republican government to be radically defective."[62] In any event, on June 18, 1787, Hamilton made a celebrated speech in the Philadelphia Convention, in which, according to Madison, he said that "he had no scruple in declaring . . . that the British Govt. was the best in the world: and that he doubted much whether anything short of it would do in America."[63] England of course was not a judiciary state, and monarchy men would not have supported a judiciary state in the Constitutional Convention, although they could well have rallied to such an idea subsequently to the defeat of their favored conception. Madison records that Hamilton at this early period in the Convention also submitted his "sketch" of a form of government providing for an executive "to serve during good behaviour"[64] or "for life," as he said in the speech.[65] As the British state was not a judiciary state it was consistent for Hamilton to provide that his executive have "a negative on all laws"[66] and that "all laws of the particular States contrary to the Constitution or laws of the United States to be utterly void; and the better to prevent such laws being passed, the Governour or president of each state shall be appointed by the General Government and shall have a negative upon the laws. . . ."[67] To speak with the utmost generality,[68] Hamilton's position, with its emphasis on the executive, thus veers somewhat toward the position of John Adams, whose Massachusetts constitution explicitly provided,[69] it seems to the writer, that the judiciary should enjoy merely an advisory role, when it was requested, on matters of constitutionality.[70]

At no time during the Convention did Hamilton change over to the judiciary state. It can be said without dispute that Hamilton played no part in the events leading to the formulation of the text of the Constitution concerning the judiciary power.[71] In this connection August 27 was the decisive day, for on it Madison made his authentic "construction," which was incarnated in the constitutional words "cases in law and equity," that "cases" not of a "judiciary nature" were excluded from the scope of the judiciary power.[72] Mr. Farrand shows, in connection with the date of August 27, that Hamilton left the Convention on June 29, appeared to have been in Philadelphia on July 13, attended the Convention on August 13,[73] and was in New York during the critical period of August 20-September 2.[74]

Hamilton was appointed to the Committee on Style on September 8;[75] but this played no substantial role in formulating the text on the scope of the judiciary power. On September 6 he expressed his antagonism toward the proposed constitutional plan,[76] and it may be assumed that this was his matured opinion. And on September 17, the last day of the Philadelphia Convention, he said "No man's ideas were more removed from the plan than his own were known to be; but is it possible to deliberate between anarchy and Convulsion on one side, and the chance of good to be expected from the plan on the other."[77] This, then, was Hamilton's role in the Convention itself. In summary it may be said that Hamilton was never the representative of the judiciary state at the Constitutional Convention.

In tracing the subsequent development of Hamilton into the protagonist of the judiciary state, it is proper to call some attention at this point to the post-convention role of James Wilson, a delegate to the Constitutional Convention from Pennsylvania; for Wilson possibly was the only delegate to the Constitutional Convention who participated in the decisive formulation of August 27,[78] who signed the constitutional plan and who supported the judiciary state in a state ratifying body. Thus he is a really qualified antagonist of Madison, and in due course possibly may have influenced Hamilton.

On December 1, 1787, Wilson, in the Pennsylvania discussion over ratification, said that it was the duty of the justices to pronounce void a congressional "transgression" because the judges, "independent, and not obliged to look to every session for a continuance of their salaries will behave with intrepidity."[79] On December 7, 1787, in another speech Wilson quoted the pertinent constitutional text relating to the judiciary power, stating it in full, unlike Chief Justice Marshall subsequently in *Marbury v. Madison*, but in such way that the printed version italicizes the concluding words "arising under the Constitution." Then Wilson continued, saying that the "judges, as a consequence of the independence, and the particular powers of government being defined will declare . . . null" laws "inconsistent with the Constitution."[80] Thus James Wilson essentially derived the judiciary state from the "intrepidity" of "independent" justices; but did not discuss the phrase "cases in law and equity" which had been intended by Madison to exclude the theory of unassociated judicial supremacy. In the Convention, both Madison and Wilson had favored an associated judiciary revisionary power. When this had failed Madison seemed determined to oppose the idea, much more drastic, of unassociated judicial supremacy, while Wilson perhaps clung to it, although Madison's records decidedly indicate the contrary, or revived it after the Constitutional convention ended. The phrase "cases in law and equity" thus may sum up Madison's victory over Wilson in the new situation arising after the defeat of the conception of the associated judiciary revisionary power. If so, Wilson's reasoning at the Pennsylvania ratifying convention seems essentially based on an omission. In any event Wilson has to be taken account of as an influence in Hamilton's development into the supporter of the judiciary state.

Federalist Number 33, to which Mr. Corwin called attention in showing Hamilton's conversion to judicial supremacy,[81] appeared on January 3, 1788, a few weeks after Wilson's speeches. However, at this time there is as yet no attempt by Hamilton to defend the judiciary state. It seems to the writer that in this paper there is antagonism by Hamilton to the judiciary state.[82] But in *Federalist* Number 78, as Mr. Corwin said, Hamilton's "conversion" to the judiciary state is announced. Together with *Federalist* Numbers 79 to 85, this appeared for the first time in New York on May 28, 1788, as the concluding part of the second volume of the first edition of the *Federalist* papers as a book.[83] The earlier essays of course had been first published at different times in fugitive form. Although the Constitution already had been adopted in ten states,[84] the outcome in New York could be vital. Finally the Constitution was ratified by New York on July 26, 1788, by a vote of 30 to 27.

Hamilton's support of the judiciary state therefore appears for the first time in *Federalist* Number 78 during his struggle with

Brutus-Yates over the ratification of the Constitution in New York, and seems "inspired" by this opponent's letters. It should be noticed that Hamilton seems to have indicated his conversion in the *Federalist* essays and no place else. In his speeches in the New York ratifying convention after June 20, 1788, that is, after the pertinent *Federalist* papers had been published, Hamilton does not seem to advert, to the writer's knowledge, to the judiciary state.[86] Hamilton's idea of the judiciary state indeed did not become politically important until about fifteen years later when Jefferson came into power in what Jefferson himself called "the revolution of 1800" which "was as real a revolution in the principles of our government as that of 1776 was in its form."[87] The judiciary state was then brought forward in 1803 through *Marbury v. Madison*[88] as a counterrevolutionary measure.

The precise interaction between Brutus-Yates in his *Letters* and Hamilton-Publius in *Federalist* Numbers 78, 80 and 81 may now be briefly noticed. As it was Brutus' purpose in this situation to defeat ratification of the Constitution and Hamilton's purpose to compel ratification of it, Hamilton could accept only so much of Brutus' conception, which had been put forth to alarm New York, as would put an end to that fear, and yet attain the now desired judiciary state. This is the extent to which Brutus-Yates "inspired"[89] Publius-Hamilton. The question then is whether Hamilton could borrow from his opponent without involving himself in contradiction.

Federalist Number 78, the first pertinent essay by Hamilton, seems to the writer to be a remarkable document. In part of it Hamilton seems consciously to be mediating between Montesquieu and Rousseau[90] and to be arranging a "reconciliation" between these great opponents, so as to make the judiciary seem innocuous and "weak." Then, it seems, Hamilton works over Montesquieu's theory of intermediate powers[91] so that this "weak" judiciary power nevertheless may overcome and check a stronger power. Hence Hamilton maintained in this essay that it was the duty of the "weak" court under a "limited constitution" to declare "all acts contrary to the manifest tenor of the constitution void." He derived this in part from the independence of the justices under a limited constitution and perhaps indirectly hinted that this was a "natural presumption."

But in *Federalist* Number 80 Hamilton attempted, so it seems, to derive the general and unqualified power to declare constitutionality from the very phrase "cases in law and equity." He seems to entertain this position, *pur et simple,* at the same time he insists, correctly, it is believed, that "equity" connoted the "formal and technical distinction between LAW and EQUITY." The mode and form of expression were both emphatic. However, the only extended illustration he gave of the judicial power over constitutionality was that of the judiciary power to declare state legislation unconstitutional. To this extent Hamilton would not perhaps have offended the then beliefs of Madison.[92] In *Federalist* Number 80 Hamilton does not, however, give as an illustration judiciary power to declare the constitutionality of congressional action. This suggests either an unstated, undeveloped and "strange" distinction, or that his "illustrations" were only illustrative. Chief Justice Marshall in *Marbury v. Madison* obviously took it as meaning the latter. But it was clear that Hamilton, despite his attempted caution and despite his attempted exploitation of the "rules" of "construction"[93] had become involved in a contradiction; for he also was firmly and strongly insisting on the "formal and technical distinction between LAW and EQUITY," as a result of which both judicial supremacy over the Congress and judicial supremacy over the states were in effect precluded. What Hamilton intended as a fetter on legislation he thus unwillingly admitted was a fetter on the judiciary. As will be indicated, it seems to have been Brutus who put Hamilton in this embarrassing situation.

So in *Federalist* Number 81 Hamilton seems to embark on another mode of thought. He now justifies judicial supremacy on the ground that it need not be "deducible from any circumstance peculiar to the plan of the convention; but from the general theory of a limited constitution." This seems to be a return, perhaps, to *Federalist* Number 78 and a virtual abandonment of *Federalist* Number 80, at least in the latter's most general signification, in so far as it had sought to establish the judiciary state on the basis of the very text which specifically controlled the extent and the scope of the judiciary power. The judicial power over constitutionality, which Hamilton in *Federalist* Number 80 seemed to attempt to derive from the constitutional text itself, at least to the extent of so indicating to Chief Justice Marshall, was defended alone on an extra-constitutional "general theory" in *Federalist* Number 81. To a certain extent through *Federalist* Number 81 Hamilton improved his position. He must have believed that it freed him of the criticism of Madison.[94] He might have believed that he found a theory with which to introduce the conception of judicial supremacy into the different state constitutions as well as into the federal Constitution; for he perceived the danger to the judiciary state deriving from the various state constitutions, and here suggested a mode of conquering them—and their spokesman, John Adams. Moreover, he might have believed that he found a theory for the recall of Coke and the rule of law, exiled a century from England, as well as for the use of those sporadic cases in which the American courts are said to have overthrown legislation during the period of the American Revolution, cases which, however, may mean no more than that the American courts collaborated "legally" in the American Revolution.[95] But on the whole Hamilton's position was much worsened by *Federalist* Number 81, for he had to contradict or seem to contradict *Federalist* 80, and, above all, he had been driven away from the constitutional text itself. He had been brought to this situation, it seems, by Brutus.

The basis for Hamilton's seeming vacillation, which ends as a fatal concession that the Constitution itself does not provide for judicial supremacy, may have been the result of Brutus' conception of a praetorian judiciary, particularly through his use of the word "equity." Because of Brutus, Hamilton may have fled from the Constitution. Hamilton in *Federalist* Number 80 had to insist on the "formal and technical distinction between LAW and EQUITY." He began *Federalist* Number 81 by writing "there is not a syllable in the plan which *directly* empowers the national courts to construe the laws according to the spirit of the Constitution." Obviously this may have been intended as a response to Brutus' conception of constitutional "equity," based, as Brutus had said, on the "reasoning spirit"[96] of the Constitution. This may connote that Brutus' attack had alarmed the supporters of the Constitution, and that it was Hamilton's task to allay fear that the Constitution provided for its own destruction by the judiciary.[97]

Brutus thus may have forced Hamilton, in order to save New York for the Constitution, into insisting on the extremely "technical" character of "equity." This is the situation from which Hamilton never truly escaped. If Brutus forced Hamilton to maintain the extremely "technical" meaning of "equity" this signified that the whole phrase "law and equity," which described a unity of opposites, was also extremely "technical." Hamilton was compelled to admit this. However, if the entire phrase "law and equity" were completely "technical," as Hamilton properly said, the whole case for judicial supremacy on the basis of these words completely collapsed, for judicial supremacy was not indicated by a "technical" conception of them. A different ground for judicial supremacy thus would become a necessity.

Federalist Number 81 may represent, then, Hamilton's attempt to satisfy this necessity, which he now found in the weak "general theory" of "limited constitutions" in general; for Brutus had isolated and quarantined him from the constitutional text itself. Therefore under cover of condemning Brutus' idea that the natural law as judicially conceived reigned over the Constitution, Hamilton in fact was forced to embrace such a natural law theory himself. Brutus, however, had maintained his opinion because he believed it to be derived from the Constitution, but Hamilton held his view because it was not to be founded in the Constitution.

If these surmises as to the significance of *Federalist* Numbers 78, 80 and 81 are correct, it may be repeated[98] that Chief Justice Marshall, who appreciated the weakness of grounding the collationary *Marbury v. Madison* [99] on Hamilton's "general theory" alone rather than in the Constitution, sought once again to discover the power of the Supreme Court in the constitutional text itself by resolving Hamilton's contradiction in *Federalist* Number 80. But he failed because he had to erase four vital words from the Constitution. This was the very praetorianism of which Brutus had written.

5

The impact between the two American praetors, Brutus-Yates and Publius-Hamilton, also may have developed to involve Publius-Madison even before it affected Chief Justice Marshall. This relation possesses a certain importance in considering the judiciary state, for it was Madison, of course, who had induced the Convention to accept his "construction" that the judiciary power should only extend to "cases of a judiciary nature" and who had concretized his "construction" in the constitutional text that the judicial power should only extend to "cases in law and equity."[100] Madison thus excluded the reception of the judiciary state and therefore he is opposed to both Yates and Hamilton. Thus, the impact of Madison and its effect should be considered also.

Outside the Convention, however, Madison could not and would not have attempted to impose the Convention meaning of a constitutional text on the ratifying state conventions. Madison said he held fast to two principles of constitutional interpretation: first, that the opinions of the members "fully developed into their matured practical shapes" gave the sense of the Convention itself;[101] second, that "if the meaning of the Constitution is to be sought out of itself, it is not in the proceedings of the Body that proposed it, but in those of the State Conventions which gave it all the validity and authority it possesses."[102]

These two principles help unfold the importance of Madison's statement of October, 1788, made a few months after *Federalist* Numbers 78, 80 and 81 were first published, in which he said:

> In the State Constitutions & indeed in the Fedl one also, no provision is made for the case of a disagreement in expounding them; and as the Courts are generally the last in making ye decision, it results to them by refusing or not refusing to execute a law, to stamp it with its final character. This makes the Judiciary Dept paramount in fact to the Legislature, which was never intended and can never be proper. [103]

Madison's dogmatic last sentence seems to be a rebuke addressed primarily to those who knew or should have known of the intention of the Philadelphia Convention; and was made by Madison at a time when the proceedings of the Convention were still subject to the resolution of secrecy as to its deliberations. Because of Madison's view of the paramount role of the ratifying state conventions, this rebuke cannot have been pointed toward them. Madison therefore seems to be criticizing those who were disloyal to the matured results reached at Philadelphia. Ordinarily no one more than Madison respected the views of fellow delegates as to the true sense of the Convention and no one realized more than he the difficulties of grasping the meaning of the Constitution. Yet at this time, Madison spoke sharply and firmly to deny the existence of judiciary supremacy.

Madison seems, then, to be condemning various proponents of the judiciary state who knew or should have known that the judiciary state had been excluded from the constitutional plan. This might include Wilson, whose theory of the judiciary state derived from the constitutional intrepidity and independence of the justices. This might include Hamilton, whose theory of the judiciary state derived from his general theory of limited constitutions. This might include Yates, whose theory of the judiciary state derived from his conception of "equity" and whose theory showed disregard for the "matured practical shape" of the thought on which he based his theory. Of these theories of judicial supremacy, Hamilton's perhaps "experimental proposition" as expressed in the *Federalist* was "truest"—from the point of view of pragmatism. Nevertheless, Madison not only seems to have condemned Hamilton's spurious results in 1788, but never seems to have forgiven Hamilton for "experimenting" generally with the Constitution.[104]

From Madison it is necessary to pass for a moment to Jefferson, the most determined opponent of the judiciary state. Jefferson was not at the Philadelphia Convention, but the close relation between Jefferson and Madison should not be forgotten. Moreover, Jefferson had access to Madison's records of the Constitutional Convention and possessed a transcript of them. Jefferson sought to have Madison publish the records of the Constitution before Madison died, a suggestion which Hamilton opposed.[105] Madison died in 1836, but it was not until 1840 that his notes were published.[106] Under these circumstances the dogmatism and confidence with which Jefferson, who died in 1826, opposed the constitutionality of the judiciary state is worthy of notice. To Jefferson the theory of the judiciary state was one not "meriting any respect."[107]

It seems to the writer that it was John Taylor[108] of Caroline, one of the greatest Jeffersonians, who overcame all theories of the judiciary state. He did this largely by grasping firmly not Madison's records of the Constitutional Convention, which were still unpublished, nor the records of the different state ratifying conventions, which naturally enough, even when were available, were practically silent, but the Constitution itself.

In 1814 Taylor wrote that the power to declare constitutionality makes the judiciary "a greater legislative power," that "a power of construing is nearly equivalent to a power of legislating," that the connection between legislating and judging is such "that one may be easily run into the other; and that it is impossible to keep these powers separate and distinct as our theory requires," and asked "why should construction of law be quite independent of sovereign will, when law itself is made completely subservient to it," for (as if answering Wilson) "The power of construction is a supremacy over the legislature and the sovereign."[109]

In 1823 Taylor took hold of the Constitution itself. He considers the meaning of the constitutional text as to "cases in law and equity." "A power to try cases in law and equity," he says, "has never been understood to comprise a power of altering constitutions or forms of government." This could have been aimed at the reasoning of Brutus.

> The English judiciary try cases in law and equity, but this does not comprise a power to alter the rights of the English political departments. . . . Controversies may arise under the Constitution between political departments, in relation to their powers . . . but they would not be cases in law and equity, nor is any power to decide them given to the federal judiciary. [110]

This could have been addressed to Hamilton and Marshall.

As Taylor was first of all interested in repelling judicial supremacy over the states, he was also thrown into controversy with Madison as to the meaning of the phrase "cases in law and equity." As might be expected, after the constitutional formulation of August 27, which was so decisive, practically all discussion relative to the judiciary state ceased, except for certain statements by Madison in the last six days of the Convention. The question then arose as to the mode of control of abuses of the states of the power granted them by the Constitution to lay inspection charges on exports. At first Madison believed that the Congress would relieve against state oppressions by acting under the commerce clause.[111] But shortly afterward Madison seems to have abandoned the belief that this was the mode of control, perhaps, as he said three days later, because the commerce clause was "vague."[112] In abandoning reliance on the commerce clause, Madison expressed his regret that the Convention had rejected earlier the idea of a "negative on the state laws" and said that now "The jurisdiction of the supreme court must be the source of redress."[113] Perhaps this view was the same as that of Rutledge on the critical date of August 27.[114] However, the Convention refused to follow Madison's statement and explicitly gave power to the Congress to control the states in their levy of inspection fees on exports.[115] Taylor's answer to Madison rests then not only on the significance of the constitutional phrase "cases in law and equity," but also on the explicit constitutional provision that the

Congress has power to prevent the states from abusing their power to impose inspection fees on exports.[116]

Taylor also spoke once of the "mysteriarchs"[117] who had gained control of the Constitution. He might have added that the school of constitutional mystification was also the school for American praetors, among whom, however, contradiction reigned. Wilson justified the judiciary state because the judges being "independent" and "the particular powers of government being defined" could be "intrepid." But Hamilton upheld the judiciary state because the, for him, unintrepid and "weak" judges, who were "next to nothing," could assert the unwritten "general theory of limited constitutions" over a written constitution that the perhaps careless Wilson said possessed the character of "the particular powers of government being defined." The "intrepid" and "weak" Marshall, however, made Hamilton's unwritten "general theory of limited constitutions" into the written theory of a particular Constitution by erasing the constitutional phrase "cases in law and equity" from the Constitution, one of Wilson's "particular powers of government being defined" as unlimited thereby.

These jurists contradict themselves. Against them must be set the school of Jefferson which rests on the essence of the idea of Jefferson, Paine, Madison, John Taylor, Livingston and of John Adams and perhaps of the earlier or intermediate Hamilton. This school derives from the Constitutional Convention and the constitutional text itself, and so overcomes its own contradictions. Because he insisted on holding fast to the Constitution, Brutus perhaps also belongs to the school of Jefferson, for if in essence he justified praetorianism, perhaps as a "bugaboo" or as an "experimental proposition" of his own, he did so nevertheless on the basis of his conception of a specific and decisive constitutional text, so that even in his failure he remains, because of the correctness of his legal method, a great opponent of the American judiciary state as well as a great American prophet.

NOTES

1. Franklin, *The Constitutional Struggle*; 1938, 1 *Nat. Lawy. G. Quar.* 357 (1938). See Haines, "The Adaptation of Administrative Law and Procedure to Constitutional Theories and Principles," 34 *Am. Pol. Sci. Rev.* 1 (1940). On the classic instance of Aebutianism, which is the formulation of substantive law

attained through control over legal procedure, see Buckland and McNair, *Roman Law and Common Law* (1936) 3.

2. Corwin, *Court over Constitution* (1938).

3. On the use of "Roman" names in the New York at this time, see Spaulding, "The Ratification of the Federal Constitution," 5 *History of the State of New York* (1934) 31, 48. It is well known that the Americans and the Frenchmen of the eighteenth century disguised themselves as Romans. Hence it may be noted that legal development may take both the form of emancipation from a text (*e.g.*, Roman equity, twentieth century "free law"), and of a return to a text (an emancipation from an emancipation, *e.g.*, legal humanism in the renaissance, the present-day revulsion against the judiciary state based on the demand of a restored text of the Constitution).

4. See Corwin, *op. cit. supra* note 2, at pp. 35, 45. For further information about Robert Yates, see Webster, *The Weakness of Brutus Exposed* (1787), in Ford, *Pamphlets on the Constitution of the Untied States* (1888) 117; Ford, *op. cit.*, at p. 424; 3 Farrand, *Records of the Federal Convention of 1787* (rev. ed. 1937) 90; 20 *Dict. Am. Biog.* (1936) 601. For information about Robert Yates in relation to Livingston, discussed in Part 3 of this paper, see Hatcher, *Edward Livingston* (1940), c. 2, 3.

5. Madison to Trist, Dec., 1831, 9 *Writing of Madison* (Hunt's ed. 1910) 471, 474. On the ratification of the Constitution in New York, see 1 Alexander, *A Political History of the State of New York* (1906) 28–36; Spaulding, *op. cit. supra* note 3.

6. Madison to Trist, Dec., 1831, *supra* note 5.

7. Beard, *Economic Origins of Jeffersonian Democracy* (1915) 72–3.

8. 2 *Dict. Amer. Hist.* (1940) 28, 29.

9. Yates, *Secret Proceedings and Debates of the Convention* . . . (1821). See 1 Farrand, *op. cit. supra* note 4, at pp. xiv–xv.

10. Corwin, *op. cit. supra* note 2, at p. 45.

11. "Perhaps the judicial power," he wrote, "will not be able, by direct and positive decrees, ever to direct the legislature. . . . But it is easy to see, that in their adjudications they may establish certain principles, which being received by the legislature, will enlarge the sphere of their power beyond all bounds." Corwin, *op. cit. supra* note 2, at p. 244.

12. *U. S. Const.*, Art. 3 § 2, cl. 1. Corwin, *op. cit. supra* note 2, at p. 234.

13. 1 Cranch 137, 2 L., Ed. 135 (U. S. 1803).

14. Therefore, Chief Justice Marshall was satisfied to say that "The judicial power of the United States is extended to all cases arising under the constitution. Could it be the intention of those who gave this power, to say, that in using it, the constitution should not be looked into? . . . This is too extravagant to be maintained. . . . And if they can open it at all, what part of it are they forbidden to read or to obey? . . ." See *Marbury v. Madison*, 1 Cranch 137, 178–9, 2 L. Ed. 135, 178 (U. S. 1803).

15. Corwin, *op. cit. supra* note 2, at p. 234.

16. Corwin, *op. cit. supra* note 2, at p. 236; *cf. id.* at pp. 237, 243, 246.

17. Corwin, *op. cit. supra* note 2, at p. 237.

18. Corwin, *op. cit. supra* note 2, at p. 251.

19. Corwin, *op. cit. supra* note 2, at pp. 244–6.

20. Corwin, *op. cit. supra* note 2, at p. 243.

21. Corwin, *op. cit. supra* note 2, at p. 246.

22. *Ibid.*

23. See *supra* note 15.

24. Corwin, *op. cit. supra* note 2, at p. 236. See 1 *Chitty's Blackstone* 58, 3 *id.* 431; see also 2 Austin, *Lectures on Jurisprudence* (4th ed. 1879) 598.

25. Franklin, "The Judiciary State I," 2 *Nat. Lawy. G. Quar.* 244, 253–261 (1940) (p. 31 and section 4 in this volume).

26. Cf. *supra* note 6.

27. Franklin, "The Judiciary State I," at p. 256 (p. 44 in this volume); 2 Farrand, *op. cit. supra* note 4, at p. 430; see also *id.*, at p. 423.

28. 2 Farrand, *op. cit. supra* note 4, at p. 430.

29. *Ibid.*

30. Madison to Trist, Dec., 1831, *loc. cit. supra* note 5, at p. 477.

31. Franklin, "The Judiciary State I," at p. 259 (p. 47 in this volume); 2 Farrand, *op. cit. supra* note 4, at p. 425.

32. The New Yorker, Brutus, was quite in error in speaking generally of ". . . the power . . . of courts of equity, in the manner in which these powers are usually exercised in the different states." Corwin, *op. cit. supra* note 2, p. 234. For instance, in Massachusetts, a neighbor of New York, complete equity power was not received until the last quarter of the nineteenth century, and in Pennsylvania, another neighbor of New York, complete equity power was not given to the judiciary, until the end of the first third of the nineteenth century and in Brutus' time could be exercised, when it wished, by the legislature itself. Hamilton, *Federalist* No. 82 (1788). Wilson, "Courts of Chancery in the American Colonies," 2 *Select Essays in Anglo-American Legal History* (1908) 810; Pound, *The formative era of American Law* (1938) 155; Cowan, "Legislative Equity in Pennsylvania," 4 *Univ. Pitt. L. Rev.* 1 (1937); see also Corwin, *op. cit. supra* note 2, at p. 13.

33. 1 Holdsworth, *A History of English Law* (3d ed. 1922) 463, 464.

34. Madison to Washington, Oct. 18, 1787, 3 Farrand, *op. cit. supra* note 4, at pp. 129. 130. A "republic" is a "government by its citizens in mass," and has "the element of popular election and control. . . ." Jefferson to John Taylor, May 28, 1816. 15 *The Writings of Thomas Jefferson* (Library ed. 1904) 17, 19, 23.

35. 2 Farrand, *op. cit. supra* note 4, at p. 430.

36. *Supra* note 15.

37. It may lead to one-sidedness to ignore the interaction between eighteenth century France and eighteenth century America. See Chinard, *Jefferson et les idéologues* (1925). c. 5; *cf.* Hegel, *Philosophy of History* (Sibree's tr. 1840) 143. However, it is not pretended that there is any immediate or direct interaction between the Constitution and the *Code civil,* so far as the subject of this paper is concerned. Yet it may be of some interest to note that the first edition of the *Federalist* papers was published in New York in 1788, and that the second edition, with two printings, and the third edition were published in France in 1792 and 1795, both seemingly subject to official censorship. The fourth edition appeared in New York in 1799. 11 *Hamilton's Works* (Lodge's ed. 1904) xxxi–xxiv.

In Louisiana, of course, the reception of French thought has been more obviously immediate and direct. When Livingston, in his scheme of unemployment relief, told the Louisiana legislature about 1825 that "Political society owes perfect protection to all its members . . . it also owes necessary subsistence to those who cannot procure it for themselves. . . . This relief must be given by providing means of employment for the industrious, and gratuitous support for the helpless," 1 Livingston, *Complete Works on Criminal Jurisprudence* (1873) 528–530, he was repeating in substance Art. 21 of the French Constitution of 1793, in which Paine had some share, 15 *Dict. Nat. Bio.* 69, 75, and which provided that "assistance is a sacred duty. Society owes subsistence to unfortunate citizens either in procuring them work or in assuring the means of existence to those who are unemployed." See also 3 *The Writings of Thomas Paine* (Conway ed. 1895) 128, 130; Hatcher, *op. cit. supra* note 4, at pp. 82–3, 277. As late as 1872, argument in the Slaughter-House Cases, which arose in Louisiana, drew heavily on French sources. See Slaughter-House, 16 Wall. 35, 45, 21 L. Ed. 394. (U. S. 1873).

38. *Encyclopédie, ou dictionnaire raisonné des sciences, des arts et des métiers* I (1751) xx.

39. *Encyclopédie, supra* note 38, (1755) V, 131.

40. "Sometimes equity is confounded with justice," said the essay on equity in the Encyclopaedia, "but the latter appears rather designed to recompense or to punish conformably to some law or established rules than conformably to the varying circumstances of an action. It is for this reason that the English have a court of chancery or of equity to temper the severity of the letter of the law and to consider the matter which is brought there, uniquely according to the rule of equity and conscience. This court of chancery is one of the good institutions that there are in England, and one of the most worthy of being imitated by civilized nations. In fact, the interest of a sovereign and his love for his peoples which requires him to beware that nothing be done in his empire contrary to the general good also demand that he redress, that he rectify and that he correct what can have been made so. So equity, taken in this particular sense, is a will of the prince, disposed by the rules of wisdom, to correct what is found in a law of his state, or in a civil judgement of the magistrature established by his orders, when things have not been regulated as the view of the general good would require in the circumstances contemplated. . . . [N]atural law is the true source of equity worthy of all our attention. . . . In fact, it is not on human and arbitrary agreement that equity depends; its origin is eternal and inalterable in a way that if we were free of the yoke of religion we should not be from that of equity." *Encyclopédie, supra* note 38, V, 894–5. The writer concludes by recalling Montesquieu's praise of equity. ". . . yes, Rhedi," wrote the author of the *Persian Letters*, "were I certain of following invariably this equity that I have before my eyes I should regard myself the foremost of men." *Lettres persanes* (1721) lxxxiv. *Cf.* Rousseau, *Considérations sur le gouvernement de Pologne et sur la reformation projetée* (1722) c. 10. Rousseau praised the Roman praetorship "of the good times of Rome" which gave the legal power "to interpret and to supplement at need by the natural light of reason and common sense. Nothing is more puerile than the precautions taken on this point by the English." English law, he said, was a vast labyrinth where both memory and reason were lost.

41. Before proceeding it would be unfair not to correct within limits the usual opinion that these eighteenth century jurists were entirely incapable of conceiving the movement of history. If they at the most recognized only

repetitions and machine-like movement, it was not entirely because the best of these thinkers did not acknowledge history, but because under the circumstances historical development in France had to proceed by establishing a fixed conception of human nature which in the France of their time had been degraded and ought to be restored. So if Diderot and d'Alembert said "Nature is always the same" it should be remembered that the Encyclopaedia itself, which was established on a conception of the unity of knowledge and of the many-sided relations of its parts, occasionally showed otherwise. If the Encyclopaedia in general conceived of equity and natural law as perpetual and invariable, it also gave elsewhere a beautifully written account of natural law in which was almost attained a conception of dialectical relation. *Encyclopédie*, *supra* note 38, IX, 665.

42. Fenet, *Recueil complet des travaux préparatoires du Code civil II* (1827) 7.

43. Substantially in this form, it has been part of the Louisiana Civil Code since 1808, and is today the basis for *L'équité Louisianaise.* Art. 21, *La. Civil Code* of 1870; see Franklin, "Equity in Louisiana," 9 *Tulane L. Rev.* 485 (1935).

44. "One of the orators has pretended that we were giving to the judges a power denied by the Constitution. 'I think,' he has told us, 'that we have no tribunals of equity which may dispense with the statutes. There is a court of equity in England; in Rome the praetor was a judge of equity; in France the king had the right to give dispensation, and the *Parlemens* often deviated from the letter of the statute. But, among us, the calling of the judge is confined to the faithful application of the statutes.'

"All these objections, establish nothing against the article; they prove only that the article has not been understood.

"The author of the objection would be sound if we should allow the judges the liberty of putting natural equity in place of law. Thus in Rome the praetor did not apply the law when he believed it contrary to natural equity. He introduced the actions of good faith in order to escape the laws which had established exact formulae for each action; in England the court of equity and in France the courts of the sovereign often made law in order to modify the laws; but this is not how the article works. Our article only fits the cases where the law is obscure or insufficient and the cases where is even no law. In these several instances should the judge surrender his calling or fulfill it?" Locré, *La legislation de la France* I (1827) 480, 481. *Cf.* 2 Austin, *op. cit. supra* note 24, at pp. 634–5.

45. ". . . In England" (under the last kings of the House of Stuart), Hegel writes, ". . . it was an accepted principle that the ruler was responsible for his actions to God only. . . . This also involves the assumption that it is the ruler alone who knows for certain what is essential and necessary to the state; for in him . . . is contained the principle that he is an immediate revelation of God. This principle, however, when further logically developed, reaches the point at which it turns round into its direct opposite, for the distinction between priests and laymen does not exist among Protestants." Then Hegel writes, after considering the possession of divine revelation, nor does "there exist any such privilege which can belong exclusively to a layman. To the principle of the divine authorization of the ruler there is accordingly opposed the principle of this same authorization which is held to be inherent in the laity in general. . . ." 1 Hegel, *Lectures on the Philosophy of Religion* (Speirs' tr.1895) 249. But *cf.* Pound, *The*

Spirit of the Common Law (1921) 60–1; Pound, *Contemporary Juristic Theory* (1940) 26. *Cf.* also the famous article on Geneva in *Encyclopédie*, *supra* note 38, XV (1777) 959.

46. See Franklin, "Concerning the Historic Importance of Edward Livingston," 11 *Tulane L. Rev.* 163 (1937).

47. Harris, in Pound, *op. cit. supra* note 32, at pp. ix–x. *Cf.* Acheson, Taney: "Notes Upon Judicial Self Restraint," 31 *Ill. L. Rev.* 705, 706–7 (1937).

48. Franklin, "Some Observations on the Influence of French Law on the Early Civil Codes of Louisiana," *Journées du droit civil français* 833 (1936).

49. Franklin, "The Judiciary State II," 3 Nat. Lawy, G. Quar. 27 (1940) 27–41 (pp. 57–78. in this volume).

50. Madison to Washington, Oct. 18, 1787, *loc. cit. supra* note 34.

51. *Supra* note 43.

52. *Supra* note 44.

53. Franklin, *loc. cit. supra* note 46. Livingston rejects the mechanistic conception of legislation, characteristic of the eighteenth century in general, according to which formulation alone is the chief task of legislation. "The legislative power," Locke wrote, "is that, which has a right to direct how the force of the Commonwealth shall be employed. . . . But because those laws which are so constantly to be executed, and whose force is always to continue, may be made in a little time, therefore there is no need that the legislature be always in being, not having any business to do." 5 Locke, *Works* (1923) 424. But Livingston's conception of legislature in permanence is a historical conception, for he also raises the questions of reformation of legislation. There may then be some reason for relating his thought to Hegel's for whom the organism of the state "is the development of the idea into its differences, which are objectively actualized." Hegel, *infra* note 108, § 269.

54. Jefferson to Livingston, March 25, 1825, 7 *The Writings of Thomas Jefferson* (Washington ed. 1854) 402.

55. *Ibid.*

56. *Supra* note 15.

57. *Supra* note 14.

58. See p. 96. It may be suggested that Chief Justice Marshall did not care to ground judicial supremacy alone on unreceived ideas as to the rule of law, for after all the Constitution was a written document, the result of a Constitutional Convention in which every grant of power was suspiciously and jealously regarded, and of a period detesting English judicial ideas, even without the theory of the supremacy of the law, as "antirepublican." *Supra* note 34. Marshall may have been forced, if he thought of the matter at all, into anchoring his result in part in a constitutional text from which he omitted the basic words, "law and equity."

59. *Supra* note 8.

60. Corwin, "Book Review," 7 *Am. Pol. Sci. Rev.* 329, 331 (1913). See Haines, *The American Doctrine of Judicial Supremacy* (2d ed. 1932) 135n.

61. 3 Farrand, *op. cit. supra* note 4, at pp. 396, 397.

62. 3 Farrand, *op. cit. supra* note 4, at p. 418.

63. 1 Farrand, *op. cit. supra* note 4, at p. 288.

64. 1 Farrand, *op. cit. supra* note 4, at p. 292.

65. 1 Farrand, *op. cit. supra* note 4, at p. 289.

66. 1 Farrand, *op. cit. supra* note 4, at p. 292.

67. 1 Farrand, *op. cit. supra* note 4, at p. 293; see also *id.*, at p. 304; 3 *id.* at p. 617.

68. Later Hamilton himself disputed whether this account of his conception was correct or not. Hamilton to Pickering, Sept. 16, 1803, 3 Farrand, *op. cit. supra* note 4, at p. 397; see 2 Hockett, *Constitutional History of the United States* (1939) 61. In any event it was quite proper for him, in his own defense, to say that "neither the proposition thrown out for debate, nor even those voted on in the earlier stages of deliberation were considered as evidences of a definitive opinion . . . it appeared to me to be in some sort understood, that with a view to free investigation, experimental propositions might be made, which were to be received merely as suggestions for consideration." Hamilton to Pickering, Sept. 16, 1803, *loc. cit. supra*, at p. 398. This statement is entirely in accordance with Madison's statement that Brutus-Yates could not speak of the determinations of the Convention with definiteness because the latter had left it on July 5, "before the opinions of the members were fully developed into their matured practical shapes." Both Madison and Hamilton in this fashion cast doubt on the authentic nature of Brutus' theory of the praetorian judiciary. It is regrettable that Mr. Beard concluded mechanically that the majority of the Convention "tacitly" accepted the judiciary state, without considering the thought and formulations of these men and their schools in their historical development and unfolding. Beard, *The Supreme Court and the Constitution* (1912) c. 2. See Melvin, "The Judicial Bulwark of the Constitution," 8 *Am. Pol. Sci. Rev.* 167 (1914).

69. *Mass. Const.* (1780) 2. 3. 2.

70. Franklin, "The Judiciary State I," at pp. 250–53 (39–41 in this volume). See Walsh, *The Political Science of John Adams* (1915) c. 13.

71. "While the record of the convention may contain no opinion upon this subject by Oliver Ellsworth of Connecticut or Alexander Hamilton of New York, they were leading advocates of the doctrine of judicial control. . . ." Dougherty, *Power of Federal Judiciary over Legislation* (1912) 60.

72. *Supra* notes 28–31.

73. 2 Farrand, *op. cit. supra* note 4, at p. 268.

74. 3 Farrand, *op. cit. supra* note 4, at p. 588. See also Spaulding, *op. cit. supra* note 3, at p. 42; Corwin, *op. cit. supra* note 2, at p. 48.

On August. 20, 1787, Hamilton wrote to King from New York: ". . . if any material alteration should happen to be made in the plan now before the Convention, I will be obliged to you for a communication of it. I will also be obliged to you to let me know when your *conclusion* is at hand; for I would choose to be present at that time." 3 Farrand, *op. cit. supra* note 4, at p. 70. On Aug. 28, 1787, Hamilton wrote to King from New York: "I wrote to you some days since to request you to inform me when there was a prospect of your finishing, as I intended to be with you, for certain reasons, before the conclusion. It is whispered here that some late changes in your scheme have taken place which give it a higher tone. Is this the case?" 3 Farrand, *op. cit. supra* note 4, at p. 75.

75. 2 Farrand, *op. cit. supra* note 4, at p. 553.

76. 2 Farrand, *op. cit. supra* note 4, at p. 524.

77. 2 Farrand, *op. cit. supra* note 4, at pp. 645–6.

78. 2 Farrand, *op. cit. supra* note 4, at pp. 426, 427, 429, 431.

79. 2 Elliot, *The Debates in the Several State Conventions* (2d ed. 1876) 446.

80. 2 Elliot, *op. cit. supra* note 79, at p. 489.

Wilson also upheld the idea of the judicial power to declare constitutionality in his law lectures at the University of Pennsylvania. He did not discuss, however, the constitutional phrase "cases in law and equity." Wilson in part reached his conclusion because the judges, under the Constitution, were "independent," because legislation may be "controlled by natural or revealed law," and because he obeyed Coke. 1 Wilson, *Works* (Wilson ed. 1804) 455–63. See also 2 *id.* 215–6, 260–77. See also *infra* note 86.

81. *Supra* note 60.

82. In discussing the constitutional text relating to the supremacy of the Constitution and the laws of the United States, Hamilton said that the national government must judge the propriety of its laws "in the first instance" and that if it should overpass the just bounds of its authority "the people . . . must . . . take such measures to redress the injury done to the Constitution as the exigency may suggest and prudence justify." *Federalist* No. 33.

83. 11 Hamilton, *op. cit. supra* note 37, at p. xxxii.

84. *Supra* note 8.

85. *Ibid.*

86. 2 Hamilton, *op. cit. supra* note 37, at p. 3–100; *cf.* p. 94. Sumners' discussion of the New York state constitutional convention has been summarized with the statement that "there is comparatively little about the Supreme Court." 1 Alexander, *op. cit. supra* note 5, at p. 34. Sumner says of what he calls the "sleeping giant" in the Constitution that neither Hamilton nor anybody else "foresaw that the function of the Court would build upon the written Constitution a body of living constitutional law." 1 Alexander, *op. cit. supra* note 5, at pl. 34. Perhaps this may mean that Hamilton was not so much "converted" to the judiciary state as that he was again indulging in one of his "experimental propositions." Certainly New York at that time was no place vigorously to push ideas that were essentially Thermidorian. Hamilton, himself regarded the situation as one which would lead to "convulsion" if the Constitution which was so obnoxious to him personally, were not accepted. *Supra* note 77.

Moreover, early theorists of the judiciary state may not always have been entirely consistent in their support of it. For instance, Mr. Burdick seems to have had an impression that Hamilton planned a Roman-French system of codification. Burdick, *Principles of Roman Law* (1938) 38. Wilson, as early as 1791, undertook to prepare a code for the legislature of Pennsylvania, in which the body of the common law would be "reduced into a just and regular system," in consequence of which he made some rather interesting remarks concerning legal classification and the teaching of law in the universities. He seems perhaps to have forecast the "institutional" or "commentary" method of the private codes or restatements of the American Law Institute. 1 Wilson, *op. cit. supra* note 80, at pp. iii–xiv. Wilson's law professorship at the University of Pennsylvania was the occasion for his defense of the judiciary state. See *supra* note 80.

87. Jefferson to Roane, Sept. 6, 1819, *loc. sit. supra* note 54, VII, 133.

88. *Supra* note 13. "The nation declared its will by dismissing functionaries of one principle and electing those of another, in the two branches, executive and legislative, submitted to their election. Over the judiciary department, the

constitution had deprived them of their control. That, therefore, has continued the reprobated system. . . ." Jefferson to Roane, *loc. cit. supra* note 87.

89. Corwin, *op. cit. supra* note 2, at p. 45.

90. See *infra* note 108.

91. Montesquieu, *De l'esprit des lois* (1748) 2. 4. Montesquieu conceived of the nobility and the clergy as intermediate powers, weaker than the monarch, yet nevertheless able to check and overcome him; and hence they were necessary in the state. The freedom-loving Montesquieu who justified the separation of powers because it secured English freedom, *id.*, 11.6, seemed to regret that the English loved freedom so much that they had impaired these intermediate powers. On Montesquieu's influence in England, particularly on Paine and Burke, see Fletcher, *Montesquieu and English Politics* (1939). On Helvétius' opposition to Montesquieu and on the presentation of Helvétius' criticism to Americans through Jefferson, see *infra* note 108. Jefferson as early as 1790 was aware of Helvétius' private letter showing his hostile position toward Montesquieu. Chinard, *Pensées choisies de Montesquieu tirées du "Common-Place Book" de Thomas Jefferson* (1925) 15, n, 1. In arranging in 1810 for the translation and publication of Destutt de Tracy's critique of Montesquieu, Jefferson wrote that "Helvétius' letter, on the same works should be annexed, if it can possibly be procured. It was contained in a late edition of the work of Helvétius published by the Abbe de la Roche. Probably the edition might be found. . . . I am glad to hear of everything which reduces that author [Montesquieu] to his just level, as his predilection for monarchy, and the English monarchy in particular, has done mischief everywhere, and here also, to a certain degree. . . ." Jefferson to Duane Sept. 16 1810, in Chinard, *op. cit. supra* note 37, at p. 59. See also 1 Grimm and Diderot, *Historical and Literary Memoirs and Anecdotes* (1772, tr. 1814) 143, 146, 152. Helvétius wrote Montesquieu: "The idea of perfection amuses our contemporaries; but it instructs the youth and aids posterity. . . . I doubt . . . that they will adopt . . . your complicated balances of intermediate powers . . . before long . . . these are the tyrants of the people . . . one sees the danger of an equilibrium which it is necessary to rupture ceaselessly in order to accelerate or retard the movements of a machine so complicated." Helvétius to Montesquieu, 3 *Oeuvres complètes d'Helvétius* (nouvelle *ed.* 1818) 256, 261, 262. Helvétius wrote Saurin, concerning Montesquieu: "Professional feeling *(l'esprit de corps)* overflows everywhere. Under the name of 'French' there exist only corporations and individuals, and not a citizen who merits this title. The philosophers themselves would form corporations; but if they flatter the particular interest at the expense of the general interest, I predict their reign will not be long." Helvétius to Saurin, *op. cit. supra*, at pp. 265, 267.

92. *Infra* note 113.

93. See Madison in *Federalist* No. 41 and Hamilton in No. 83. See also Madison in Nos. 40, 44, and Hamilton in No. 32.

94. *Infra* note 113.

95. See 9 Adams, *Works* (1851) 390.

96. *Supra* notes 16, 17.

97. *Cf. supra* note 10.

98. *Supra* note 58.

99. *Supra* note 13.

100. *Supra* notes 26–31. For something of the impact between Madison and Marshall, see Sumners, "The Constitution Today," 26, *Am. Bar Ass'n Jour.* 285, 288 (1940).

101. *Supra* note 6. For an elaborate application by Madison of his own historical method, see his letter to Stevenson, Nov. 17, 1830, 3 Farrand, *op. cit. supra* note 4, p. 483.

102. Madison, *supra* note 30; see Hockett, *supra* note 68.

103. Observations on "The Draught of a Constitution for Virginia" . . . (1788), 5 Madison, *op. cit. supra* note 5, at p. 284.

104. In 1834, Trist records a statement concerning Hamilton made to him by Madison: " . . . the divergence between us took place—from his wishing to *administration,* or rather to administer the Government (these were Mr. M.'s very words) into what he thought it ought to be; while, on my part, I endeavored to make it conform to the Constitution as understood by the Convention that produced and recommended it, and particularly by the state conventions that *adopted* it." Memorandum by Trist, Montpellier, Sept. 27, 1834, 3 Farrand, *op. cit. supra* note 4, at pp. 533, 534. See in considerable detail, Walsh, *op. cit. supra* note 70, at pp. 285–8, especially at p. 286, n. 4.

105. See 2 Hockett, *op. cit. supra* note 68, c. 4.

106. *Ibid.* see 1 Farrand, *op. cit. supra* note 4, at pp. xv–xix.

107. 6 Jefferson, *op. cit. supra* note 54, at p. 462.

108. Mr. Chinard hints that an account of John Taylor would be one-sided if it did not take account of the influence of eighteenth century French thought on him. Chinard, *op. cit. supra* note 37, at p. 227. See in general, Beard, *op. cit. supra* note 7, c. 7, 12; Chinard, *Thomas Jefferson* (2d ed. 1939) v–xvi. It is certain that before Taylor, Rousseau, in opposing Montesquieu's exclusively political theory of the separation of powers, had inquired whether there could be a separation of powers, a division *"en force et en volonté,"* a split between theory and practice. ". . . after having dismembered the social body . . . one does not know how they reassemble the pieces." Rousseau, *Du contrat social* (1762) 2.2. See in general, Tchernoff, "Montesquieu et J.-J. Rousseau," 20 *Revue du droit publique* 49, 61–77 (1903). Taylor's contemporary, Hegel, for whom the Absolute Idea was the unity of theory and practice, Wallace, *The Logic of Hegel* (Tr. 2d ed. 1892) § 236, possibly with the aid of Fichte, Fichte, *The Science of Rights* (1796, Kroeger's tr. 1889) 243–7, overcame Kant's efforts to buttress Montesquieu, Kant, *The Philosophy of Law* (1796, Hastie's tr. 1887) 165, 170–3, and in effect pursued Rousseau's inquiry. Hegel concluded that each power possessed the character or "moments" of all the others, predicted the failure of the division as well as a struggle among them for supremacy. Hegel, *Philosophy of Right [Law]* (Dyde's tr. 1896)§§ 269, 269 add., 272, 272 add, 272 n., 273, 275, 300, 300, add. See Franklin, *loc. cit. supra* note 25, at pp. 245–6. Moreover, in 1811 conceivably with Taylor's inspiration or sympathy, see Chinard, *supra,* Jefferson had caused to be translated and published at Philadelphia. Helvétius' private criticism of Montesquieu, Destutt de Tracy, *A Commentary and Review of Montesquieu's Spirit of Laws* (1811) 285. See Carcassonne, *Montesquieu et le problème de la constitution française* (1927) 299–301. The effect of this was to burst the political bounds of Montesquieu's conception, at least for English-speaking thinkers who knew the social struggles *of seventeenth century England.*

On John Taylor in general, see Beard, *op. cit. supra;* 2 Parrington, *Main Currents in American Thought* (1927) 14–9 150, 277, 336; Simms, *Life of John Taylor* (1932); Chinard, *op. cit. supra;* Jefferson to Taylor, Feb. 14, 1821, *loc. cit. supra* note 34, XVIII, 312; 18 *Dict. Amer. Bio.* (1936) 331; Lerner, John "Marshall and the Campaign of History," 39 *Col. L. Rev.* 396, 430–1 (1939).

109. Taylor, *An Inquiry into the Principles and Policies of the Government* (1814) 204, 206, 208, 224.

110. Taylor, *New Views on the Constitution* (1823) 134. ". . . we must determine, whether the enumeration of federal judicial powers, is not a limitation and restriction like the enumeration of the federal legislative powers. . . . The federal judicial power is extended only 'to all cases in law and equity arising under the Constitution.' The analogy . . . is considerable." *Id.*, at p. 133. A power to try "Cases in law and equity" implies "no right to try and modify the powers themselves." *Id.,* at p. 155.

Writing under the name of Curtius, Taylor attacked *Marbury v. Madison, supra* note 13, almost as soon as this case was decided. "It is not a little extraordinary," said Curtius-Taylor, ". . . that the word 'independence,' as applicable to the judiciary, is not to be found in the constitution. That wise system, so far from countenancing the independence of any public agents, legislative, executive or judicial, has provided the most efficient checks to make them all dependent. By declaring that the judge shall hold his office during good behaviour, it has made him independent of the executive; but that circumstance, so far from creating a claim to legislative independence, really produces a necessity in several cases for legislative interference. . . . We all know that the judges have assumed the power of pronouncing laws unconstitutional . . . and thereby jeopardize life and property, all the peace of the country. Are the legislature, in this case, to submit? Are they to give an absolute control over the laws to the judiciary? . . . This absolute authority is opposed to the whole theory of our government, and opposes all responsibility to public opinion. Grant the legislature to be in error . . . Unless supported by the enlightened and permanent impressions of the people it will be short lived. . . . But an error of the judges, if paramount, will be of great duration, and will admit of no remedy until the existing judges die and new ones are appointed. Before this all occur, the liberties of the people may be destroyed." Curtius, *A Defence of the Measures of the Administration of Thomas Jefferson* (1804) 35–7; see 18 *Dict. Amer. Bio.* (1936) 331, 332. See also Simms, *op. cit. supra* note 108, at pp. 111–2.

This presentation of the school of Jefferson relative to *Marbury v. Madison* reflects two somewhat related conceptions of this school. In the first place, the school has maintained that judicial "independence" should connote independence only of the executive power. This position may derive from the Declaration of Independence, in which was set forth "a history of repeated injuries and usurpations, all having in direct object the establishment of an absolute Tyranny," and in which the crown was accused of having made "Judges dependent on his Will alone." In 1819 Jefferson complained because the judiciary continued "the reprobated system" after the electoral "revolution of 1800." Jefferson to Roan, *loc. cit. supra* note 87. In 1820 Jefferson said that "A judiciary independent of a king or executive alone, is a good thing; but independence of the will of the nation is a solecism, at least in a republican government." Jefferson, *op. cit. supra* note 54, at pp. 133–4. In 1821 Jefferson said, "It is a misnomer to call a government republican, in which a branch of the supreme power is independent of the nation." 10 Jefferson, *op. cit. supra* note 54, at p. 199.

In the second place, the school of Jefferson has insisted on "responsibility to public opinion." This claim derives from the Reformation, from seventeenth century English political history and from eighteenth century French thought. 3 Hegel, *Lectures on the History of Philosophy* (Tr. Haldane and Simson 1896) 379, 390, 397–8. Hegel said that "French philosophy does away with the lay or outside position in regard alike to politics, religion and philosophy . . . there should not be in legal matters an exclusive caste and society (not even a class of professional lawyers). . . . To treat barbarians as laymen is quite as it should be . . . but to treat thinking men as laymen is very hard. . . ." See also *supra* note 45. It may be noted here that Mr. Corwin says that, "To the end of his life Madison gave no assent to the dogma that the Supreme Court's view of the Constitution had a peculiar sanctity and finality attached to it. His position was that any reading of the Constitution was subject, and properly subject, to the operation of public opinion. It is the attitude of a layman rather than of one who felt himself to belong to an order laying claim to a special skill and insight." Corwin, "The Posthumous Career of James Madison as Lawyer," 25 *Am. Bar Ass'n Jour.* 821, 824 (1939). Further in this connection, attention should be called to *United States v. Hudson*, 7 Cranch 32, 3 L. Ed. 259 (U. S. 1812). This case not only weakens *Marbury v. Madison* in that it held that there are no federal common law crimes, thus seeming to reflect a technical conception of the constitutional phrase "cases in law and equity," but in that Johnson, J., said that the court considered the question "as having been long since settled in public opinion." The view of the school of Jefferson as to the decisive role of public opinion led to its general deep concern as to problems and systems of education. Jefferson himself held, as against the judiciary state, which regards the people as "not enlightened enough to exercise their control with a wholesome direction" that a regime of "the people themselves" whose "discretion" had been informed "by education . . . is the true corrective of abuses of constitutional power." 7 Jefferson, *op. cit supra* note 54, 178–9.

For an effort to reconcile the claims of the judiciary state with the claims of public opinion, see Lowell, *Public Opinion and Popular Government* (1913) 9–10. See Dicey, *Lectures on the Relation Between Law and Public Opinion in England* (1917) 9; and *cf.* Dicey, *Introduction to the Study of Law of the Constitution* (7th ed. 1908) c. 4, 13.

Curtius' condemnation of the judiciary state weakens Mr. Beveridge's and Mr. Warren's belief that Jefferson at first received *Marbury v. Madison* in silence. 3 Beveridge, *Life of John Marshall* (1919) 143–4; Warren, *Congress, The Constitution and the Supreme Court* (1925) 195.

111. 2 Farrand, *op. cit. supra* note 4, at p. 588.

112. 2 Farrand, *op. cit. supra* note 4, at p. 625.

113. 2 Farrand, *op. cit. supra* note 4, at p. 589.

114. 2 Farrand, *op. cit. supra* note 4, at p. 428. This seems, perhaps, the

same position that Madison held a few years later in his Virginia Report against the alien and sedition bills, where he maintained that the phrase "cases in law and equity" justified judicial power over the states (as distinguished from the Congress). 4 Elliot, *op. cit. supra* note 79, at p. 564.

115. *U. S. Const.*, Art. 1, § 10, cl. 2.

116. Taylor, *op. cit. supra* note 110, at p. 158.

117. *Ibid.*

Infamy and Constitutional Civil Liberties

(1954)

1

During the period since the ending of the Second World War an unparalleled reign of political and social repression has developed in the United States. A similar situation on a much reduced scale existed at the close of the eighteenth century, when the Alien and Sedition laws were introduced. The words of Edward Livingston, who, as a Jeffersonian leader in the Congress, fought these measures, well describe the present day state of affairs:

> After such manifest violation of the principles of our Constitution, the form will not long be sacred; presently every vestige of it will be lost and swallowed up in the gulf of despotism. But, should the evil proceed no further than the execution of the present law, what a fearful picture will our country present! The system of *espionage* being thus established, the country will swarm with informers, spies, delators, and all that odious reptile tribe that breed in the sunshine of despotic power; that suck the blood of the unfortunate, and creep into the bosom of sleeping innocence, only to awake it with a burning wound. The hours of the most unsuspecting confidence, the intimacies of friendship, or the recesses of domestic retirement, afford no security. The companion whom you must trust, the friend in whom you must confide, the domestic who waits in your chamber, are all tempted to betray your imprudence or unguarded follies; to misrepresent your words; to convey them, distorted by calumny, to the secret tribunal where jealousy presides—where fear officiates as accuser, and suspicion is the only evidence that is heard.[1]

It is not possible to exaggerate the scope of present day political and social terror. Professor Emerson and Professor Haber, of the Yale Law School, estimate that up to January 1952 four million persons in or seeking federal employment had been checked for their loyalty.[2] Professor Emerson has estimated that ten million persons in the United States are subject to loyalty oaths.[3] But it is not at all possible to measure the indirect and more subtle intimidating effects on the entire American people of these and other actions. Only the other day an editorial writer of *The New York Times* noted that for ". . . tens of thousands of individuals in the professions, in academic life, in the arts and sciences, in private and public affairs and of course in politics too . . . there is the consciousness that to stray from the orthodox safety-line is to invite, sooner or later, open denunciation or sly innuendo from the fanatics who make an organized business of intellectual vigilantism. . . . Nobody likes to be called a Communist or a pro-Communist no matter how unjustly; many people will trim their positions in the desire to avoid the calumny of the extremists. Some will do it consciously; more, probably, unconsciously."[4]

Although many congressional and presidential devices have been utilized to intimidate the American people, the general legal conception which these particular means of mass repression reflect collectively is that which makes persons nationally unworthy or nationally disgraced and subject by virtue of their dishonorable position in American life to a variety of public effects therefor. This contemporary American idea of national degradation by means of, or as a result of congressional and executive action, may be called infamy. Such idea of national censure, or of the qualities and effects thereof, is historically analogous to the institution of *infamia* in Roman law.

Greenidge says that Roman *infamia* was

> . . . a moral censure pronounced by a competent authority in the State on individual members of the community, as a result of certain actions which they had committed, or certain modes of life which they had pursued, this censure involving disqualification for certain rights both in public and in private law.[5]

Buckland says that the *infames* "appear in Justinian's law as a sharply defined group who, by reason of wrongful or unseemly conduct, are subjected to serious disabilities. Shameful trades, condemnation in certain actions and criminal charges, dismissal in disgrace from the army, and misconduct in family relations are the chief cases."[6]

American infamy also seems related to Roman *capitis deminutio,* the idea of the impairment of legal personality itself.[7]

As will be indicated in more detail later, the idea of *infamia* was received from Roman law by feudal law. Moreover, the qualities and effects of feudal infamy obtained during the colonial period of the history of the United States, especially during the witchcraft frenzy in seventeenth century Massachusetts. In 1662 "Unice" Cole, a widow, was indicted by a grand jury for Massachusetts "for not having the fear of God before her eyes and being instigated by the devil" entered "into covenant with the devil and since have had familiarity with the devil contrary to the peace of our sovereign the king. . . ." At the trial it was found that the defendant was "not legally guilty according to indictment, but just ground of vehement suspicion of her having had familiarity with the devil" existed. Although she was not "legally" guilty of witchcraft she was "vehemently suspected" thereof, that is, infamed, and accordingly legally banished by the Massachusetts court.[8] The case of "Unice" Cole is a seventeenth century anticipation of contemporary American infamy by congressional and presidential action.

2

However, the Roman, feudal and colonial idea of *infamia* is excluded by the Bill of Rights, that is, by the first ten amendments to the Constitution of the United States, which initiated our Second Constitution in 1789. The infaming of Americans and the intimidation of millions of Americans who fear that they may be infamed by accusations of Communism, thus becoming subject to the effects of infamy, may therefore be criticized or condemned as unconstitutional.

The contemporary mission of infamy is illuminated by the contrast to be found in eighteenth century American social theory as it is formulated in the Bill of Rights or in the Second Constitution. Chief attention must be directed to the First Amendment. In a single sentence this provides:

> Congress shall make no law respecting an establishment of religion, or prohibiting the free exercise thereof; or abridging the freedom of speech, or of the press; or of the right of the people peaceably to assemble, and to petition the Government for a redress of grievances

In his dissenting opinion in *Dennis v. United States,* the case in which the leaders of the American Communist party were convicted for violation of the Smith Act, Mr. Justice Black said "I have always believed that the First Amendment is the keystone of our Government, that the freedoms it guarantees provide the best insurance against destruction of all freedom."[9] Mr. Justice Black's evaluation of the First Amendment is justified. However, American legal scholarship has not yet realized the force of his position, nor shown why it is correct. It will not suffice to rest with Professor Meiklejohn, who in effect defends the First Amendment on grounds derived from Plato.[10] It will not do to conclude with Professor Chafee, with Professor Emerson, or with Mr. Justice Frankfurter, in his concurring opinion in *Dennis v. United States,* who explain the First Amendment almost exclusively in reference to English political and legal history.[11] A true appreciation of the origins and purposes of the Bill of Rights, and particularly of the First Amendment, may indicate more clearly the incompatibility of modern *infamia* and the Constitution.

The First Amendment primarily consecrates the political and legal theory of the eighteenth century French *Encyclopédistes* as received and developed in the United States by the American adherents of French *Encyclopédisme* who gathered about Jefferson.[12] In a letter Jefferson said:

> I deride with you the ordinary doctrine, that we brought with us from England the *common law rights.* This narrow notion was a favorite in the first moment of rallying to our rights against Great Britain. But it was that of men who felt their rights before they had thought of their explanation. The truth is, that we brought with us the *rights of men;* of expatriated men.[13]

John Adams once summed up the differences between himself and Jefferson relative to eighteenth century French thought. Adams recalled to Jefferson "when Lafayette harangued, you, and me, and John Quincy Adams, through a whole evening in your hotel in the *Cul de Sac*, at Paris, and developed the plans now in operation to reform France. . . ." Adams said he was repelled by Lafayette, as he had been before by Turgot, Rochefoucauld, Condorcet and Franklin. "I have never read reasoning more absurd, sophistry more gross, in proof of the Athanasian creed, or transubstantiation," Adams said, "than the subtle labors of Helvétius and Rousseau to demonstrate the natural equality of mankind." But, as to the impact of French thought on Jefferson, Adams said: "Your steady defence of democratical principles, and your invariable favorable opinion of the French revolution, laid the foundation of your unbounded popularity."[14]

It is the historical relationship between the First Amendment and French and American *Encyclopédisme* which explains why Mr. Justice Black is justified in holding that the First Amendment is the keystone of the Constitution of the United States.

Eighteenth century French and American *Encyclopédisme* was the outcome of a long complicated struggle during which feudal fetters on political freedom were broken or transcended. Because French and American *Encyclopédisme* was directed against feudalism, it was the philosophy of Enlightenment, in opposition to obscurantism. The First Amendment consecrates the Enlightened State of French and American *Encyclopédisme* and establishes the forms of existence of the Enlightened State. In accordance with the outcome of *Encyclopédisme* these are stated as a series of absolute freedoms or negations—the Congress shall make no law respecting an establishment of religion, nor abridging freedom of speech or of the press, nor of the right of the people peaceably to assemble and to petition the government for redress of grievances. Such freedoms pass readily from the negative into the correlative positive, and as such the negations of the First Amendment consecrate or posit the American Public Opinion State.

Encyclopédisme accepted and justified natural law. But since natural law was also the basis for scholasticism and feudalism, it must first be understood that the natural law of scholasticism and that of *Encyclopédisme* are in opposition. Jocob Gemmel says that "the extra-scholastic natural law of the eighteenth century has only the name in common with scholastic natural law."[15] Emil Marmy says that what passed under the name of natural law during the eighteenth century was not natural law, but the "caricature" thereof made by eighteenth century rationalism.[16]

Scholastic natural law was related to theology and was philosophically idealistic. Rommen says that the "individualistic" natural law of the eighteenth century differed from scholastic natural law because of its "nominalism," that is, "in the separation of the eternal law (*lex aeterna*) and the natural law (*lax naturalis*)."[17] Cassirer writes that ". . . the middle ages could no more admit the complete autonomy of natural law than it could admit the autonomy of natural reason. Reason remains the servant of revelation. Its task within the realm of the mind and soul is to lead to, and to help prepare the way for, revelation. Natural law is therefore subordinated to divine law even though it was granted a relatively large degree of recognition."[18] However, the natural law of *Encyclopédisme* was materialistic. Hegel says that in the French Enlightenment "We see . . . materialism freely emerge."[19] Grotius, for instance, said that "Natural law is so immutable that it cannot be changed by God himself. For though the power of God be immense, there are some things to which it does not extend."[20]

Anti-feudal French materialism, part of the history of which derived from earlier English materialism as exemplified by Bacon, Hobbes and Locke, asked the question, why, if man is rational, did man live in an irrational or feudal society. Idealistic legal theory concerning natural law often got no further than establishing natural law in the hearts of men, but anti-feudal French materialism asked why natural law was not established in the heart of society. Rousseau, in effect, posed this problem when he wrote in the famous first sentence of the first chapter of *Contract social* that "Man is born free, and everywhere he is in chains."[21] Jefferson echoed this when he claimed for the Americans "the *rights of men*; of expatriated men." Jefferson again echoed Rousseau in his First Inaugural Address in 1801, speaking of "the agonizing spasms of infuriated man, seeking through blood and slaughter his long-lost liberty."[22]

Thus, from the point of view of the rationalism of materialistic natural law, the problem more precisely was, why was man alienated or estranged from his reason, so that he lived irrationally. The answer of *Encyclopédisme* was that human life was irrational because of the feudal or irrational circumstances or environment of human life. It was necessary, therefore, to change these irrational circumstances through the force of rational education. The feudal circumstances must be swept away through education. Education, largely through legislation, would enlighten man by changing the circumstances in which man existed. Hence, Diderot said "If the laws are good, morals are good; if the laws are bad, morals are bad. . . ."[23] The justification of the French civil code reflects this theory of the educational mission of law. In turn, enlightened man would govern the legislator through his public opinion. Public opinion was to rule the state. Hence Jefferson said that "The good opinion of mankind, like the lever of Archimedes, with the given fulcrum, moves the world."[24] At the end of his life, Jefferson wrote Lafayette that "The force of public opinion cannot be resisted, when permitted freely to be expressed. The agitation it produces must be submitted to."[25] Indeed, Jefferson conceived that rule through public opinion could make the state itself superfluous, writing that "I am convinced that these societies (as the Indians) which live without government, enjoy in their general mass an infinitely greater degree of happiness than those who live under the European governments. Among the former, public opinion is in the place of law, and restrains morals as powerfully as laws ever did anywhere."[26]

However, because *Encyclopédiste* theory was mechanistic it created real difficulty. If feudal or irrational circumstances dictated feudal or irrational consciousness feudal circumstances could not and would not seem irrational, and enlightened consciousness capable of overcoming feudal circumstances and feudal consciousness by the force of rational education or by the force of rational public opinion could not and would not develop. This historical difficulty could by surmounted, if it could be assumed that somehow or other there existed an enlightened educator who was free of the historic alienating or fettering circumstances, who was therefore rational, and who through his power of education and his laws would overcome the feudal circumstances and introduce into social life the force of rational public opinion thus created. This solution, which forgets that the educator himself must be educated, divides society into two parts, the educator towering over and directing those to be educated. Thus, a new alienation is introduced. This, indeed, is the theory of those who today seek to dominate and to dictate American public opinion. They claim a monopoly of American political life as well as of American economic life. Hence, they seek—through the idea of infamy—to transfer the power to make public opinion from the people to themselves. This result has been sought more than once in contemporary world history.

But the First Amendment was designed to reject the solution by which an educator educates the alienated or fettered people. It is the theory of the First Amendment that the determination to educate or to create public opinion is a self-determination of each particular educator. In other words, there is freedom to educate public opinion. This is why the First Amendment forbids the state—or Congress—to abridge freedom of speech and of the press. Because the act of political education is based on a self-determination by the one educated, the Congress is forbidden to abridge the right of the people peaceably to assemble and to petition the government for a redress of grievances. Moreover, the freedom to educate is a freedom to educate not merely opinion alone, but public opinion, so that the force of opinion may be a real and an effective force. Hence the First Amendment guarantees that the self-determined educator shall have self-determined access or free access to the consciousness of those to be educated. In other words, the First Amendment guarantees the protection of the means of educating public opinion—speech, press, peaceable assembly, petition.

The theory of the First Amendment, therefore, is a theory guaranteeing the position of the self-determined political educator, or political party, that of the self-determining political student, or people, and securing the means of access by the consciousness of the self-determining political student. It is not surprising that the First Amendment consecrates the theory of the self-determined educator instead of a theory by which society is divided into two parts, the dominant educator and the dominated, alienated, or fettered people, who are to be educated. Although *Encyclopédisme* was a mechanical materialism, it developed, as Hegel points out, from the history of Protestantism, which advanced the idea of the autonomy or self-determination of the individual conscience or subject of religion. What Hegel says is probably especially true of American *Encyclopédisme*:

> French philosophy does away with the lay or outside position in regard alike to politics, religion and philosophy. . . . What the philosophers brought forward and maintained was, speaking generally, that men should no longer be in the position of laymen, either with regard to religion or to law; so that in religious matters there should not be a hierarchy, a

> limited and selected number of priests, and in the same way that there should not be in legal matters an exclusive caste and society (not even a class of professional lawyers), in whom should reside, and to whom should be restricted, the knowledge of what is eternal, divine, true, and right, and by whom other men should be commanded and directed: but that human reason should have the right of giving its assent and its opinion. To treat barbarians as laymen is quite as it should be—barbarians are nothing but laymen; but to treat thinking men as laymen is very hard. This great claim made by man to subjective freedom, perception and conviction, the philosophers in question contended for heroically and with splendid genius, with warmth and fire, with spirit and courage, maintaining that a man's own self, the human spirit, is the source from which is derived all that is to be respected by him. . . . Thought was raised like a standard among the nations, liberty of conviction and of conscience in me. . . . Thus in another form they completed the Reformation that Luther began.[27]

Because the First Amendment reflects Hegel's formulation, the constitutional text has general and absolute force. It is not subject to impairment or alienation by introducing ideas such as infamy with its effects into American public life. Nevertheless, in his majority opinion in *Dennis v. United States*, Mr. Chief Justice Vinson upheld the idea that the state could alienate public opinion from the public, saying that "the societal value of speech must, on occasion, be subordinated to other values and considerations."[28]

Yet the text of the First Amendment is indeed both general and absolute. In one sentence it separates church and state and guarantees free opinion. If, as Mr. Chief Justice Vinson says, free opinion is a relative and not an absolute civil liberty, then the separation of church and state is also a relative and not an absolute separation. This warning was expressed by Edward Livingston, the American *Encyclopédiste* codifier and constitutional lawyer, in his struggle in the Congress of 1798 against the Alien and Sedition laws. Referring to the First Amendment, Livingston said that the Constitution anticipated situations in which a congressional majority might "wish to pass laws to suppress the only means by which its corrupt views might be made known to the people, and therefore says, *no* law shall be passed to abridge the liberty of speech and of the press. This privilege is connected with another dear and valuable privilege—the liberty of conscience. What is liberty of conscience? Gentlemen may tomorrow establish a national religion agreeably to the opinion of a majority of this House, on the ground of an uniformity of worship being more consistent with public happiness than a diversity of worship. The doing of this is not less forbidden than the act which the House are about to do."[29]

The supporters of the Alien and Sedition legislation in effect sought to overcome Livingston's conception that the First Amendment sets absolute and general limits on the power of the Congress by suggesting that the force of the Constitution was relative to historical circumstances. Otis attacked Livingston, saying:

> Have not the French heretofore pushed their intrigues into some of the first offices of our Government? Do not our bad citizens correspond with the agents of the Directory, and does not that Directory boast of its diplomatic means[?]. . . Are not . . . the victories of France, her influence, and facility in revolution-making to be imputed to the system of espionage which she has so well digested, rather than to any other cause?[30]

Hence, in his concurring opinion in *Dennis v. United States,* Mr. Justice Jackson echoed the theory of the Alien and Sedition laws when he said it was required "to reappraise, in the light of our own times and conditions, constitutional doctrines devised under other circumstances to strike a balance between authority and liberty."[31]

But Jefferson, whose *Encyclopédisme* justifies the First Amendment, and against whom the Alien and Sedition Laws were hurled by the ancestors of those who now seek to replace Jefferson's Enlightened State with the Infaming State, asserted the absoluteness of the First Amendment. In his First Inaugural Address, made in 1801, after he had defeated and politically ruined the forces of John Adams and of those who were responsible for the Alien and Sedition laws, he said:

> During the contest of opinion through which we have passed, the animation of discussion and of exertions has sometimes

worn an aspect which might impose on strangers, unused to think freely, and to speak and to write what they think. . . . All . . . will bear in mind this sacred principle, that, though the will of the majority is in all cases to prevail, that will, to be rightful, must be reasonable; that the minority possess their equal rights, which equal laws must protect, and to violate which would be oppression. . . . And let us reflect that having banished from our land that religious intolerance under which mankind so long bled and suffered, we have yet gained little if we countenance a political intolerance as despotic, as wicked, and capable of as bitter and bloody persecutions. During the throes and convulsions of the ancient world, during the agonizing spasms of infuriated man, seeking through blood and slaughter his long-lost liberty, it was not wonderful that the agitation of the billows should reach even this distant and peaceful shore; that this should be more felt and feared by some and less by others; that this should divide opinions as to measures of safety. But every difference of opinion is not a difference of principle. We have called by different names brethren of the same principle. We are all republicans; we are all federalists. If there be any among us who would wish to dissolve this Union, or to change its republican form, let them stand, undisturbed, as monuments of the safety with which error of opinion may be tolerated where reason is left free to combat it. I know, indeed, that some honest men fear that a republican government cannot be strong; that this government is not strong enough. But would the honest patriot, in the full tide of successful experiment, abandon a government which has so far kept us free and firm, on the theoretic and visionary fear that this Government, the world's best hope, may, by possibility, want energy to preserve itself? I trust not. I believe this, on the contrary, the strongest government on earth. I believe it is the only one where every man, at the call of the law, would fly to the standard of the law, would meet invasions of the public order as his own personal concern.[32]

In this Inaugural Address Jefferson thus makes it precise that the First Amendment has general and absolute force, so that attempts to exclude particular social forces from participating as educators in the formation of public opinion, such as is attempted through the idea of infamy or of national unworthiness, are unconstitutional. The Amendment explicitly destroys the historic monopoly of religion; but all future monopolies in regard to opinion are also forbidden or excluded by the freedoms or safeguards—freedom of speech, press, peaceable assembly and petition—thrown up to protect and to justify the self-determined political educator of public opinion. These safeguards are absolute and general in order to prevent a secular monopoly, reminiscent of the monopoly of religion.

The First Amendment, then, is unqualified in guaranteeing the educational activity and the means of educational activity of the self-determined educator of public opinion. Such education, as Jefferson says, should be "reasonable," that is, rational or an appeal to the reason of the self-determining political students, the people. It must not be education through terror. It must not be education through other forms of intimidation and fear, as it is through infamy. It should be education based on scientific truth.

Encyclopédisme founded itself on the great development of science which had taken place before it and which had made possible the undermining of feudalism. *Encyclopédisme* held that scientific knowledge alone was knowledge, and that such knowledge was knowledge of an objectively existing world. Hence, Jefferson said "Difference of opinion leads to inquiry, and inquiry to truth."[33] This means that *Encyclopédisme* did not justify knowledge based on secular faith—although this is a presupposition of contemporary American infamy—any more than it justified knowledge based on religious faith.

Once it is grasped that the First Amendment has introduced the Public Opinion State, the state based on the hegemony of public opinion, it becomes clear that the effect of contemporary American congressional or presidential mass infamy is to attack and to weaken the Public Opinion State by intimidating and silencing the public opinion which should govern American public life. Because Communism has been infamed by the state, millions of persons, almost all of them not Communists, fear being infamed as Communists, fear the consequences or effects of such infamy, and under such pressure have become mute, narcotized, hypocritical or opportunistic.

Therefore, contemporary American infamy, infamy by executive or congressional activity, may be said to have the aim of alienating or of estranging the American people from making and declaring American opinion. A false opinion, the opinion of the infamers, is thereby substituted for the opinion of the people whose rational opinion is supposed to govern American public life under the First Amendment. As such, contemporary American congressional or presidential infamy alienates the consciousness, will and opinion of the people from the people themselves. The consequence, then, of contemporary American infamy is that American public life has been divided into two parts, one of which, the state, towers over, controls and directs the other, the people. In this fashion the state has been put in the position from which it had been excluded by the First Amendment, which subordinated the state to the public opinion of the people.

3

Jefferson was justified in suggesting in his First Inaugural Address that the attacks which had been made on the American Public Opinion State by the Alien and Sedition laws were linked to the "bitter and bloody persecution" of the history of medieval religious rivalry. Because the Bill of Rights is inspired by *Encyclopédiste* theory it is not surprising that it reprobates all the devices of medievalism, such as infamy.[34] These ten amendments are a constitutional *precis* of eighteenth century American *Encyclopédiste* criticism of feudalism and of the means of feudalism. Hence, the idea of infamy as an exclusionary force affecting public opinion encounters not only the condemnation of the First Amendment, but also is forbidden by the Fifth Amendment, the text of which in part says that "No person shall be held to answer for a capital, or otherwise infamous crime, unless on a presentment or indictment of a grand jury. . . ." Thus, the Constitution fetters the power of infamy, so that the idea of national unworthiness may not be invoked to destroy the Public Opinion State. This part of the Fifth Amendment buttresses the First Amendment and is itself buttressed by the First Amendment.

The Fifth Amendment restricts the role of infamy entirely to the formal criminal law. The "infamous crime" or "infaming crime" of the Fifth Amendment is a crime for which there are two distinct sanctions—the principal punishment, the constitutionally justified imposition of which also justifies the subsidiary punishment, that is constitutional infamy or constitutional national disgrace. Infamy is so far-reaching in its effects that constitutionally it may only be supplementary to a principal punishment for a crime consecrated or justified by the Constitution. Infamy is so destructive that an "infamous crime" or the "infaming crime" be based exclusively on a presentment or indictment of a grand jury. As infamy may be inspired by lies, suspicion and rumor, the Fifth Amendment excludes it unless there is a criminal conviction following the action of the grand jury. Infamy is so reprobated constitutionally that only the particular individual accused and convicted can be constitutionally infamed. Hence, the entire contemporary American system of mass infamy collapses under the force of the Fifth Amendment. Moreover, because the First Amendment reflects on the Fifth Amendment, the scope and effects of infamy visited on the particular individual convicted under the Fifth Amendment are further restricted by the theory of the Public Opinion State established in the First Amendment, the keystone of the Constitution.

In delimiting the scope of infamy the Fifth Amendment has been paralleled by the development in the modern Roman or modern civil law. Thus, under Articles 32-36 of the German criminal code, and under Articles 8, 28, 34 and 35 of the French penal code, the mission of infamy is restricted to the force of a supplemental or auxiliary punishment for certain important crimes. But in these criminal codes the legal effects of infamy are precisely detailed.

Because of the weakness of American comparative law and of American legal history, the purpose of the text of the Fifth Amendment relating to "infamous crimes" has not been well understood. This part of the amendment was received into the Bill of Rights on the initiative of Massachusetts,[35] where, as has been shown, the qualities or effects of infamy—for witchcraft—had been known during the seventeenth century. The formulation of the Fifth Amendment concerning capital and infamous crimes represents a development from the less satisfactory text of the Body of Liberties of colonial Massachusetts, which as early as 1641 provided in response to the destructive force of religious infamy or excommunication in

Puritan theology that "No mans life shall be taken away, no mans honour or good name shall be stayned [stained] . . . nor any wayes punished . . . unless it be by vertue or equitie of some express law of the Country waranting the same, established by a general Court and sufficiently published, or in case of the defect of a law in any partecular case by the word of God." However, in the middle of the nineteenth century, Mr. Chief Justice Shaw, of Massachusetts, unfortunately said that it was not "easy to perceive precisely what was intended in the article by the term 'infamous punishment.'"[36] The subsequent opinions of the Supreme Court of the United States relating to "infamous crimes" under the Fifth Amendment, on the whole, reflect the difficulties of Mr. Chief Justice Shaw and the failure to recognize that the phrase "infamous crimes" means "infaming crime" and that it was an outcome and criticism of the history of infamy in Roman, feudal and American colonial law.

The Supreme Court of the United States has on occasion grasped that the text of the Fifth Amendment concerning "infamous crimes" touches the Public Opinion State consecrated by the First Amendment. Thus, Mr. Justice Gray said in *Ex parte Wilson* that "what punishments shall be considered as infamous may be affected by the changes of public opinion from one age to another."[37] In a dissenting opinion, Mr. Justice Brandeis stated that "The protection contained in the Fifth Amendment refers to infamous crimes—a term obviously inviting interpretation in harmony with conditions and opinion prevailing from time to time."[38]

Thus, it may be said that the Public Opinion State of the First Amendment and the text of the Fifth Amendment relating to "infamous crimes" are inseparably interrelated. As it is the mission of both amendments to maintain the Public Opinion State, there is no place for mediate or immediate congressional or executive infamy, open or disguised, in the area of American public opinion.

This directs attention to what Mr. Justice Gray said in *Ex parte Wilson:*

> Nor can we accede to the proposition, which has been sometimes maintained that no crime is infamous, within the meaning of the Fifth Amendment, that has not been so declared by Congress. . . . The purpose of the Amendment was to limit the power of the Legislature, as well as of the prosecuting officers, of the United States. We are not indeed

> disposed to deny that a crime, to the conviction and punishment of which Congress has superadded a disqualification to hold office, is thereby made infamous. . . . But the Constitution protecting every one from being prosecuted, without the intervention of a grand jury, for any crime which is subject by law to an infamous punishment, no declaration of Congress is needed to secure, or competent to defeat, the constitutional safeguard.[39]

Edward Livingston makes it evident that the phrase "infamous crime," as used in the Fifth Amendment, connotes an "infaming crime," as used in Roman and feudal ideas of infamy. Livingston's thinking was formulated in his introductory report to the Louisiana legislature in 1822, in which he submitted his *projet* of a criminal code on *Encyclopédiste* principles. In his report he criticized *Las Siete Partidas*, the thirteenth century Spanish Code, because of its system of infamy. Concerning infamy, Livingston said:

> It operates on the condition or standing in society of those who come within its purview. It is called in the Spanish law, 'Enfamamiento'; and, from its definition, is a species of dishonour attached to persons, as well from their birth or course of life, as from having incurred the animadversion of the magistrates, without being convicted or even accused of any offence; as from the condemnation for an infamous crime. Political disabilities attended this state, which our institutions have, in some instances, virtually repealed; but the note of ill fame may still remain, and greatly influence the comfort and respectability of those to whom it is thus attached by law, if those laws are still in force. The subject forms the sixth title of the seventh books of the Partidas. By the second law of this title, the innocent fruit of an illegal marriage, the son whom the father may justly or unjustly have accused in his testament, the suitor to whom the judge may, in court, have addressed an admonition to amend his life, the advocate who may have been warned not to bring a false accusation, the man of good credit who availed himself of his character to ruin that of another by slanders, and the unfaithful depositary, were all declared infamous. By the third law, not only the wife unfaithful to a living husband, but she who forgets a dead one in the arms of a second before her

> year of mourning is expired, together with her father, if he consent to the marriage, and the too impatient successor of the deceased, come within the penalties of the law. The following law confounds in the same indiscriminate class of infamy, procurers, comedians, mountebanks, gamblers and buffoons. The exclusion from office of all these ill-associated descriptions of persons is, perhaps, remedied by our constitutional laws. . . . Let it be remembered that these disabilities attach not upon conviction only, but from the fact.[40]

From Livingston's discussion of infamy in *Las Siete Partidas* its relation to the "infamous crime" of the Fifth Amendment explicitly appears. Moreover, his discussion also indicates that the Fifth Amendment takes account of the complicated historical subcategories, historical distinctions, historical sources and historical justifications for infamy known in Roman law, and expels all of them, save as a subsidiary sanction of a criminal conviction of a particular accused, as to which it is limited in its political effects by the First Amendment.

Cuq,[41] like Girard,[42] points out that in Roman law there was an important distinction between *l'infamie de droit* and *l'infamie de fait*, that is, between infamy derived from law and infamy derived from fact. But Sohm gives more details concerning the sub-categories and distinction of Roman *infamia*. He writes: "There were, more particularly, two groups of cases which were contrasted with one another, the cases of 'infamia immediate,' and of 'infamia mediata.' Infamy was said to be 'immediate,' if it attached to a person at once, ipso jure, on the commission of some act which deserved to be visited with social disgrace. Thus it attached to persons engaged in a disreputable trade. . . . On the other hand, infamy was said to be 'mediate,' if it did not attach directly, but only after a court of law had passed judgment on the delinquent on the ground of some act which deserved to be visited with social disgrace. Such was the effect above all things of every criminal sentence touching life, limb, or liberty. A similar result however followed condemnation in certain civil cases, especially if judgement were given against a person in civil action on account of a dishonorable breach of duty. . . . No codification of the law of honour can, in the nature of things, be complete. It was necessary, therefore, to allow the Roman judges a discretionary power to take account of such cases of infamy as had not been specified in any statute or in the praetorian edict. Looked at from this point of view, there were two kinds of *existimationis minutio*, '*infamia*' and '*turpitudo*.' In the case of 'infamy' the conditions under which it should attach were fixed, not by the law, but by the free discretion of the judge acting, in each individual case, on the verdict of public opinion, in other words, on the verdict of society."[43]

As Livingston brings out, there were several significant subcategories of Spanish infamy. Thus, Partidas 7.6.1 says that "There are two kinds of defamation, one of which arises solely from an act which is performed, and the other derived from the law which declares persons to be infamous on account of the acts which they commit." As an example of infamy from the fact, Partidas 7.6.2 says "A person not born of lawful marriage is infamous from that very fact, as ordained by the Holy Church." As an example of infamy derived from the law, Partidas 7.6.3 mentions the woman who "is found in some place in which she has committed adultery with another person." Partidas 7.6.5 mentions the offenses for which persons are infamed after criminal judgment, saying "when a sentence is pronounced against a party by an ordinary judge, condemning him on account of treason, forgery, adultery, or any other crime which he has committed, such sentence renders the condemned party infamous."[44]

The Italian feudal law of infamy seems to have been similar to the Roman and Spanish law.[45]

German feudalism had a very complicated system of infamy. This included *Rechtlosigkeit*, due to dishonorable acts, which "attached to persons who were proved guilty of such acts as made them impossible among reputable men. Here belong (a) those who had suffered condemnation to a *degrading punishment*. . . . (b) Those who had committed a deed which betrayed a *base or depraved disposition*." The latter lost their honor "even though no condemnation was suffered." German medieval law also knew *Rechtlosigkeit* "due to personal relations or social callings." Persons thus infamed were those born out of wedlock or those who carried on ignominious trades, the latter representing class distinctions.[46]

French feudal law also recognized distinctions of infamy. It could result as a matter of law from certain penal sentences, such as a term at the galleys, and it was also connected with the exercise of certain professions.[47]

The mission of the Fifth Amendment may now be seen as that of suppressing infamy, whether Roman, feudal or American colonial, save in criminal law under the conditions stated in the amendment and as excluded by the force of the First Amendment. The Fifth Amendment blocks and excludes mass infamy. In short, the Fifth Amendment fortifies the First Amendment by protecting forces of American public opinion from intimidation and elimination. It thus appears that contemporary American presidential or congressional infamy represents an illegitimate assault on the Public Opinion State created by the Bill of Rights.

4

As has been said, the Bill of Rights is an interrelated system, each text of which illuminates and is illuminated by the others. Hence, it may be mentioned that Mr. Justice Gray introduced discussion of the problem of the relation between the infamous or infaming crime of the Fifth Amendment and the Eighth Amendment, forbidding "cruel and unusual punishments."[48]

Similarly, Article I, 9, cl. 3, of the Constitution says that "No Bill of Attainder or ex post facto law shall be passed"; and Article I, 10, cl. 1, forbids bills of attainder by the states. These texts have been taken by the courts to mean that legislative action which imposes punishment without judicial trial for past activity is forbidden. To the extent that bills of attainder were infaming or were based on infaming presuppositions, and to the extent that bills of attainder were mass condemnations, as when the Stuart Parliament of 1688 attained over 2,000 persons in a single bill,[49] and to the extent that bills of attainder attached mass infamy, the requirements of the Fifth Amendment relating to infamous or infaming crimes are an advance over the original Constitution. This is because the Fifth Amendment not only clarifies the old texts, but excludes prospective, immediate congressional or presidential infamy and prevents prospective mass infamy.

5

Unless refuge is taken in pragmatic subjectivism or formalism, the American Infaming State cannot endure the scrutiny or inspection of the Constitution. The gravity of the present-day aggression against the American Public Opinion State imposes heavy responsibilities. In particular, the judiciary has the important task of defending the Constitution. Of course Jefferson fought against the power of Judicial review of congressional action as asserted by Mr. Chief Justice Marshall in *Marbury v. Madison*,[50] and President Franklin D. Roosevelt weakened the Judiciary State. However, as Jefferson's attack on judiciary supremacy was inspired by his attachment to the Public Opinion State and to the Constitution which introduced the Public Opinion State, he criticized the Supreme Court not because it was independent, but because it was independent of the Constitution. Hence, in 1789, Jefferson held that the judiciary had a responsibility to maintain the Bill of Rights against the Congress and the President. He so wrote Madison from Paris on 15 March 1789, saying:

> In the arguments in favor of a declaration of rights, you omit one which has great weight with me; the legal check which it puts into the hands of the judiciary. This is a body, which if rendered independent and kept strictly to their own department, merits great confidence for their learning and integrity.

Later in the letter Jefferson told Madison:

> The inconvenience of the declaration [of rights] are, that it may cramp government in its useful exertions. But the evil of this is short-lived, moderate and reparable. The inconveniences of the want of a declaration are permanent, afflicting and irreparable. They are in a constant progression from bad to worse. The executive, in our governments, is not the sole, it is scarcely the principal object of my jealousy. The tyranny of the legislatures is the most formidable dread at present, and will be for many years. That of the executive will come in its turn, but it will at a remote period. . . . I am much pleased with the prospect that a declaration of rights will be added.[51]

The justification for the present historic responsibilities of the judiciary in regard to the Bill of Rights is thus set forth by Jefferson. Because Jefferson firmly maintained and fixedly held before him the validity of the Public Opinion State, he asserted the power of the judiciary to defend the Bill of Rights.[52] He avoided the error of Mr. Justice Frankfurter, who in concurring in *Dennis v. United States*, said "Primary responsibility for adjusting the interests which compete in the situation before us of necessity belongs to the Congress."[53] This means that the Congress determines public opinion and is not determined by public opinion. The power of opinion is thus subordinated to the opinion of power. Ultimately, Mr. Justice Frankfurter says that "Civil liberties draw at best only limited strength from legal guarantees."[54] But Jefferson, with his usual sensitivity to historical development, had foreseen that if the judiciary were free of the Public Opinion Constitution, the constitution of public opinion would cease to be free; and urged the responsibility of the judiciary to defend the Bill of Rights.

NOTES

1. *Annals of the Congress of the United States* (1851) 2010, 2011.
2. Emerson and Haber, *Political and Civil Rights in the United States* (1952) 563.
3. "Report on Guild Activities," 13 *Lawyers Guild Review* 38, 40 (1953).
4. Oates, "This is the Real, the Lasting Damage." *The New York Times Magazine,* March 7, 1954, p. 9.
5. Greenidge, *Infamia* (1894) 37.
6. Buckland, *A Text-Book of Roman Law from Augustus to Justinian* (2d ed., 1932) 91.
7. Greenidge, *op. cit. supra* note 5, at p. 6; Buckland, *op. cit. supra* note 6, at p. 134; Schulz, *Classical Roman Law* (1951) 72. The conception of *capitis deminutio media* underlies President Eisenhower's proposal for forfeiture of citizenship, made in his message concerning the state of the Union on January 7, 1954. *The New York Times*, January 8, 1954, p. 10, c. 3. When enslavement or deprivation of freedom is added to such loss of citizenship, *capitis deminutio media* becomes *capitis deminutio maxima*, virtually civil death.
8. Records of the Court of Assistants of the Colony of the Massachusetts Bay, 1630–1692 (Cronin's ed., 1928) III, 253.
9. *Dennis v. United States,* 341 U.S. 494, 580 (1951).
10. Meiklejohn, *Free Speech* (1948) 20.
11. Emerson and Haber, *op cit. supra* note 2 at p. 361 Frankfurter, J., concurring, in *Dennis v. United States,* in U.S. 494, 524 (1951); Chafee, *Free Speech in the United States* (1941) c. 1.
12. Franklin, "The Judiciary State I," 3 *National Lawyers Guild Quarterly* 27, 28 (1940); also in this volume.
13. *The Writings of Jefferson* (Washington's ed. 1854), VI, 65.
14. *The Works of John Adams* (1856), X, 52.
15. Gemmel, in Brugger, *Philosophisches Wörterbuch* (1948) 132.
16. Marmy, in Rommen, *Le Droit naturel* (Marmy tr.,1946) 10.
17. Rommen, *op. cit. supra* note 16, at p.117.
18. Cassirer, *The Philosophy of the Enlightenment* (Koelln's and Pettegrove's tr., 1951) 241.
19. Hegel, *Lectures on the History of Philosophy* (Haldane's and Simson's tr., 1896) III, 381.

20. Grotius, *De jure belli ac pacis* (Whewell's ed., 1853) 4.
21. Rousseau, *Du contrat social* (1762) 1.1.
22. *The Writings of* Jefferson (Washington's ed., 1854) II, 2.
23. Diderot, *Interpreter of Nature: Selected Writings* (Stewart's and Kemp's tr. 1937) 181.
24. *The Writings of Jefferson* (Washington's ed., 1854) VI, 405.
25. *The Writings of Jefferson* (Washington's ed., 1854) VII, 325.
26. *The Writings of Jefferson* (Washington's ed., 1853) II, 100.
27. Hegel, *op. cit. supra* note 19, at pp. 379, 390, 397–8.
28. *Dennis v. United States*, 341 U. S. 494, 503 (1951).
29. *Annals*, *op. cit. supra* note 1, at p. 2154.
30. *Annals*, *op, cit. supra* note 1. at p. 2017.
31. *Dennis v. United States,* 341 U.S. 494, 561 (1951).
32. *Loc. cit. supra* note 22. The election of 1800 which carried Jefferson into the presidency was called by him the "revolution of 1800," saying that it "was as real a revolution in the principles of our government as that of 1776 was in its form; not effected indeed by the sword, as that, but by the rational and peaceable instrument of reform, the suffrage of the people." *The Writings of Thomas Jefferson* (Library ed., 1904), XV, 212.
33. *The Writings of Jefferson* (Washington's ed., 1854), VI, 447.
34. The discussion of *infamia* in the Encyclopedia was rich in detail, setting forth the significant sub-categories. *Encyclopédie, ou dictionnaire raisoné des sciences, des arts et des métiers* (nouvelle ed., 1778), XVIII, 652–654. See notes 40–47, *infra*.
35. Oppenheimer, "Infamous Crimes and the Moreland Case," 36 *Harvard Law Review* 299, 300 (1923).
36. *Jones v. Robbins,* 8 Gray 329, 347 (1857).
37. *Ex parte Wilson*, 114 U.S. 417, 427 (1885).
38. *United States v. Moreland*, 258 U.S. 433, 451 (1992).
39. *Ex parte Wilson*, 114 U.S. 417, 426 (1885).
40. Livingston, *A System of Penal Law for the State of Louisiana* (1833) 63.
41. Cuq, *Manuel des institutions juridiques des romains* (2e ed., 1929) 63.
42. Girard, *Manuel élémentaire de droit romain* (8e ed 1929) 216.
43. Sohm, *The Institutes* (Ledlie's tr., 1907) 184. See, further, Czyhlarz, *Lehrbuch der Institutionen des Romischen Fechtes* (18. Auf. 1924) 84; Savigny, *Traité de droit romain* (Guenoux tr., 1841), II, n or LXXVI–LXXXIV; Dernburg, *Fandekten* (4. Auf. 1894), I, 133; Windscheid, *Lehrbuch des Fandektenrechts*, 9. Auf. (Kipp's), 1906, I, 246; Arndts, *Lehrbuch der Pandekten* (13. Auf. 1886) 39; Pothier, *Oeuvres* (3 id. (Bugnet) 1890), IX, 43; Petropoulos, *Istoria kai eisighisis romackou thikeou* (1944) 420. See both the discussion and bibliography in Pommeray, *Études sur l'infamie en droit* (1937).
44. *Las Siete Partidas* (Scott's tr., 1931).
45. Calisse, *A History of Italian Law* (Register's tr., 1928) 423.
46. Huebner, *A History of Italian Law* (Philbrick's tr., 1918) 103.
47. Brissaud, *A History of Germanic Private Law* (Howell's tr., 1912) 885. On the relation of canonist excommunication to infamy and *capitis deminutio*, see p. 883.

48. *Ex parte Wilson*, 114 U.S. 417, 425 (1883).

49. Cooley, *A Treatise on the Constitutional Limitations* (8th ed., 1927), I 937, note 1.

50. 1 Cranch 137 (1803).

51. *The Writings of Jefferson* (Washington's ed., 1853), III, 3.

52. As John Taylor, one of the most powerful Jeffersonian jurists, attacked the idea of judiciary supremacy declared in *Marbury v. Madison*, because it "opposes all responsibility to public opinion," the contemporary force of his reasoning justifies judiciary intervention to defend the Public Opinion State as consecrated by the Bill of Rights. See Curtius, *A Defence of the Measures of the Administration of Thomas Jefferson* (1804) 35–37. See, further, Franklin, "Brutus the American Praetor," 15 *Tulane Law Review* 16, 47, note 110 (1940); also in this volume. "In Jeffersonian thought the power that must struggle through the force of public opinion to gain the paramount place in the state, so that its hegemony is recognized, accepted and followed by the other powers, is the power that at a given historical moment will best defend that American people and their democratic and national attainments; and public opinion becomes a force in Jeffersonian theory 'while the spirit of the people is up,' that is, while it is active and ceases to be contemplative." Franklin, "War Power of the President: A Historical Justification of Mr. Roosevelt's Message of 7 Sept 1942," 17 *Tulane Law Rev*. 217, 248 (1942). See also Franklin, "War-Time Powers of the American Presidency as Conceived by Thomas Jefferson," 2 *Lawyers Guild Rev*. 13, (1942). On Jefferson's *"habilité dialectique"*, see Barca Trelles, "La Doctrine de Monroe," Academie de droit international, *Recueil des cours*, XXXII, 391, 429 (1930).

53. *Dennis v. United States*, 341 U.S. 404, 555 (1951).

54. *Ibid*.

The *Encyclopédiste* Origin and Meaning of the Fifth Amendment[1]

(1955)

1

The present intense popular interest in the Fifth Amendment reflects the crisis in the American Bill of Rights which has developed under President Truman and President Eisenhower. There is a feeling in the United States that the Bill of Rights has been subverted by the government.

The Fifth Amendment cannot be understood apart from the entire Bill of Rights, that is, apart from the first ten amendments of the Constitution.

It will be recalled that the original Constitution of 1787 had no Bill of Rights; and that, in order to secure the acceptance of the Constitution, a Bill of Rights was added in 1789. The latter may be called the Second Constitution because it profoundly changed the character of the Constitution of 1787. The influence of Jeffersonianism appears prominently here, even though the content of the Bill of Rights in large measure is borrowed from various state constitutions introduced during the period of the American Revolution.

The chief idea of the Bill of Rights is the democratic conception, contained in the First Amendment, that public opinion and public will, rather than authority, both secular and religious, should govern the American State. This hegemony of public opinion is realized in the First Amendment through the following formulation:

> Congress shall make no law respecting an establishment of religion, or prohibiting the free exercise thereof; or abridging the freedom of speech, or of the press: or the right of the people peaceably to assemble, and to petition the Government for a redress of grievances.

Mr. Justice Black quite properly has called the First Amendment "the keystone of our Government."[2]

In order to maintain the priority of public opinion in the Public Opinion State, the government must behave legally. This requirement of the subordination of the government to legality (or to the rule of law) was designed to overcome the arbitrariness of the feudal State. As feudal arbitrariness had been subject to the rivalry of religion, the Bill of Rights, which in the First Amendment has absolutely separated Church and State, consequently subjected the State to a new check, that of legality. The conception is that if the State respects legality, the force of democratic public opinion, which is supposed to control the American State under the First Amendment, could flourish and become effective. Hence, if it can be said that the First Amendment establishes the Public Opinion State, the other amendments in effect subject the State to ideas of legality, to legal limits which it must not overcome or affront.

2

These texts of the Bill of Rights, more precisely, are a criticism of general feudal arbitrariness. They are historical texts, and as such constitute a *précis* or summary of the abuses of feudalism throughout Europe. It is usually believed that the Bill of Rights is a condemnation solely of English feudalism. This is a serious error, which has had the effect of weakening the Bill of Rights.

The Bill of Rights is largely an American *précis* of the criticism of European feudalism in general, as made by the French *Encyclopédistes* of the eighteenth century during the period prior to the French and American Revolutions. The Bill of Rights reflects criticism not merely of English feudalism, but of European feudalism as a whole, as it had been made by the French *Encyclopédistes* and received in America, especially by Jefferson and the Jeffersonians.

3

Certainly, the force of the Fifth Amendment is lost unless it is understood as a text criticizing European feudalism. It is not a text condemning English feudalism alone.

The Fifth Amendment, it will be noticed from reading it, falls into four parts, each of which is separated by a semi-colon:

> No person shall be held to answer for a capital, or otherwise infamous crime, unless on a presentment or indictment of a Grand Jury, except in cases arising in the land or naval forces, or in the Militia, when in actual service in time of War or public danger; nor shall any person be subject for the same offence to be twice put in jeopardy of life or limb; nor shall be compelled in any criminal case to be a witness against himself, nor be deprived of life, liberty, or property, without due process of law; nor shall private property be taken for public use, without just compensation.

The first part of the amendment deals with infamous crimes, the second part with the problem of double jeopardy, the third part (which has two clauses) with the matter of self-incrimination and of due process, and the fourth part with the matter of eminent domain.

Primary interest must center on the first part of the amendment, dealing with the matter of "infamous" crimes. The phrase "infamous" crimes means "infaming" crimes and connotes a reference to the institution of "infamy," as it had developed largely in Roman law and later in feudal Europe, but not as such in England.

In Roman law the idea obtained that a person could be civilly unworthy or dishonored or disgraced or infamed (Bentham mentions about thirty-three English synonyms for infamy[3]) as a result of a judgment against him, or even without a judgment against him.

Under feudalism the Roman conception of infamy was maintained, but in addition thereto, the parallel idea of religious infamy or of excommunication was developed.

The first rumbling against excommunication appears with Luther, who in effect maintains that no living person could be excluded by a living person from the "invisible" communion, that is, subjected to excommunication, except by his own determination. Hence he should not be excommunicated by the church.

> 1. We have seen that the sacrament of the holy body of Christ [Luther said in 1520] is a sign of the communion of all saints, therefore it becomes necessary to know also what the ban is which is employed in the Church. For its chief and peculiar function and power is to deprive guilty Christians of the holy sacrament. . . . Therefore the one cannot be understood apart from the other, because the one is the opposite of the other; for the Latin word

communio means fellowship, and thus do the learned designate the Holy Sacrament. Its opposite is the word *excommunicatio*, which means exclusion from the fellowship, and so do the learned term the ban. . . .

2. There is a twofold fellowship, corresponding to the two things in the sacrament, the sign and the thing signified . . . the first is an inner, spiritual and invisible fellowship of the heart, by which one is incorporated by true faith, hope and love in the fellowship of Christ and of all saints. . . . This fellowship can neither be given nor taken away by anyone, be he bishop, pope or angel or any creature. . . . This fellowship no ban can touch or affect, but only the unbelief or sin of the person himself; by these he can excommunicate himself, and thus separate himself from the grace, life and salvation of the fellowship.[4]

In 1521 Luther said:

> Excommunication is only an external penalty and does not deprive men of the common prayers of the Church.
>
> Behold how the pope strives to be God. In the preceding articles he has assumed authority to save souls by means of indulgences, and in this article he assumes authority to damn souls by means of the ban. Neither of these thing can be done by any creature, but only by the high divine Majesty.[5]

In 1530, almost a decade later, Luther said:

> Once upon a time, popes, bishops, priests and monks had such authority that, with their little letters of excommunication they could force and drive kings and princes wherever they wished without resistance or defense. Nay, kings and princes could not ruffle a hair of any monk or priest, no matter how insignificant the maggot was. They had to put up with it when a rude jackass in the pulpit would vilify a king and a prince and make fun of them as his wanton will suggested. . . . The worldly rulers were completely subject to these clerical giants and tyrants and these dissolute, rude fellows walked all over them . . . none of the worldly lords knew how to revenge himself upon the clergy, except by being too hostile to them, speaking evil of them, and when he

could, playing secret tricks on them, or winking at what others did.[6]

Luther's thought "externalized" and restated in secular terms meant that no one could be excluded by the State from the community or from the Public Opinion State by infaming him or by declaring him nationally disgraced or dishonored.

However, John Calvin retained excommunication for exclusionary and disciplinary reasons. "Those, I say, who trust that churches can long stand without this bond of discipline are mistaken. . . ." Calvin maintained, ". . . that there may be nothing in the Church to bring disgrace on his [God's] sacred name, those whose turpitude might throw infamy on the name must be expelled from his family." A purpose of excommunication, aside from shaming the sinner into repentance, Calvin said, is "that the good may not, as usually happens, be corrupted by constant communication with the wicked. For such is our proneness to go astray, that nothing is easier than to seduce us from the right course by bad example."[7] Because of Calvin excommunication appears as a basic institution in theocratic, Puritan Massachusetts. But as early as 1641 it was delimited by the Massachusetts Body of Liberties as the result of popular resentment against such undemocratic exclusionary ideas. Unfortunately this very complicated colonial history has long since been forgotten or ignored.

Infamy and excommunication have always been powerful weapons of criminal law. Hence, the *Encyclopédie* said that punishment could "affect life, body, esteem or property. . . ."[8] In his *Lettres persanes,* [9] Montesquieu referred to the ruinous force of infamy in feudal Europe, saying, "the hopelessness of infamy causes torment to a Frenchman condemned to a punishment which would not deprive a Turk of a quarter hour of sleep." Eden, the English criminal jurist associated with the Enlightenment, explains the penal power of civic degradation, saying "virtue, though of a social nature, will not associate with infamy."[19]

Luther's condemnation of excommunication was "externalized," secularized and developed to condemn infamy by French *Encyclopédisme* during the eighteenth century, and passed from it into the Constitution of Massachusetts of 1781 and then into the Fifth Amendment in 1789. The great name here is Beccaria, the Italian jurist of the eighteenth century, who was the spokesman for the *Encyclopédistes* in their attacks on feudal criminal law throughout Europe. Jefferson studied Beccaria's discussion of infamy in the Italian text, as his extracts from Beccaria show. Jefferson also extracted the discussion of infamy which appeared in Eden's eighteenth century commentary on English criminal law. Eden was the most important English follower of Beccaria. Beccaria's legal influence extended to the leading American theorist of criminal law through his power over Edward Livingston. Without question, Beccaria is one of the decisive personalities in the history of law.

Professor Adhémar Esmein agrees that Beccaria's pamphlet "was a petition which Europe used to present to its sovereigns."[11] Because the United States had no sovereign, it may be said that Beccaria's writing was presented to its Constitution.

Beccaria, in effect, anticipated the Fifth Amendment through his criticism of feudal ideas of infamy. In the first place, it may be mentioned that Beccaria condemned the imposition of infamy by the state. ". . . [I]nfamy," he said, "is a sentiment regulated neither by the laws nor by reason, but entirely by opinion."[12]

The great French *Encyclopédiste* jurist, Brissot de Warville, developed Beccaria's position, when he said:

> . . . It is more the power of moral custom rather than in the hands of legislators that there resides this terrible weapon of infamy, this kind of civil excommunication, which deprives the victim of all consideration, which ruptures all the ties which attach his fellow citizens to him, which isolates him in the midst of society. [13]

Even in elementary French student legal literature of the present century the matter is fresh. "The naming of infaming punishments," a *vocabulaire de droit* says, "has given rise to sharp criticism. It is wrong, it is held, that the legislator pretend to attach disgrace to the condemnation; furthermore, it goes beyond his right, for it does not dispose of public opinion."[14]

Pastoret, moreover, warned that the state might seek to inflict infamy by itself creating appropriate public opinion. He said:

> One can correct men by a variety of means, and shame is no less powerful than pain or captivity. Infamy, being the result of opinion, exists independently of the legislator; but he can

employ it adroitly to cause it to emerge as a salutary punishment.[15]

Bentham, like Pastoret, realized that a great problem existed. He said that infamy was "determined altogether by the persons to whom it belongs ultimately to dispense it, unassisted and uncontrolled by the political magistrate. In this state it acted before the formation of political society, before the creation of that artificial body of which the political magistrate is the head . . . it was an engine, to the power of which the political magistrate was a witness, before the construction of that which is of his own immediate workmanship. It then was, it still is, and it ever must be, an engine of great power, in whatever direction it be applied; whether it be applied to counteract or to promote his measures. No wonder, then, he should have sought by various contrivances to press it into his service. When thus fitted up and set to work by the political magistrate, it becomes a part of the vast system of machinery to which we have given the name of the political sanction."[16]

But in accordance with the conception of *Encyclopédisme* that the infliction of infamy must be determined by self-determined public opinion, the Fifth Amendment requires both a grand jury indictment and a jury conviction, the two concurring juries thus declaring public opinion. It excludes presidential and congressional infamy, such as has developed in the United States since the ending of the Second World War. It excludes the abuse described by Pastoret and mentioned by Bentham, by declaring the contemporary system of presidential and congressional infamy unconstitutional and illegal.

This is the American outcome of the revolt against Roman feudal infamy. However, even the history of infamy in ancient Roman law seems to have been a struggle between two opposed conceptions of infamy, the original one being "a mode of expression of popular justice . . . even before the establishment of the State," as the French scholar Pommeray, like Bentham, says in his recent extraordinarily important history of Roman infamy,[17] and the other being state infamy. Pommeray seems to say that, with the overthrow of the Roman state in the West, infamy almost disappeared until it was resuscitated by canonist infamy.[18] Brissot de Warville related

Encyclopédiste theory of infamy to Roman popular infamy, when he said:

> Happy the people where the sentiment of honor can be the only law! There is scarcely any need of legislation: there infamy is its criminal code. . . .[19]

And in the United States, Jefferson praised the American Indians, because among them "public opinion is in the place of law, and restrains morals as laws ever did anywhere."[20]

In the second place, Beccaria criticized mass infamy. He said:

> The punishment of infamy should not be too frequent, for the power of opinion grows weaker by repetition; nor should it be inflicted on a number of persons at the same time, for the infamy of many resolves itself into the infamy of none.[21]

Eden, the English follower of *Encyclopédiste* ideas relating to infamy, in effect, echoed Beccaria's attack on mass infamy. He said infamy or ". . . shame loses its effect, when it is inflicted without just and cautious distinction; or, when by the wantonness of oppression, it is made familiar to the eye. . . ."[22]

In his influential notes concerning Beccaria's essay, Diderot, the most important of the *Encyclopédistes,* added:

> I wish that the author [Beccaria] had made known the imprudence of rendering a man infamous and of leaving him free. This absurd method peoples our forests with murderers. [23]

The Fifth Amendment is the outcome of Beccaria's thought as developed by Diderot and Pastoret. It does so by confining the role of infamy to that of a supplemental or secondary punishment for a crime, the repression of which is justified under the Constitution, following the grand jury indictment and jury conviction of the particular defendant.[24] It excludes presidential or congressional infamy. It thus excludes mass infamy, as demanded by Beccaria.

During recent years this part of the Fifth Amendment has been violated because the President and the Congress have infamed Communists and those whom they accuse of Communism, contrary to the limitations set forth in the Fifth Amendment. For instance, there exists legislation requiring administrative registration of organizations and members of organizations declared infamous by the executive and legislative authorities.

4

This discussion of infamy, which explains the meaning of the first part of the Fifth Amendment and which gives this clause of the amendment an importance which has not yet been realized, also clarifies the second part of the Fifth Amendment, forbidding double jeopardy, and the third part of the amendment, which, it will be recalled, reads as follows:

> . . . nor shall [any person] be compelled in any criminal case to be a witness against himself. . . .

The question that today arises from this test is whether the privilege recognized therein against self-incrimination, as it is usually called, is also a privilege against incriminating third persons.

To answer this question, it is necessary to realize that the Administration of European feudal criminal justice was based on the use of the informer or of the delator. In the Congress of 1798, Edward Livingston, the New York and Louisiana *Encyclopédiste* jurist and political heir of Jefferson, whose *projet* of a criminal code for Louisiana links him to Beccaria, attacked the alien and sedition legislation because it introduced the informer into American political life. His words may be reproduced because they described the outcome of the informing system as it existed in Europe during the middle ages and as it exists in the United States today:

> . . . the country will swarm with informers, spies, delators, and all that odious reptile tribe that breed in the sunshine of despotic power; that suck the blood of the unfortunate, and creep into the bosom of sleeping innocence, only to awake it with a burning wound. . . . The companion whom you must trust, the friend in whom you confide, the domestic who waits in your chamber, are all tempted to betray your imprudence or unguarded follies; to misrepresent your words; to convey them, distorted by calumny, to the secret tribunal where jealousy presides—where fear officiates as accuser, and suspicion is the only evidence that is heard. [25]

Through the institution of monitories the medieval church also was involved in the system of informing. At the request of the state the church could order its followers to inform, excommunication being the penalty for failure to do so.[26] Pothier, the most important French jurist of the eighteenth century, devoted himself elaborately to the technical legal problems arising out of the use of monitories.[27]

The outcome of this general system was popular hatred of the informer. If the church threatened excommunication of those who did not obey the warning to inform, the people felt that the informer infamed himself by informing. Beccaria said:

> Secret accusations are a manifest abuse, but consecrated by custom in many nations, where, from the weakness of the government, they are necessary. This custom makes men false and treacherous. Whoever suspects another to be an informer, beholds in him an enemy. [28]

Then Beccaria asks:

> By what arguments is it pretended that *secret* accusations may be justified?" [29]

And then he inquires whether secret accusations do not flow from "the necessity of protecting the informer from infamy."[30]

Thus, Beccaria explains why it must be said that the privilege against self-incrimination is also a privilege against informing; for one cannot incriminate another without incriminating or infaming oneself. Indeed, Beccaria's thought makes it possible to suggest that the privilege against self-incrimination, consecrated by the Fifth Amendment, may also be described as a general privilege against any kind of self-infamy. The privilege guaranteed by this amendment is related to the history of torture,[31] an object of which may have been to force the tortured person to infame himself.

Beccaria says:

> The torture of a criminal, during the course of his trial, is a cruelty, consecrated by custom in most nations. It is used with an intent either to make him confess his crime, or explain some contradictions, into which he had been led during his examination; or discover his accomplices; or for some kind of metaphysical and incomprehensible purgation

> of infamy, or finally, in order to discover other crimes of which he is not accused, but of which he might be guilty.[32]

Among his reflections on this, Beccaria says:

> There is another ridiculous motive for torture, namely, to purge a man from infamy. Ought such an abuse to be tolerated in the eighteenth century? . . . It is not difficult to trace this senseless law to its origin. . . . This custom seems to be the offspring of religion, by which mankind, in all nations and in all ages, are so generally influenced. We are taught by our infallible church, that those stains of sin . . . are to be purged away in another life by an incomprehensible fire. Now infamy is a stain, and if the punishments and fire of purgatory can take away all spiritual stains, why should not the pain of torture take away those of a civil nature? I imagine that the confession of a criminal, which in some tribunals is required as being essential to his condemnation, has a similar origin, and has been taken from the mysterious tribunal of penitence, where the confession of sins is a necessary part of the sacrament.[33]

Beccaria then continues:

> . . . infamy is a sentiment regulated neither by the laws nor by reason, but entirely by opinion. But torture renders the victim infamous, and therefore cannot take infamy away.[34]

Beccaria accomplished two important things by his attack on torture: (1) Torture infames the tortured person whether he incriminates himself or another. (2) But the visitation of such infamy is determined not by the law, but by public opinion. When the third part of the Fifth Amendment says, appropriately enough in scriptural language (considering that Beccaria was condemning a medieval theological idea), that no person shall be compelled "to be a witness against himself," it gives force to the critical thought of Beccaria by recognizing a privilege against self-infamy, including self-infamy by informing, the reality of such infamy being determined by public opinion and not by the law.

Beccaria's idea that the informer was infamed also appears in the *Encyclopédie,* but only within limits. "Following the laws of the digest and of the code, delators were odious . . .", it said,

". . . though in several cases they were not reputed infamous."[35] A somewhat similar idea in a different area of criminal law appears in the thought of the greatest American opponent of the informer system, Edward Livingston, who, speaking of Louisiana law, said:

> [It] now calls for the punishment of acts, which, if not strictly virtues, are certainly too nearly allied to them to be designated as crimes. The ferocious legislation which first enacted this law, demands . . . the sacrifice of all feelings of nature, of all the sentiments of humanity; breaks the ties of gratitude and honor; make obedience to the law consist in a dereliction of every principle that gives dignity to man, and leaves the unfortunate wretch, who has himself been guilty of no offence, to decide between a life of infamy and self-reproach, or a death of dishonor. Dreadful as this picture is, the original is found in the law of accessories after the fact. If the father commit treason, the son must abandon, or deliver him up to the executioner. If the son be guilty of a crime, the stern dictates of our law require, that his parent. . . should barbarously discover his retreat . . . men are required to be faithless, treacherous, unnatural and cruel, in order to prove that they are good citizens, and worthy members of society.[36]

In declaring the informer infamed by public opinion, Beccaria accepts the idea implicit in *Encyclopédisme* that feudal criminal law was a form of social rivalry. Beccaria's statement, noted once before, that "Whoever suspects another to be an informer, beholds in him an enemy,"[37] should be taken literally. Diderot, who distinguishes the accuser and the denouncer of crimes from the delator or informer, states that nevertheless "these three persons are equally odious in the eyes of the people."[38] Diderot described criminal law as "war."[39] Robespierre first sought attention, when as a young lawyer, he attacked the scope of infamy because it was a form of aggression directed against the people. "The ancient French laws," it was pointed out, "prosecuted the actor, only punishing the crimes of nobles by the loss of their privileges, corporeal penalties being reserved for the non-noble, the prejudice of dishonor only attaching to that part of the nation disgraced by servitude."[40] Robespierre thus showed that the law of infamy had been a contradiction, for the rulers of France who had declared themselves to be honorable could not be dishonored, whereas the serfs, who were declared to have no honor, could be deprived of honor or infamed. Perhaps it is a characteristic of Bentham to uphold what Robespiere condemned. He said that "Among the poorer classes, among men who live by their daily labour, sensibility to honour is in general less acute. A day labourer, if he be industrious, though his character be not unspotted, will be at no loss for work. His companions are companions of labour, not of pleasure. . . . His wants are confined to the mere necessaries of life."[41] Pastoret says that criminals, who were sensible to honour because of education, "are the least infamous"[42] and, not unlike Condorcet, treats of class distinctions in the criminal law of infamy.[43] Huebner says that German feudal infamy also represented "class distinctions."[44] The political role which infamy thus enjoyed in the middle ages explains why the informer was infamed by public opinion or by the opinion of the people, and why full force should be given to the Fifth Amendment as a privilege against self-infamy.

It may also be mentioned that Beccaria condemned self-infamy because it violated the basic principle of the judicial process that legal determination should be founded on genuinely contentious procedure. He said

> . . . it is confounding all relations, to expect that a man should be both the accuser and the accused. . . .[45]

The *Encyclopédie* said that

> The natural instinct which attaches a man to life, and the sentiment which excites him to flee from infamy, does not permit one to put a criminal under the obligation of accusing himself even voluntarily and of presenting himself to torture out of sheer wantonness.[46]

Hence the Beccarian conception of the third part of the Fifth Amendment is buttressed by general legal ideas relating to the judicial process. This thought seems justified because the third part of the Fifth Amendment, which begins with the privilege against self-incrimination, concludes with the due process clause, providing that no person shall be "deprived of life, liberty, or property, without due process of law." The two clauses are significantly related because they are only separated by a comma, whereas the other clauses of the Fifth Amendment are separated by semi-colons.

5

It is necessary to repeat once more that Beccaria held that "infamy is a sentiment regulated neither by the laws, nor by reason, but entirely by opinion."[47] For instance, in feudal France a person tortured by the law was not thereby infamed as a matter of law.[48] Nevertheless, as has been shown, Beccaria said that such person was indeed infamed by public opinion, and it would follow under the Fifth Amendment that he should not be tortured to infame himself before public opinion.

Because the informer is infamed by public opinion, rather than by the law itself, and because the Fifth Amendment guarantees a privilege against self-infamy, the witness cannot constitutionally be required to inform on others in return for immunity given him by the State. The State cannot immunize the informer from his infamy, for the informer is infamed by public opinion. As Luther might say, the State cannot assume "authority to save souls by means of indulgences."[49]

This conclusion is consistent with certain *Encyclopédiste* theory. Certain jurists of the Enlightenment condemned compromise with the criminal by which he gained immunity from punishment in exchange for his information. Such arbitrary compromise violated the idea of legality or of the rule of law, and the idea of equality before the law. Even during the period introduced by the eighteenth *brumaire,* Bexon said:

> A government founded on strict justice, on the equality of men before the law, cannot admit when it has decided by the magistrates invested with its power, that there exists the privileges of respite, of pardon, of grace. . . .[50]

He says that such privileges connote "traces of arbitrary power."[51]

In England, Eden, who was under Beccarian influence, criticized compromise of crime in exchange for information. He said:

> It was formerly usual for the prisoner . . . to confess the indictment, and be admitted, on his own request, to become an approver against others of the same felony; upon the conviction of whom he was entitled to his pardon. This practice was never prohibited by law, but gradually discouraged and disused; "for the truth is (saith Sir M. Hale) that

> more mischief hath come thereof by false accusations of desperate villains, than benefit to the public by the discovery, and conviction of real offenders." . . . It may be good policy to raise mutual jealousies among villains; but there is something very shocking in the idea of murder, by law established.[52]

Voltaire wrote that "The laws of England do not consider as guilty of conspiracy those who are privy to it, and do not inform. They suppose the informer as infamous as the conspirator is culpable."[53]

Such resentment against compromise with the criminal may explain why the humane, generous and lenient Beccaria, who opposed capital punishment, nevertheless also felt that the throne should be deprived of the power of pardon. In this Jefferson followed Beccaria in the penal *projet* introduced for him and others by Madison into the Virginia legislature in 1785, four years before the Bill of Rights was formulated. This text provided:

> Pardon and Privilege of Clergy shall henceforth be abolished, that none may be induced to injure through hope of impunity.[54]

As has been said, certain jurists of the Enlightenment were hostile to the idea of pardon, not only because under feudalism it was an arbitrary device to overcome legality and equality before the law, but because pardon could not remove infamy, which rested on public opinion. In quite a different connection, Bentham said, ". . . any kind of infamy, howsoever inflicted or contracted, may chance to prove perpetual; since the idea of the offence, or, what comes to the same thing, of the punishment, may very well chance to remain more or less fresh in men's minds to the end of the delinquent's life. . . ."[55] Pastoret criticized Montesquieu because the latter was friendly to the concept of pardon, and pointed out that in England social struggles had occurred between the Crown and the commons over the power of pardon. He quotes Blackstone as saying that the pardoning power absolves the criminal, purifies him and restores him to his civil rights. However, in France, Pastoret continues, "the absolution itself consecrates" the criminal "to infamy." He says that the clemency of the monarch "does not ward off shame." "The prince spared the punishment," Pastoret says, "without rehabilitating the culpable person in his honor. . . ." "The law itself, the accomplice of opinion," he continues, "always held him under the anathema of infamy."[56] However, Bexon, writing after the eighteenth *brumaire,* which established Napoleon's power in France, said: "Release from a punishment for a crime in favor of an accomplice who denounces it, to me seems just, even moral."[57]

The text of the third part of the Fifth Amendment does not require solutions such as that involved in the denial of the power of pardon, suggested by Beccaria, Jefferson and Pastoret. The Fifth Amendment itself establishes a privilege against self-infamy, which is a self-determined privilege. It is a privilege which can only be renounced by the person exposed to the threat of self-infamy. The privilege guaranteed by the Fifth Amendment cannot be withdrawn by the determination of the State, even in exchange for penal immunity, for the State cannot immunize the person whose honor is involved from being infamed by public opinion, which under the First Amendment is prior to the State. The privilege consecrated by the Fifth Amendment is an *Encyclopédiste* "externalization," secularization, development and enforcement of Luther's conception:

> This fellowship can neither be given nor taken away by anyone, be he bishop, pope or angel or any creature. . . . This fellowship no ban can touch or affect, but only the unbelief or sin of the person himself; by these he can excommunicate himself, and thus separate himself from the grace, life and salvation of the fellowship.[58]

Hegel pointed out that the French Enlightenment "completed the Reformation that Luther began" because it maintained "that a man's own self, the human spirit, is the source from which it derived all that is to be respected by him."[59] This thought, which is consecrated in the privilege against self-infamy, is recognized elsewhere in eighteenth century theory of the criminal law. For instance, almost two centuries before the Second World War, Benjamin Franklin said that a soldier had no duty to obey an illegal order of superior office,[60] and Edward Livingston, in the early nineteenth century, provided in his *project* of a code of criminal law, that "The order of a military superior is no justification or excuse for the commission of a crime," as distinguished from a misdemeanor.[61]

Finally, it should be mentioned that Beccaria himself criticized "tribunals" in which "a pardon is offered to an accomplice in a great crime, if he discover his associates." He says:

> This expedient has its advantages. The disadvantages are, that the law authorizes treachery, which is detested even by the villains themselves; and introduces crimes of cowardice, which are more pernicious to a nation than crimes of courage. Courage is not common, and only wants a benevolent power to direct it to the public good. Cowardice, on the contrary, is a frequent self-interested, and contagious evil, which can never be improved into a virtue. Besides, the tribunal, which has recourse to this method, betrays its fallibility, and the laws their weakness, by imploring the assistance of those by whom they are violated.
>
> The advantages are, that it prevents great crimes, the effects of which being public, and the perpetrators concealed, terrify the people.[62]

Beccaria then says that he would prefer "a general law, promising a reward to every accomplice who discovers his associates" than a "special declaration in every case" (though he feels that a State which would pass such a law would also dishonorably betray the informer and "drag to punishment who hath accepted of their invitation.")[63] Beccaria proceeds:

> But it is in vain, that I torment myself with endeavoring to extinguish the remorse I feel in attempting to induce the sacred laws, the monument of public confidence, the foundation of human morality, to authorize dissimulation and perfidy.[64]

In his note to this discussion, Diderot criticizes Beccaria's thinking, saying that the latter has forgotten "public policy" *(l'ordre public).* [65]

Here the thought of Pastoret becomes important. Pastoret follows Beccaria. Pastoret attacked the idea of immunizing the witness in return for his information, because this system is employed in hysteria-ridden societies which have become demoralized, which have turned inward, which are living in a world of myth or imagination, in a world of fear and trembling, in a world which, in contemporary ideology, has become existentialist. He begins by asking:

> Should one compensate punishment for admission of a crime by one of the accomplices? Nothing merits less favor from the laws than delation; and if it can ever be authorized or rather supported, if impunity in this case can ever become useful, it would be in moments of disturbance and of sedition where there are great calamities to prevent and great outrages to uncover; but, on the other hand, in these moments, the ordinary exaggeration of feeling, the readiness to believe what one suspects, the fears of weak men, the hidden interests of evil men, the universal lack of confidence, I do not know what mistrustful inquietude from which virtue itself is not shielded, if it possesses more kindness than courage, a kind of rapid electricity with which all sensations are communicated and which always diverts reflection and thought; all contribute to make delation even more dangerous in the midst of public disturbances than for ordinary crimes.[66]

This passage from Pastoret perhaps may be the background or inspiration for the thought in the great attack against delation which was made in Congress by Edward Livingston in 1798 at the time of the crisis of the alien and sedition laws. It may be said that because Jefferson in 1785, during the crisis of post-revolution itself, and Livingston, during the crisis of 1798 (which led to what Jefferson called the "revolution of 1800"),[67] followed the thought of Beccaria and of Pastoret rather than Diderot's note, the so-called privilege against self-incrimination, embodied in the Fifth Amendment, recognizes a self-determined privilege against self-infamy through informing.

But if it is kept in mind that the function of the Fifth Amendment links it to the First Amendment, consecrating the Public Opinion State, perhaps the disagreement between Beccaria and Diderot diminishes in importance. Indeed, Diderot said "good princes never had delators," saying also that delators under one emperor "rarely escaped infamy."[68]

As has been shown, Pastoret had warned that the State "adroitly" might seek to direct and control the public opinion which is supposed to direct and control the State. The State may demoralize social life and create and stimulate the world of fear and trembling.

Pastoret had indicated that the power of opinion might be veered into the opinion of power. Hence, in the passage just reproduced, Pastoret justifies his attack on compensation of the informer by putting it in a political setting, in a world of "public disturbances," instead of a world of "ordinary crimes." Although he is not discussing the problem of forced denunciation, Professor Griswold's thought here becomes very important. ". . . The significance of the privilege over the years," he says, "has perhaps been greatest in connection with resistance to prosecution for such offenses as heresy or political crimes. In these areas the privilege against self-incrimination has been a protection for freedom of thought and a hindrance to any government which might wish to prosecute for thoughts and opinions alone."[69] Of course, Pastoret breaks the limitation connoted by Professor Griswold because the former shows that the attack on freedom of opinion by the State justifies not only the privilege against self-incrimination, but also the privilege against delation.

Because Beccaria had not put his attack against compensated delation in the political setting discussed by Pastoret and Griswold, he perhaps exposed himself to Diderot's criticism. However, the Fifth Amendment itself consecrates Beccaria's rather than Diderot's narrower conception of *ordre public*. Beccaria would support the thought of Griswold as developed by Pastoret. But he also attacked compensated delation because delation infamed the delator and ruined him before public opinion. Moreover, he knew that compensated delation violated eighteenth century ideas of the education mission of the law-maker. This imposed moral responsibilities on the legislator, which were violated by a state-created informer system. Beccaria's thought here reunites with that of Diderot, who held that "If the laws are good, morals are good; if the laws are bad, morals are bad." [70] This Diderotian-Beccarian conception of the laws differentiates *Encyclopédiste* theory of the constitution and of the codes from Austin's imperative conception of law. Beccaria also agrees with Diderot that customary morality is "susceptible of rule and direction."[71] This Diderotian-Beccarian conception of the laws differentiates *Encyclopédiste* theory of the constitution and the codes from Savigny and his conception of the customary basis of law.

This discussion may explain why the Fifth Amendment is not textually part of the Sixth Amendment, which is devoted to "all criminal prosecutions." The Fifth Amendment is addressed to the criminal law of infamy, but may have been set off from the Sixth Amendment, because the role and effects of Romanist infamy were not entirely problems of the formal criminal law, with which the Sixth Amendment is concerned, but were also problems of the Public Opinion State, established by the First Amendment.

The relation or tie between the First and Fifth Amendments is brought out by de Servan in his *projet* of a declaration of rights of man and of the citizen presented at the National Assembly on 30 July 1789. The eighth article says that the object of civil society can be reduced to civil liberty, which is the power of the citizen to exercise all faculties not forbidden by law. The ninth article says that the faculties of the citizen are reduced to the disposition of his thought, of his person and of his property. This means that intellectual freedom is as free as economic freedom. The tenth article proposed that all true legislation should be nothing but a system of laws directed toward and conducing to civil liberty at their common center. Article eleven is a long disquisition. The political and constitutional laws, as well as the civil laws, should lead to civil liberty. The criminal laws are related to civil liberty, when each person can act without fear of unjust punishment, and when the guilty can be judged without fear of excessive punishment. Religious laws conform to civil liberty if they do not endanger the liberty of men by dogma and creed and if they promote the principles of morality. "Finally," de Servan says, "the laws, especially the laws of opinion, maintain civil liberty when in the actions where the positive laws have nothing to prescribe, each directs himself toward the public good entirely by the law of opinion, which punishes by disgrace, and rewards by esteem." In the twelfth article de Servan says, "In accordance with these principles, in every civil society legitimately governed, each citizen should be free to communicate and to make known his thoughts on objects which are not forbidden by the laws."[72]

6

At this point it should be reiterated that the Bill of Rights is essentially an American *précis* or summary, magnificently formulated, of the criticism of European feudalism, in general, as made by the French *Encyclopédistes* during the period prior to the French and American Revolutions. This has been shown in regard to the Fifth Amendment, which is devoted to the problem of European Romanist infamy, an institution, which, however, does not enjoy a really important role as such in the history of English criminal law, perhaps because it was excluded or held down by Magna Carta, as was suggested in Massachusetts during the period of the formulation of the Body of Liberties in 1641. In his work of comparative criminal law, published in 1800, Bexon says that "civic degradation, properly called, does not appear to me established in the criminal laws of England. I see only the penalty of disqualifications for any office, for any public employ, to inherit, to be testamentary executor. This degradation, as one sees it, is not as extensive as that established by the French laws . . . civic degradation truly can be a grave and terrible penalty only in a republic."[73] Eden, who is aware of the role of infamy in Romanist feudal Europe, sums up the limited role and history of English infamy as follows:

> There are two kinds of infamy, the one founded in the opinions of the people respecting the mode of punishment, the other in the construction of law respecting the future credibility of the delinquent; the law of England was erroneous, when it declared the latter a consequence of the punishment, not of the crime.—There still exist some unrepealed statutes, which inflict perpetual infamy on offenses of civil institution. But in general the rigour of this doctrine is now reduced to reason; and it is holden that, unless a man be put in the pillory, or stigmatized, for *crimen falsi*, as for perjury, forgery, or the like, it infers no blemish on his attestation. It may be highly penal to engross corn, or to publish a pamphlet offensive to government, but mercantile avarice, and political sedition, have no connection with the competence of testimony, the credit of an oath can only be overbalanced by the nature and weight of the inequity.[74]

However, the idea that the Bill of Rights is essentially an American *précis* of French *Encyclopédiste* theory affecting European feudalism is contested by Professor George Jellinek, the important German legal theorist of the nineteenth century. Jellinek holds the contrary thesis that the declarations of rights in the American state constitutions, formulated during the period of the American Revolution, not only antedate the French declaration of the rights of man and of the citizen, but were received in the texts of the latter during the French Revolution.[75]

It is indeed true that the French texts were influenced by this American constitutional history. The names of Brissot de Warville and of Condorcet may be mentioned in this connection.[76] But links such as these strengthen the idea that the Fifth Amendment itself reflects earlier *Encyclopédiste* thought which explains the texts of the bill of rights in the American state constitutions, the Bill of Rights of the United States Constitution and the French texts.

As has been shown, Brissot de Warville condemned infamy, or civil excommunication, as he called it, because it severed social relations which were required in the Pubic Opinion State.[77] Condorcet was a theorist of the Public Opinion State and of its constitutional form. The ties between these intellectuals and the American state constitutions obtained only to the extent that the American bills of rights, including the Fifth Amendment, reflected earlier French thought of the eighteenth century. When American political and constitutional thought of their period did not correspond to *Encyclopédiste* principles, these French theorists supported the Enlightenment and condemned American institutions.

Indeed, Brissot de Warville and Condorcet were aware that the American state bills of rights had precipitated an American crisis, for the Americans were only willing to condemn European feudalism, but not to overcome American slavery. Despite the American declarations of inalienable human rights, the freedom of American human beings was in truth alienated by American slavery. These French friends of America were not friends of American slavery, and joined forces with the American Quaker anti-slavery movement. Brissot de Warville founded the powerful *Société des Amis des Noirs*. Condorcet also condemned slavery. He said *Encyclopédiste* principles "required the destruction of slavery."[78] During the French Revolution he demanded the exclusion of French slave-holders from the revolutionary assembly,[79] and thus anticipated the later activity of his friend, Paine, in regard to the Louisiana slave-holders, following the American purchase of Louisiana.[80] Condorcet criticized the United States because a law excluding American slave-holders from the Congress had been defeated.[81] He said that in destroying slavery the State should not "compensate" the masters of the slaves.[82] In effect, this was a criticism of a certain meaning of the last part of the Fifth Amendment which forbids the taking of private property for public use "without just compensation," the background for which, in part, may have been the proposal advanced in America that the masters of slaves should be compensated and slavery thus ended.[83] The outcome is that the Fifth Amendment may have been a contradiction, in which the amendment in the first part strikes at impairment of the legal personality of the subjects of the Bill of Rights *(capitis deminutio,* civil death) and at civic degradation *(infamia)*, but elsewhere ambiguously regarded slaves as objects, but not as subjects of, the Second Constitution. This crisis was not solved until the introduction of the Third Constitution (Thirteenth, Fourteenth and Fifteenth Amendments) after the American Civil War.

In this situation, it must be said that the French *Encyclopédistes* gave their support to the American bills of rights only insofar as they thereby furthered and strengthened *Encyclopédiste* principles.

Although Jellinek holds that American thought was not inspired by French *Encyclopédisme,* he does not conclude that such American formulations were the outcome of English history and of English thought. The American texts, he says, "enumerate a much larger number of rights as innate and inalienable. Whence comes this conception in American law? It is not from the English law."[84] The result of Jellinek's work is that the American Bills of Rights were neither French nor English. But he connected them to nineteenth-century racial, Germanic conceptions of history.[85] This means that Jellinek has solved nothing.

Jellinek made the mistake of not relating the American Bills of Rights to American social history and to the impact thereon of French *Encyclopédiste* thought of the earlier eighteenth century, which does, indeed, antedate the American constitutional formulations and which explains both the American and French constitutional guarantees. As Jellinek ignored American social history and French *Encyclopédisme,* he concerned himself only with the influence of what might be called "terminal" texts; he missed the historic force of the ideas which were reflected in such texts. Hence he did not perceive the French influence on American thinking.

Jellinek's mistaken conception, in effect, underlies Professor Wigmore's erroneous understanding of the Fifth Amendment, with the result that this influential American legal scholar holds that the so-called privilege against self-incrimination guaranteed by this amendment is of American common law, and not of French, origin.

However, he reached this conclusion hesitatingly. He asks "How then did it come to make its appearance in the constitutional discussions and the Bill of Rights of 1787–1789"[86] He admits "The novelty and recentness of it all in common-law tradition, is apparent, not only in the very gradual progress of the recognition in criminal trials after 1641, but also in the fact that it remained an unknown doctrine for that whole generation in the colony of Massachusetts—a colony not only familiar enough with common legal proceedings, but knowing enough to send over for Sir Edward Coke's reports and other law books to inform its Court and keep abreast of the times."[87] Professor Wigmore also says of the privilege against self-incrimination that "Whatever it was worth to the American constitution-makers of 1789, it was not worth mentioning to the English constitution-menders of 1689."[88] Wigmore then asked whether the privilege developed out of French legal history, an opinion which he held in the first two editions of his masterpiece, but which he repudiated in his third edition.[89] Here he maintained that the privilege developed out of American legal history, "fortified no doubt by the legal learning brought back by the Colonial lawyers who had gone to the Inns of Court for their education. So the proposals agitated in France in the 1780's were based explicitly on an acquaintance with the constitutions of the prior decade in the new American States."[90] Hence, Professor Wigmore concludes by following Jellinek's theory.

7

Because Professor Wigmore's understanding of the origin of the Fifth Amendment is faulty, he does not realize that the so-called privilege against self-incrimination is also a privilege against self-infamy. In his dissenting opinion in *Brown v. Walker,*[91] where the constitutionality of a legislative system of *denonciateurs forcés* was the problem, Mr. Justice Field said that the Fifth Amendment protects a witness "from all compulsory testimony which would expose him to infamy and disgrace, though the facts disclosed might not lead to a criminal prosecution."[92] Professor Wigmore replies abusively to Mr. Justice Field, saying:

> It is, to be sure, of little avail to suggest reasons against a view which ignores all precedent and all history. It is simple enough to create a constitutional doctrine "instanter," if we may snatch it, like a magician's white rabbit, full-grown, out of empty space, and place it living and panting before the

> astonished spectators. But such is not the accepted judicial habit.
>
> Quite apart from the errors of logic and history, a greater fault in the opinion above quoted is its singular appeal to false sentiment. . . . Were it not so serious in its implications, it would be as ludicrous a spectacle as if one were to devote a colossal fortune to founding a hospital for the care of able-bodied vagrants, or to recite Milton's Ode to the Nativity at the birth of a favorite feline's litter.
>
> The doctrine of the minority opinion in *Brown v. Walker* rests on a misconception so radical that only the exalted source of its promulgation makes it necessary to be thus noticed.[93]

The weakness in Professor Wigmore's thought stems from his failure to heed the signal of the first words of the Fifth Amendment that its content related to the problem of Romanist feudal infamy. He ignored the warning that the meaning of the Fifth Amendment might not be explained solely in terms of the Anglo-American common law. And Mr. Justice Field made himself vulnerable to Professor Wigmore's attack because he, too, justified his correct formulation entirely on "' . . . sentiment . . . which has inhabited the breasts of English speaking peoples for centuries. . . .'"[94]

American interest in *Encyclopédisme* and in such *Encyclopédiste* texts as the Fifth Amendment was the outcome of American social history. However, Professor Wigmore does not offer this history, even though he maintains an American colonial origin for the so-called privilege against self-incrimination. He introduces an English origin of the privilege through such colonial history, although, as has been shown, the force of his own discussion of the English origins of this concept is that it had no firm place in the English common law. He mentions the very important case of John Lilburne as justifying the privilege in the history of the English common law. However, Professor Wigmore's treatment of Lilburne does not show that the privilege emerged in the common law at the time because Lilburne represented the strength and interest of the English Levellers during the seventeenth century revolution. Hence, although Lilburne gave "indomitable leadership" to the Levellers[95] and although "it is difficult to disentangle the Leveller movement from the personality of the arch Leveller," Lilburne,[96] Professor

Wigmore disposes of him by saying that "John Lilburne, an obstreperous and forward opponent of the Stuarts (popularly known as 'Freeborn John'), constituted somewhere between a patriot and a demagogue, had the obstinacy to force the issue."[97] Because Lilburne represented the Levellers, the English genesis of the privilege against self-incrimination must be related to paragraph XVI of the Levellers text of 1 May 1649, entitled *An Agreement of the Free People of England,* a prototype constitution, which provided that ". . . it shall not be in the power of any Representative, to punish, or cause to be punished, any person or persons for refusing to answer to questions against themselves in Criminall cases."[98]

Professor Wigmore's lack of interest in the Leveller movement means that he ignores much that is really important.

Leveller literature repeatedly justifies the privilege against self-incrimination as a political privilege.[99] In *The Fountain of Slaunder Discovered,* William Walwyn, like Luther, defends it on grounds of "judgment and conscience."[100] In *The Just Defence of John Lilburn,* the privilege against self-incrimination is related to "true law and due proceedings,"[101] a significant statement because the text of the Fifth Amendment itself also closely relates the due process clause to the privilege.

Moreover, *The Just Defence of John Lilburn* is also very important because the privilege against self-incrimination is there stated and upheld as a privilege against informing. Hence the following deserves close attention:

> The ancient known right and law of England being, that no man be put to his defence at law, upon any mans bare saying, or upon his own oath, but by presentment of lawful men, and by faithful witnesses brought for the same face to face; a law and known right, without which any that are in power may at pleasure rake into the brests of every man for matter to destroy life, liberty, or estate, when according to true law and due proceedings, there is nought against them; now it being my lot to be drawn out and required to take an oath, and to be required to answer to questions against myself and others whom I honored, and whom I knew no evil by, though I might know such things by them as the oppossors and persecutors would have punished them for, in that I stood firm to our true English liberty, as resolvedly persisted therein, enduring a

> most cruel whipping, pilloring, gagging, and barbarous punishment, rather than betray the rights and liberties of every man; did I deserve for so doing to be accounted turbulent? . . . who assists not in such cases, betrays his own rights, and is overrun, and of a free man made a slave when he thinks not of it, or regards it not, and so shunning the censure of turbulency, incurs the guilt of treachery to the present and future generations.[102]

In *The Picture of the Councel of State,* Lilburne says:

> . . for my part, Gentlemen, I do utterly refuse to make answer unto any thing in relation to my own person, or any man or men under heaven; but do humbly desire, that if you intend by way of Charge to proceed to any Triall of me, that it may be . . . in some ordinary Court of Justice appointed for such cases (extraordinary waies being never to be used, but abominated, where ordinarie waies may be had). . . .[103]

There is, of course, also an American social history which justifies the Fifth Amendment. Indeed the American attack on infamy goes back almost to the founding of Boston. It goes back to what is probably the first economic and social crisis in American history. It goes back to the restlessness of the people of Massachusetts (perhaps under Leveller influence), who were excluded from political and social life by the Calvinist theocracy of the Bay Colony, which, unlike Luther, employed excommunication. But the outcome of this struggle was the Massachusetts Body of Liberties of 1641 and the subsequent formulation. These texts were the work of Nathaniel Ward, probably the only common lawyer in the Bay Colony (if Lechford may be ignored). Ward was not only a common lawyer, but had lived for years in Germany, where it may be assumed that he learned as a clergyman of Lutheran hostility to excommunication and as a lawyer of the role of civilian infamy. The Body of Liberties begins by restricting the force of infamy and excommunication. "No mans life shall be taken away," it says, "no mans honour or good name shall be stayned [stained]," (a word also used by Beccaria and Bentham to describe infamy), except on grounds which were largely legislative and promulgated. Another paragraph says that "excommunication" shall not disturb the power of the excommunicated person to alienate property. A third paragraph says that "No church censure shall degrade or depose any man from any civil dignitie, office, or Authoritie he shall have in the Commonwealth." A fourth texts says that "No man shall be forced by Torture to confesse any Crime against himselfe nor any other," save after conviction for a capital crime. A fifth paragraph says that "No Magestrate, Juror, Officer or other man shall be bound to informe present or reveale any private crim or offence, wherein there is no perill or danger to this plantation or any member thereof, when any necessarietye of conscience binds him to secresie grounded upon the word of God, unlesse it is in case of testimony lawfully required." This recalls Luther's idea, already discussed, that, as excommunication or infamy is self-determined, the Fifth Amendment justifies a privilege, determined by conscience, against self-excommunication or self-infamy through informing. This conception may parallel paragraph X of the Leveller prototype constitution of 1 May 1649, which says that we do not impower or entrust our said representatives to continue in force, or to make any Lawes, Oaths, or Covenants, whereby to compell by penalties or otherwise any person to any thing in or about matters of faith, Religion or Gods worship. . . . ."[104]

8

Although it is obvious that these forgotten texts, and others, may be precursors of the Fifth Amendment, their enlightened development into the Fifth Amendment is unfettered and stimulated only by eighteenth century *Encyclopédisme*. Because in effect he followed Jellinek's theory (without discovering a social basis for it), Professor Wigmore cut himself off from the historical force and meaning of the Fifth Amendment. This scholar did this by ignoring French *Encyclopédiste* theory of criminal law and by confining his attention to French legal opinion after the formulation of the American state constitutions, as the theory of Jellinek in effect required him to do. He missed the force of Carette's observation that the magistrate de Servan's famous *discours* of 1788, which preceded the French *code pénal* of 1791 (destroying the French feudal system of criminal law founded on the criminal *ordonnance* of August 1670), in large part was "only the echo of the *philosophes;* for, before Servan, Beccaria had said and Voltaire had repeated . . . *it is necessary to proportion punishments to wrongs. . . .*"[105] Professor Wigmore seems to have felt that the matter of *Encyclopédiste* influence on the so-called privilege against self-incrimination could be disposed of by saying that

> It might be supposed that the explanation of the Colonial conventions' insistence on it in the 1780's was to be found in the agitation then going on in France against the inquisitorial feature of the Ordonnance of 1670. There appears no allusion, in Elliot's Debates on the Constitution, to the contemporary French movement; but the delegates who had been over there must have known of it.[106]

Among those whom Professor Wigmore might have mentioned as "over there" at the time was Jefferson, who from Paris on 23 May, 1788 wrote John Jay, the first chief justice of the Supreme Court:

> On the 8th, a bed of justice was held at Versailles, wherein were enregistered the six ordinances which had been passed in Council, on the 1st of May, and which I now send you. . . . By these ordinances, 1, the criminal law is reformed, by abolishing examination on the *sellette*, which, like our holding up the hand at the bar, remained a stigma on the party, though innocent; by substitution of an oath, instead of torture on the *question préalable*, which is used after condemnation, to make the prisoner discover his accomplices; (the torture abolished in 1789, was on the *question préparatoire*, previous to judgment, in order to make the prisoner accuse himself;) by allowing counsel to the prisoner for this defence; obligating the judges to specify in their judgments the offence for which he is condemned; and respiting execution a month, except in the case of sedition. This reformation is unquestionably good and within the ordinary legislative powers of the crown. That it should remain to be made at this day, proves that the monarch is the last person in his kingdom, who yields to the progress of philanthropy and civilization.[107]

This letter by Jefferson is very important, not only because it shows his great interest in the problem presented in American law by the content of the Fifth Amendment conceived as a text of French *Encyclopédisme,* but because it shows how readily the problem of infamy or of "stigma" related to the problem of self-infamy and of self-"stigma" through *dénonciateurs forcés*. Jefferson's ease in writing of these matters to Jay, his refusal to translate *"question préalable"* and *"question préparatoire"* into English, indicate his really good knowledge of French medieval criminal law[108] and of the *Encyclopédiste* ideas which in France were overcoming such law. And it does not seem unreasonable to suggest that Chief Justice Jay understood what Jefferson wrote to him.

But Jefferson had not always been "over there," and it is through him that the *Encyclopédiste* ideas which are at work "over here" in the Fifth Amendment became known in the United States perhaps even before the American state constitutions were given legal force. The theory of Jellinek and of Wigmore may thereby be refuted.

Jefferson may be regarded as the connecting link between Beccaria and the Fifth Amendment. Probably no jurist of modern history (not even Savigny) influenced his contemporaries more than Beccaria's small volume on the criminal law. He was greeted by the *Encyclopédistes* as their theorist of the criminal law. The giants of the progressive intellectual life of the eighteenth century welcomed him to their company. These included Diderot, Holbach, Helvetius, d'Alembert.[109] His work was translated into numerous languages. Diderot and Morellet wrote notes to Beccaria's text. Voltaire wrote a famous commentary, which was published together with the text of Beccaria. Voltaire's own intellectual development had been such that in 1765 it could be said he held "Infamy punishments should be abolished."[110] Certain writings of Bentham in French appeared in the same volume as a French translation of Beccaria.

On the other hand, the jurists of the ancient regime responded vigorously against Beccaria. Muyart de Vouglans, one of the most important of these jurists, believed that Beccaria represented an Italian attack on the French courts.[111] This makes Beccaria's writing especially important to French *Encyclopédisme*. He complained that there had been three French editions of Beccaria in less than six months, and demanded that the authorities "arrest the contagion."[112] The attack of Muyart de Vouglans on Beccaria was published as a refutation in the closing pages of the former's commentary on criminal law, a volume of almost 1,000 folio pages. But Muyart de Vouglans followed this *Réfutation du traité des délits et peines* [113] with a *mémoire* devoted exclusively to infamy—his *Mémoire sur les peines infamantes*.[114] Here the spokesman of French feudalism pretends to yield ground to the critics of infamy. After attempting to clarify the detail of the content of the French law of infamy, Muyart de Vouglans himself offers eighteen proposals for the reform of this institution. Perhaps the most important of these is the ninth,[115] but as it in general only reached the level attained in the Massachusetts Body of Liberties of 1641, it falls short of what was historically required in 1780, and hence is opposed to the Fifth Amendment. Legislation of the French National Assembly, codifying criminal law, given the force of law during the period 16–29 September 1791, approximately fifteen days after the enactment of the French constitutional declaration of the rights of man and of the citizen (3–14 September 1791), therefore appropriately rejects the proposal of Muyart de Vouglans regarding infamy and instead follows the Fifth Amendment. The four texts should be compared:

Massachusetts Body of Liberties (1641)
No mans life shall be taken away, no mans honour or good name shall be stayned . . . unlesse it be by vertu, or equitie of some expresse law of the Country, waranting the same, established by a generall Court and sufficiently published, or in case of the defect of a law in any particular case by the word of god.

Muyart De Vouglans' Ninth Proposal (1780)
. . . an infaming punishment can be pronounced only in consequence of a decree and of an extraordinary disposition. . . .

Fifth Amendment (1787)
No person shall be held to answer for a capital, or otherwise infamous crime, unless on a presentment or indictment of a Grand Jury. . . .

Codification of the National Assembly (1791)
No act of accusation can be presented to the jury [of accusation] save for a delict importing afflictive or infaming punishment (*peine afflictive ou infamante*).

Referring to the above codification of September 1791, Professor Adhémar Esmein says that the National Assembly had, "in effect, taken from the English the double form of jury, the jury of accusation and the jury of judgment, the double barrier, as Blackstone said, which defended the liberty of the English citizen." Professor Esmein presumably has in mind Blackstone's statement that in England ". . . no man can be convicted . . . of any capital offence, unless by the unanimous voice of twenty-four of his equals and neighbors: that is, by twelve at least of the grand jury, in the first place, assenting to the accusation, and afterwards by the whole petit jury of twelve more men finding him guilty upon his trial." However, as Blackstone justified the grand jury only for "capital offenses," whereas the Fifth Amendment requires it for "capital, or otherwise infamous crimes," and the National Assembly of 1791 required it for "afflictive or infaming punishment," the two latter formulations both should be described as an outcome of Beccarian and *Encyclopédiste* criticism of infamy.[116]

It may be said that in a sense the Fifth Amendment sublates the crisis in the French feudal law of infamy, precipitated by Beccaria and recognized as such by Muyart de Vouglans. It does so by excluding presidential and congressional mass infamy. However, the unconstitutional regime which obtains in the United States today is the system of infamy desired by Muyart de Vouglans, the legal theorist of French feudalism.

The force of Beccaria was as much felt in America as in Europe. There were three American translations of Beccaria, together with translations of Voltaire's commentary, published during the period culminating in the formulation of the Fifth Amendment. Two of these were published in Philadelphia, the third in Charleston.[117] In 1941 an American writer on Voltaire said:

> Beccaria's *Essay on Crimes and Punishment* with its famous commentary by Voltaire was known in America immediately after its first appearance in France and was the first of Voltaire's works to be published in America. It was popular in lending libraries and as a quickly sold item in bookstores, because of general interest in the formation of a new social order. A separate monograph would be necessary to trace the influence of this epoch-making tract.[118]

The same writer also says:

> In contrast to the seventeenth century, when sanctions of social order were religious, American thinkers in the

eighteenth century sought to discover the secular justifications for a social order. They were also seeking precedents for the state and federal penal codes which they were then busily establishing. In this search, judging from evidence found in catalogues of the period, Beccaria's *Essay on Crime and Punishment* with the famous commentary by Voltaire played an important part. . . . The various booksellers and libraries already mentioned brought the total number of times listed to forty-eight.[119]

Of course this weakens the ideological position of Professor Jellinek and Professor Wigmore. But their theory totally collapses because it can be shown that Beccaria and Beccarian ideas concerning infamy were in fact known to Jefferson. Jefferson himself copied in Italian large portions of Beccaria's volume, including the latter's attack on infamy.[120] The importance of this fact cannot be overstated.

Furthermore, Jefferson made summaries from William Eden's eighteenth century commentary on English criminal law, including infamy. This, too, is important, for it may perhaps be said that Eden, rather than Bentham, was the English spokesman of *Encyclopédiste* conceptions of criminal law. Thus, Edward Livingston, the chief American theorist of criminal law on the principles of *Encyclopédisme,* referred to "A spirit of enlightened legislation, taught by Montesquieu, Beccaria, Eden, and others; names dear to humanity! has banished some of the most atrocious [punishments] from the codes of Europe."[121]

Jefferson's knowledge of Eden's discussion of infamy seems to explain decisive aspects of the Fifth Amendment relating to infamy. As has been shown, Eden undermined the idea of mass infamy. Furthermore, Eden may be responsible for the exactness of expression of the Fifth Amendment in dealing with infamy. The text of this amendment was received from a similar text formulated in the Massachusetts constitution of 1781 (which did not appear in the *projet* of John Adams). However, there is a technical difference in the formulation of the two constitutions. The Massachusetts text in 1.12 is concerned with "infamous punishment," whereas the Fifth Amendment is devoted to "infamous crime." In many instances these are virtually interchangeable phrases. For instance, du Rousseaud de la Combe said in 1768 that ". . . the mark of infamy is incurred as of right by the quality of the punishment pronounced by the judgment against the condemned person."[122] However, as there may be "infamous crime" without "infamous punishment," it is required that the two ideas be kept separate.[123] Eden pointed this out, saying:

> There are two kinds of infamy, the one founded in the opinions of the people respecting the mode of punishment, the other in the construction of the law respecting the future credibility of the delinquent; the law of England was erroneous when it declared the latter a consequence of the punishment, not the crime.[124]

Bentham also strengthens the distinction when he said "A certain degree of infamy or disrepute, we have already remarked, is what necessarily attends on every kind of political punishment. But there are some that reflect a much larger portion of infamy than others," adding, in a footnote:

> Aware of this circumstance, the Roman lawyers have taken a distinction between the *infamia facti* and the *infamia juris*—the natural infamy resulting from the offence, and the artificial infamy produced through the means of the punishment by the law. See *Heinece Elementa Jur. Civil. Pand.* 1.3, tit. 2. sec. 399, whose explanation, however, is not very precise.[125]

Hence, by substituting the phrase "infamous crime" for the Massachusetts phrase "infamous punishment," the Fifth Amendment recognizes the force of Eden's and of Bentham's warning. However, because American jurists have not understood or heeded them, the phrase "infamous crime" has been taken to mean "infamous punishment," and the force of the Fifth Amendment as a text limiting the role of "infaming crime" has been dissipated. Moreover, what also may be emphasized is that the transition from the Massachusetts constitutional phrase "infamous punishment" to the national constitutional phrase "infamous crime" indicates that those American thinkers who were responsible for the text of the Fifth Amendment, especially the American *Encyclopédistes* gathered about Jefferson, accurately reflected delicate, vital aspects of the attacks on the Romanist feudal law of infamy.

Of course, as Professor Wigmore did not realize the force of the European Enlightenment, he missed the effect of the latter on the

Fifth Amendment, although the reference to infamy therein should have been a clear warning that the meaning of the entire Fifth Amendment might not be explained in terms of the Anglo-American common law alone.

Speaking generally, what has happened in America is that the mutilated or brusquely torn from the book of contemporary American ideology.

What American scholarship has lost is knowledge and understanding of the method, force and content of the eighteenth century Enlightenment. "The Philosophers of various nations," Condorcet wrote, "including in their meditations the interests of all humanity, without distinction of country, race or sect, form, despite the difference of their speculative opinions, a phalanx strongly united against all errors, against all kinds of tyranny. Animated by sentiment of universal philanthropy, they combat injustice, when foreign to their country, it cannot hit them; they also combat it when their own country makes them blameworthy in regard to other peoples; in Europe they arouse themselves against the crimes, the avidity of which blemishes the shores of America, of Africa and of Asia." He said that "The philosophers of England and of France deemed it an honor to take the name, to fulfill the duties of *friends* of these Negroes, whom their stupid tyrants scorned to count as men. The praises of French writers were the reward of tolerance in Russia and in Sweden, whereas Beccaria in Italy refuted the barbarous maxims of French *jurisprudence*."[126] However, by the period of Wigmore, the force of the Enlightenment, including of course Beccaria's attack on infamy, as realized in the Fifth Amendment, was lost.

9

The connecting link between the first part of the Fifth Amendment, requiring presentment or indictment of infaming crimes by grand jury, and the third part of the amendment, justifying a self-determined privilege against self-infamy and self-incrimination, is the second part of the amendment, which says:

> . . . nor shall any person be subject for the same offence to be twice put in jeopardy of life or limb . . .

This illuminating text enjoys this connecting role, because it, too, seems to reflect French *Encyclopédiste* theory of infamy, and hence is not exclusively a text of English law. Of course, it has its English and American colonial antecedents. The idea appears in the Massachusetts Body of Liberties of 1641, and is adumbrated, as will be seen, in Leveller thought. However, the relationship of the second part of the text to infamy, which explains its place as the second disposition of the Fifth Amendment, seems justified by eighteenth century French thought, which enlightens, unfetters, develops and activates other thought relating to double jeopardy.

It should first be asked, why ordinary principles of *res judicata* [the matter has already been judged] should not exclusively prevail in criminal law, or why the text of the Fifth Amendment reprobates double "jeopardy"? In answer, Professor Adhémar Esmein says "We recall the slight respect that the old [feudal] judicial practice had for '*res judicata*.'" He then continues:

> When the judgement was favorable to the accused absolution was very rarely pronounced, and when evidence was lacking the 'further inquiry' was the rule. This is one of the points against which the public conscience protested most vehemently, and the liberating and final effect of the acquittal by the jury was inserted in the Constitution of 1791. The Code of Brumaire, year IV, twice made application of it; in dealing with the grand jury, and in dealing with the petit jury. Two perfectly contrary systems were thus brought face to face.[128]

With considerable detail, Pothier, the most important jurist of the eighteenth century, describes feudal distinctions between criminal "definitive" judgments and "interlocutory" judgments. Among the types of the latter was the "judgment which orders the *question préparatoire*," that is, which orders torture designed to make the accused incriminate himself, and judgments of "further inquiry" *(judgments de plus amplement informé)*. The latter interlocutory judgment, Pothier says, was employed if the proof did not justify the *question préparatoire*, but if the judges nevertheless felt that it was inappropriate to absolve the accused because they anticipated new proofs. The interlocutory judgment thus made provided for "further inquiry." This might be within a definite term or even be "indefinite, which put the accused perpetually *in reatu* [tethered]. . . ." Sometimes the judges ordered such accused to be held "in prison." Judgments of "further inquiry," which had expired, could be renewed by the judges at their discretion.

There were two types of "definitive" judgments of absolution, one of them "putting out of court" *(hors de cour)* and the other which "vacated" *(congé)* the complaint. As the first of these was given when "the innocence of the accused was not quite fully justified" and when the accusation was not "without some foundation," the second kind of absolution was "more honorable to the accused" as it "fully justified him."[128]

The English Levellers protested against conditions which seem similar. In 1653 John Lilburne described the English situation, uniting his criticism of it with his struggle for the privilege against self-incrimination and forced delation. He said in *The Just Defense of John Lilburn:*

> As for instance, the first fundamental right I contended for in the late Kings and Bishops times, was for the freedom of mens persons, against arbitrary and illegal imprisonments, it being a thing expresly contrary to the law of the land, which requireth, That no man be attached, imprisoned, etc. (as in Magna Charta, cap. 29) but by lawful judgement of a Jury, a law so just and preservative, as without which intirely observed, every mans person is continually liable to be imprisoned at pleasure, and either to be kept there for moneths or yeers, or to be starved there, at the will of those that . . . are in power, as hath since been seen and felt abundantly, and had been more, had not some men strove against it; but it being my lot so to be imprisoned in those times, I conceive I did but my duty to manifest the injustice thereof, and claime and cry out for my right, and in so doing was serviceable to the liberties of my country, and no wayes deserve to be accounted turbulent in so doing.
>
> Another fundamental right I then contended for, was, that no mans conscience ought to be racked by oaths imposed, to answer to questions concerning himself in matters criminal, or pretended to be so.[129]

It already has been shown that torture did not result in infamy of law, but did result in popular infamy; and so it is assumed that the French feudal judgment which orders the *question préparatoire,* or torture, had the same rival results.

As will be shown, this contradiction appears repeatedly in the problem of determining the criterion of "jeopardy." The contradiction is overcome by the force of the Fifth Amendment.

Thus, the outcome of the French system of "further inquiry" and of "putting out of court" was infamy without conviction and infamy despite acquittal. Speaking of "further inquiry," Professor Esmein dryly says that "anyone once taken in the coils of this procedure must of necessity leave behind him something of his honor and his liberty."[130] Professor Glasson says that as the absolving formula "putting out of court" signified doubtful innocence, it resulted in "infamy of fact."[131] Pastoret says that "putting out of court" could be infaming, if the accusation had been a serious one; and that "further inquiry" was infaming.[132] The *Encyclopédie* said that those who have been accused of a grave crime are not "genuinely infamed" by "further inquiry" and "putting out of court," but nevertheless such situations import a kind of "infamy of fact."[133] Moreover, Beccaria (contrary to Muyart de Vouglans[134]) says that a person acquitted following imprisonment was nevertheless infamed. He says that "A person accused, imprisoned, tried, and acquitted, ought not be branded with any degree of infamy."[135] He continues:

> Among the Romans, we see that many, accused of very great crimes, and afterwards declared innocent, were respected by the people, and honoured with employments in the state. Why is the fate of an innocent person so different in our age? It is, because the present system of penal laws presents to our minds an idea of power rather than of justice. . . .[136]

Beccaria does not seem to have committed himself to a theory of double jeopardy, but to a prescriptive (or temporally limited) conception of criminal law. Hence he encounters the reproach of Pastoret that the French idea of *jamais deux fois sur le même objet* is more "humane" and "protective."[137] Nevertheless, Beccaria stimulates the idea that the constitutional guarantee against double jeopardy may be a guaranty against any further or repeated jeopardizing state-caused infamy such as contemporary American presidential or congressional infamy. The criterion of double jeopardy is not necessarily a prior formal determination, but may be the infliction of any prior state-caused peril, ascertained by its infaming effects, that is, by its effects on public opinion. It is not necessarily ascertained by the conception of the state itself as to its "jeopardizing" effect.

Beccaria's discussion, as reviewed in Diderot's note thereto, deepens the thought that the existence of such peril or of such jeopardy may be determined by the consequences of any state action on public opinion. Beccaria says that even the acquitted person is popularly infamed because "accused and convicted are thrown indiscriminately into the same prison," where as "military imprisonment," following military conviction, "in the common opinion is not so disgraceful as the civil."[138] Beccaria says that "the pomp that attends a military corps, would take off the infamy."[139] But Diderot interposes that the acquitted person is nevertheless infamed because public opinion is alarmed by the civil imprisonment; for public opinion here senses a problem of *ordre public* and public repose. That is why "shame" attaches even to the absolved person, despite his acquittal in the ordinary criminal courts. However, public opinion does not infame the military convict, Diderot says, because opinion has not been interested in breaches of military discipline.[140] Diderot relates public opinion to public interest and thus the infliction of infamy to public interest.

But Beccaria, in effect, reminds Diderot that the activity of the state may have created a false opinion, have alienated the public from the "power" to make its own opinion. Beccaria explains the absurd differences in the force of infamy because "infamy . . . like all popular opinions, is more attached to the manner and the form than to the thing itself."[141] Beccaria sharpens the idea that the infamy may in effect reflect the opinion of "power," not the power of opinion. Hence the existence of prior "jeopardy" or of prior infamy may be determined even by the effect of prior unconstitutional state action on public opinion. The exclusion of double jeopardy may become a shield against what Beccaria in the present situation calls "power rather than justice" and against what he elsewhere calls "open or disguised despotism,"[142] and against what Pastoret, in thought already discussed at length, called the "adroitness" of the state in creating public opinion.[143]

If prior infamy may be said to be a criterion of double jeopardy, its place in the text of the Fifth Amendment may be perceived. If the first part of the Fifth Amendment drastically limits the scope and role of constitutional infamy, the second part, reprobating double infamy or jeopardy, and the third part, excluding self-infamy, are weapons of defense against unconstitutional infamy. The amendment thereby fulfills its mission of fortifying the First Amendment, and is itself strengthened by the Eighth Amendment.

10

Because the force of the democratic Bill of Rights is today weakened, great responsibility is imposed on American lawyers. The task is that of breaking through to the eighteenth century sources and eighteenth century meaning of American civil liberties and civil rights. Unless such break-through to the sources is accomplished, the Bill of Rights as a democratic force in contemporary American society may diminish.

The achievement of the break-through to the constitutional sources imposes, in particular, the following responsibilities.

On the judiciary there is imposed the responsibility of maintaining its independence, acknowledging subordination only to the text of the Constitution and of the Bill of Rights.[144]

On the lawyer there is imposed the responsibility of contesting the principle of *stare decisis* [stand by things decided, i.e., precedent], so that the judiciary may be aided in its struggle to break through to the text of the Bill of Rights and to the sources and origins thereof. The principle of *stare decisis* is not justified by the content of the Constitution,[145] but it is an unconstitutional force which excludes access to the original text and to the sources of the Bill of Rights, and which also determines the content of a para-constitution which is not the same as, and which may be opposed to, the Constitution.

On the legal scholar there is imposed the task of grasping the import of the original text of the Bill of Rights, of discovering and mastering its sources and origins. It is the duty of recovering the eighteenth century materials, which have been torn from the book of American ideological history. Indeed, even during the eighteenth century itself, Thomas Cooper was forced to complain that American libraries ". . . do not contain the means of tracing the *history* of questions; this is a want which the literary people feel very much. . . ."[146]

This demand for the break-through does not require capitulation to discredited theories of natural law. Indeed, the break-through will discredit the contemporary revival of natural law, because it will bring to the front the historical method implicit in and applied by the eighteenth century theorists but excluded in the present revival of natural law.[147]

NOTES

1. This paper is a development of an earlier essay. Franklin, "Infamy and Constitutional Civil Liberties," 14 *Lawyers Guild Rev.* 1 (1954); also in this volume.

2. *Dennis v. United States*, 341 U.S. 494, 580, 71 S. Ct. 857, 602 (1951).

3. Bentham, *Principles of Penal Law*, 2 *The Works of Jeremy Bentham* (Bowring's ed., 1838) 365, 355. Milton used the word "infamy" and similar words scores of times. See 1 Patterson, *An Index to the Columbia Edition of the Works of John Milton* 952 (1940).

4. Luther, *A Treatise Concerning the Ban* (1520), 2 *Works of Martin Luther* (Holman ed.) 33, 37–8 (1915).

5. Luther, "An Argument in Defense of the Article of Dr. Martin Luther Wrongly Condemned in the Roman Bull" (1521), 3 *Works*, *supra* note 4, 5, 79 (1930).

6. Luther, "The Eighty-Second Psalm Translated and Explained" (1530), 4 *Works*, *supra* note 4, 283, 287 (1931).

7. 2 Calvin, *Institutes of the Christian Religion* (Beveridge's 1949 printing) 455–6.

8. 12 *Encylcopédie, ou dictionnaire raisonné des sciences, arts et des métiers* (1751 et seq.) 197.

9. 1 Montesquieu, *Lettres persanes* (1721) LXXX (Barckensen ed. (1913) 158.

10. Eden, *Principles of Penal Law* 52 (1771).

11. Esmein, *A History of Continental Criminal Procedure With Special Reference to France* (Simpson's tr., 1914) 614, note 1.

12. *An Essay on Crimes and Punishments by the Marquis Beccaria of Milan* [1764]. With A Commentary by M. de Voltaire [1766] (New Ed., 1872) 61.

13. 1 Brissot de Warville, *Théorie des loix criminelles* 190 (1781).

14. Soufflier, *Vocubulaire de droit* 307 (1908).

15. 1 Pastoret, *Des loix pénales*, partie 2, page 121 (1790).

16. Bentham, *op. cit. supra* note 3, at p. 456. See Condorcet, *Reflexions sur la jurisprudence criminelle*, Oeuvres, VII, 22, 24.

17. Pommeray, *Études sur l'infamie en droit romain* 269 (1937).

18. Pommeray, *op. cit. supra* note 17, at p. 276.

19. Brissot de Warville, *op. cit. supra* note 13, at p. 188.

20. 2 *The Writings of Jefferson* (Washington's ed., 1853) 100.

21. Beccaria, *op. cit. supra* note 12, at p. 83.

22. Eden, *op. cit. supra* note 10, at p. 30.

23. Beccaria, *Traité des délits et des peines . . . accompagnée de notes de Diderot et suivie d'une théorie des lois pénales par Jeremie Bentham* (Morellet ed., 1797) 95. The Italian text may be found in Beccaria, *Dei delitti e delle pene* (cura di Calamandrei, 2a ed., 1950).

24. The National Assembly legislated on 21 January 1790 that infamy "being personal" to the criminal, it should not affect his family. Carette, *Lois annotées 1789 à 1830 (continuées depuis 1845 par Delleneuve et Carette)* (n. d.) at p. 12. Robespierre's influence may be perceived here. See *infra* note 40.

25. *Annals of the Congress of the United States* 2010, 2011 (1851).

26. On this see Glasson, *Précis élémentaire de l'histoire du droit français* 588 (1904); Esmein, *op. cit. supra* note 11, at pp, 365, 400.

27. Pothier (Bugnet, 3e ed., 1890) 387, 419.

28. Beccaria, *op. cit. supra* note 12, at p. 53.

29. *Id.* at p. 56.

30. *Ibid.*

31. Griswold, *The Fifth Amendment Today* 3 (1955).

32. Beccaria, *op. cit. supra* note 12, at p. 58.

33. *Id.* at p. 60.

34. *Id.* at p. 61. But legally torture was not infaming. Glasson, *op. cit. supra* note 26, at p. 528.

35. 10 *Encyclopédie, ou dictionnaire raisonné des sciences, des arts et des métiers* (nouvelle ed., 1777) 594, 595.

36. Livingston, *A System of Penal Law for the State of Louisiana* 14 (1833).

37. Beccaria, *loc. cit. supra* note 28.

38. Diderot, *Dictionnaire encyclopédique*, 15 Oeuvres de Denis Diderot 10 (1821).

39. Diderot, *op. cit. supra* note 23, at p. 68 note.

40. Atalone, "Une oeuvre de jeunesse de Robespierre à l'Academie de Metz," *Les marches de l'Est*, Année 1911–1912. No 9, 301, 304.

41. Bentham, *op. cit. supra* note 3, p. 437.

42. Pastoret, *op. cit. supra* note 15, tome 2, partie 4, at p. 79.

43. *Id.* at p. 51. On Condorcet's outlook, see Schapiro, *Condorcet and the Rise of Liberalism* 143 (1934).

44. Huebner, *A History of Germanic Private Law* (Philorick's tr., 1981) 103. On distinctions of "rank" in Italian infamy, see Calisse, *A History of Italian Law* (Register's tr., 1928) 462.

45. Beccaria, *op. cit. supra* note 12, at p. 59.

46. Encyclopédie, *op. cit. supra* note 8, at pp. 197, 198.

47. Beccaria, *loc. cit. supra* note 12.

48. Glasson, *loc. cit. supra* note 34.

49. Luther, *loc. cit. supra* note 5.

50. Bexon, *Parallele du code pénal d'Angleterre avec les lois pénales françaises* 22 (1800).

51. *Id.*

52. Eden, *op. cit. supra* note 10, at p. 170.

53. Voltaire, *op. cit. supra* note 12, at p. 206.

54. 2 *The Papers of Thomas Jefferson* (Boyd's ed., 1950) 492, 503).

55. Bentham, *op. cit. supra* note 3, at p. 461.

56. Pastoret, *op. cit. supra* note 15, volume 1, partie 1, at p. 48.

57. Bexon, *op. cit. supra* note 50, at p. 393.

58. Luther, *op. cit. supra* not 4.

59. 3 Hegel, *Lectures on the History of Philosophy* (Haldane's and Simson's tr., 1896) 390, 398.

60. Letter to Vaughan, Passy, 14 March 1785, 11 *The Works of Benjamin Franklin* 11, 18 (1904).

61. *A Code of Crimes and Punishments* 1.3.36, Livingston, *op. cit. supra* note 36, at p. 370.

62. Beccaria, *op. cit. supra* note 12, at p. 139.

63. *Id.* at p. 140.

64. *Id.*

65. Diderot, *op. cit. supra* note 23, at p. 67 note. See also Diderot, *id.*, p. 54 note.

66. Pastoret, *op. cit. supra* note 15, tome 2, partie 4, at p. 43.

67. 15 *The Writings of Thomas Jefferson* (Library ed., 1904) 212.

68. Diderot, *op. cit. supra* note 38, at pp. 3, 4. Legislation of the French National Assembly of 16–29 September, given the force of law only a few days after the declaration of the rights of man and of the citizen, recognized a duty of "civic denunciation," but as in the case of natural ("moral" in English common law) obligations of the civil code, provided no sanctions for enforcement of such responsibility. It is not necessary to explain this legislation in terms of theory of natural law, as, in effect, the French system of 1791 thus recognizes the role of a self-determined privilege against self-infamy. See Carette, *Lois annotées 1789 à 1830 (continuées dupuis 1845 par Devilleneuve et Carette)* (n. d.) at p. 155, 156.

69. Griswold, *op. cit. supra* note 31, at p. 8.

70. Quoted in Franklin, "The Kantian Foundations of the Historical School of Law of Savigny," 22 *Revista juridica de la Universidad de Puerto Rico* 64, 79 (1952–1953).

71. Quoted in Franklin, *loc. cit. supra* note 70, at p. 78. See Beccaria, *op. cit. supra* note 12, at p. 157.

72. *Projet de déclaration des droits de l'homme et du citoyen, présenté à l'assemblée nationale, séance de Juillet 1789*, 2 *Oeuvres choisies de Joseph-Michel-Antoine de Servan* 323, 324 (1819).

73. Bexon, *op. cit. supra* note 50, at p. 86.

74. Eden, *op. cit. supra* note 10, at p. 54.

75. Jellinek, *The Declaration of the Rights of Man and of the Citizen* (Farrand's tr., 1901) 20. See also, Chinard, *The Commonplace Book of Thomas Jefferson* 63 (1926). See bibliography in Schapiro, *op. cit. supra* note 43, at p. 143.

76. Gidney, *L'influence des États-Unis d'Amerique sur Brissot, Condorcet et Mme. Roland* 10 (1930).

77. *Supra* note 13.

78. Condorcet, *Exquisse d'un tableau historique des progrès de l'esprit humain; suivie de réflexions sur l'esclavage des nègres* 317, 342 (1822).

79. Condorcet, *Sur l'admission des députés des planteurs de Saint-Domingue dans l'assemblée nationale*, *op. cit. supra* note 78, at pp. 415, 417.

80. Franklin, "The Eighteenth *Brumaire* in Louisiana: Talleyrand and the Spanish Medieval Legal system of 1806," 16 *Tulane Law Rev.* 514 (1942).

81. *Loc. cit. supra* note 79.

82. Condorcet, *op. cit. supra* note 78, at p. 348. Condorcet said that "it would be infamous to sell the liberty of other men for a sum of money." *Id.* at p. 417.

83. 4 *Recherches historiques et politiques sur les états-unis de l'Amérique septentrional par un citoyen de Virginie [Mazzei] avec quatre lettres d'un bourgeois de New-Heaven [Condorcet] sur l'unité de la législation* 129 (1788).

84. Jellinek, *op. cit. supra* note 75, at p. 56.

85. Jellinek, *op. cit. supra* note 75, at p. 97.

86. 8 Wigmore, *A Treatise on the Anglo-America System of Evidence in Trials at Common Law* (3d ed., 1940) 301.

87. *Ibid.*

88. *Ibid.*

89. Wigmore, *op. cit. supra* note 86, at p. 302, note 113.

90. *Id.* at p. 303.

91. 161 U.S. 591, 628 (1896).

92. *Id.* at p. 631.

93. Wigmore, *op. cit. supra* note 86, at pp. 328–9.

94. 161 U.S. 591, 632.

95. 9 *Encyclopedia of the Social Sciences* 421, (1933).

96. Pease, *The Leveller Movement* 86, (1916). See also p. 89.

97. Wigmore, *op. cit. supra* note 86, at p. 291.

98. Haller and Davies, *The Leveller Tracts* 1647–1653, 324 (1944).

99. *Id.* at pp. 82, 138, 152, 202, 204, 237, 457. The Diggers, who in politics were left of the Levellers, protested because Lilburne and others had been sent to the Tower "for not answering interogatories." The tyrants, they said, "still keep up the *Kingly* power, altering the title. . . ." *A Declaration of the Well-Affected in the Country of Buckinghamshire*, reprinted in *The Works of Gerrard Winstanley* (Sabine's ed., 1941) 641, 644–5.

100. *Id.* at p. 250.

101. *Id.* at p. 454.

102. *Id.* at pp. 454–5.

103. *Id.* at p. 223.

104. *Id.* at p. 323.

105. Carette, *Lois annotées 1789 à 1830 (continuées depuis 1845 par Devilleneuve et Carette)* (n. d.) 163, note 3. Professor Adhémar Esmein says: "The criminal law of ancient France was atrocious, unequal and unjust. . . . The preparation of the necessary reform was made by the writing of the *philosophes* and of the publicists: Montesquieu, Voltaire, Beccaria had posed the essential principles, and the numerous publications on the criminal procedure of the English law presented the concrete model, furnished by the nation which in this matter alone had conserved liberty and justice." Esmein, *Précis élémentaire de l'histoire du droit français de 1789 à 1814* (1911) 249.

106. Wigmore, *op. cit. supra* note 86, at p. 302.

107. Jefferson, *op. cit. supra* note 67, volume 7 at pp. 15, 16.

108. See Glasson, *op. cit. supra* note 26, at p. 530.

109. See Beccaria, *op. cit. supra* note 23, 1. On the relation between the French and Italian Enlightenments, see Cotta, *Gaetano Filangieri e il problema della legge*, e. III (1954).

110. Maestro, *Voltaire and Beccaria As Reformers of Criminal Law* 49 (1942).

111. Muyart de Vouglans, *Les lois criminelles de France dans leur ordre naturel* 816 (1780).

112. *Id.* at p. 814.

113. 1766.

114. Muyart de Vouglans, *op. cit. supra* note 111, at p. 832.

115. Id. at p. 837.

116. The French legislation of 1791 is text 1.5 of the book on "criminal justice and the institution of juries" of the Décret *concernant la police de sureté, la justice criminelle et l'établissement des jurés."* Carette, *op. cit. supra* note 105 at pp. 155, 157. On "afflictive" punishment, see von Bar, *A History of Continental Criminal Law* (Bell's tr., 1916) 273. Esmein's position is stated in his *Précis élémentaire de l'histoire du droit français de 1789 à 1814*, 110 (1911). His reference to Blackstone is presumably to Blackstone, *Commentaries of the Laws of England* 4.23.306.

117. Barr, *Voltaire in America* 1744–1800, 121–2 (1941).

118. *Id.* at p. 119.

119. *Id.* at p. 23.

120. Chard, *op. cit. supra* note 73, at p. 298, especially at p. 304. What knowledge did Jefferson have of Muyart de Vouglans' ninth proposal, which the force of the Fifth Amendment overcomes? See *supra* note 115. Although there may be no firm answer to this question, there may be internal evidence that Jefferson was aware of Muyart de Vouglans' *Réfutation* of Beccaria, which was published together with the ninth proposal. See notes 113, 114, *supra*. Jefferson's letter to Jay, quoted *supra* note 107, in part seems to be a paraphrase of Muyart de Vouglans, who wrote: "There is still a case where the *question* [torture] can be ordered, not indeed by an interlocutory judgment, but by the very definitive judgment which condemns the accused to the last punishment: this is so when the crime is of a nature which could not have been committed by the accused alone, or when there is proof from the charges and informations that he had accomplices. In that case, it is the usage to add in the judgment that the accused will be put *préalablement* to the *question* [torture] in order to gain revelation of his accomplices; this is called the *question préalable*, in order to distinguish it from that which is ordered before the definitive judgment, and which is called for that reason the *question préparatoire."* Muyart de Vouglans, *op. cit supra* note 111, at p. 817. Seealso *infra* note 128. See further, Esmein, *Précis élémentaire de l'histoire du droit français de 1789 à 1814* (1911) 10, 27.

121. Livingston, *op. cit. supra* note 36, at p. 19. Concerning Eden, see Radzinowicz. *A History of English Criminal Law and its Administration from 1750*, 301 (1948). On Jefferson's summaries of Eden, see Chinard, *op. cit. supra* note 73, at p. 323.

122. Du Rousseaud de la Combe, *Traité des matieres criminelles, suivant l'ordonnance du mois d'août* 1670 (7e ed., 1768).

123. Von Bar, *A History of Continental Criminal Law* (Bell's tr., 1916) 275. See *Encyclopédie*, *op. cit. supra* note 8, volume VIII, at pp. 575, 576.

124. Eden, *op. cit. supra* note 10, at p. 54.

125. Bentham, *op. cit. supra* note 3, at p. 460.

126. Condorcet, *op. cit. supra* note 78, at p. 213.

127. Esmein, *op. cit. supra* note 11, at p. 522.

128. Pothier, *Traité de la procédure criminelle*, 10 *Oeuvres de Pothier* (Bugnet ed., 1890) 387, 473, 475, 476.

129. Haller and Davies, *op. cit. supra* note 98. at p. 454.

130. Esmein, *op. cit. supra* note 11, at p. 239.

131. Glasson, *op. cit. supra* note 26, at p. 326.

132. Pastoret, *op. cit. supra* note 15, tome 1, partie 2, at p. 131.

133. *Encyclopédie*, *op. cit. supra* note 8. volume 8, at p. 576.

134. Muyart de Vouglans, *op. cit. supra* note 111, at p. 822.

135. Beccaria, *op. cit. supra* note 12, at p. 110.

136. *Ibid.*

137. Pastoret, *op. cit. supra* note 15, tome 2, partie 4, at p. 98.

138. Beccaria, *op. cit. supra* note 12, at pp. 110, 111.

139. *Id.* at p. 110.

140. Diderot, *op. cit. supra* note 23, at p. 24 note.

141. Beccaria, *op. cit. supra* note 12, at p. 110.

142. *Id.* at p. 114.

143. *Supra* note 15.

144. Franklin, *loc. cit. supra* note 1, at p. 10.

145. Franklin, "The Judiciary State II," 3 *National Lawyers Guild Qu.* 27, 31 (1940); also in this volume. "But the ultimate touchstone of constitutionality is the Constitution itself and not what we have said about it." Frankfurter, J., in *Graves v. New York,* 306 U.S. 466, 491–2 (1939). See Franklin, "Concerning the Historic Importance of Edward Livingston," 11 *Tulane Law Review* 163, 180 (1937).

146. Cooper, *Some Information Respecting America* 65 (1794). Muyart de Vouglans complained of the sources introduced by Beccaria. Professor Adhemar Esmein quotes the former as writing of Beccaria's book: "You, sir, no doubt, expect, like myself, to find under the title of a 'Traité des délits et des peines', an accurate and methodical study of the laws and principles relating to the subject, citations of authorities on the questions which may arise thereupon. . . . You will, however, be astonished to see that nothing of the kind is to be found in this book." Esmein, *op. cit. supra* note 11, at p. 371.

147. Franklin, "Théorie monadiste legale et ses perspectives pour un systeme de droit mondial," *Les cahiers du droit*, no 33, p. 45 (1954).

Index